Rethinking Employment Policy

D. LEE BAWDEN
FELICITY SKIDMORE
Editors

Rethinking Employment Policy

THE URBAN INSTITUTE PRESS
Washington, D.C.

THE URBAN INSTITUTE PRESS
2100 M Street, N.W.
Washington, D.C. 20037

Library of Congress Cataloging in Publication Data

Rethinking Employment Policy / D. Lee Bawden, Felicity Skidmore, editors

p. 282

Rethinking Employment Policy / Isabel V. Sawhill.—Do We Know Enough About the Unemployment Problem to Know What, If Anything, Will Help? / George Johnson.—Employer Approaches to Reducing Unemployment / Robert Eisner.—Matching Workers and Job Opportunities / Marc Bendick, Jr.—Government Training as a Means of Reducing Unemployment / Burt S. Barnow.—Worker's Rights / Ronald G. Ehrenberg.—Insuring Equal Opportunity in Employment Through Law / Leroy D. Clark—Implications of Internationalization for Labor Market Institutions and Industrial Relations Systems / Ray Marshall.—International Competition and American Jobs / Daniel Burton.—Effective Employment Policy / Forrest Chisman.

1. Manpower policy—United States. 2. Unemployment—United States. 3. Foreign trade and employment—United States. I. Bawden, D. Lee. II. Skidmore, Felicity.
HD5724.R45 1988   331.12'042'0973—dc19   88-39161
ISBN 0-87766-459-5 (casebound)
ISBN 0-87766-458-7

Printed in the United States of America

9 8 7 6 5 4 3 2 1

Distributed in the United States and Canada
by University Press of America
4720 Boston Way Lanham, MD 20706

THE URBAN INSTITUTE is a nonprofit policy research and educational organization established in Washington, D.C., in 1968. Its staff investigates the social and economic problems confronting the nation and government policies and programs designed to alleviate such problems. The Institute disseminates significant findings of its research through the publications program of its Press. The Institute has two goals for work in each of its research areas: to help shape thinking about societal problems and efforts to solve them, and to improve government decisions and performance by providing better information and analytic tools.

Through work that ranges from broad conceptual studies to administrative and technical assistance, Institute researchers contribute to the stock of knowledge available to public officials and private individuals and groups concerned with formulating and implementing more efficient and effective government policy.

Conclusions or opinions expressed in Institute publications are those of the authors and do not necessarily reflect the views of other staff members, officers or trustees of the Institute, advisory groups, or any organizations that provide financial support to the Institute.

Acknowledgments

Of the numerous people whose contributions helped make these essays and their publication possible, the following deserve special thanks: Alan Pifer and Forrest Chisman, chair and project director, respectively, of the Project on the Federal Social Role, for their substantive and moral support throughout; the members of the advisory board for the study, whose role is described in the *Introduction*; Judith Golub, who helped plan and organize the conference at which the essays were first presented; Barbara Bergmann, Charles Betsey, John Bishop, Gary Hufbauer, Sar Levitan, Arnold Packer, and David Stevens, the conference discussants whose participation contributed to the quality of the final essays; Mildred Woodhouse and Susanne White, who gave word processing support through several versions of the manuscript; Donna Grebe, who did the lion's share of the proofreading; and Christina Dietrich, who kept the production schedule on track.

CONTENTS

Tables

More than four decades after passage of the Full Employment Act of 1946 our society is still unable to provide a job for everyone who wants to work. After the "longest peacetime expansion" since World War II, more than five percent of our work force is unemployed, and this does not count the millions of persons who have been so discouraged by their failure to find a job that they are no longer looking for one.

The challenge is twofold: first, to find a way to use our potential work force more fully without creating inflationary pressures; and second, to target job training and employment programs to those who can benefit most, rather than spending resources on those who will do as well in the labor market without program help as with it. There are encouraging signs that we may be making slow progress in learning how to mediate employment swings at the macroeconomic level, but we are still groping for any kind of effective employment policy at the individual level.

The Urban Institute has placed priority on examining labor market issues almost since its founding twenty years ago. In the late 1960s Charles Holt's pioneering research into ways to reduce friction in the labor market by improving the matching of jobs to job seekers began the search for ways to improve the unemployment-inflation trade-off. This was followed by Alan Fechter's equally pathbreaking work demonstrating the high degree of fiscal substitution—using job program resources to hire workers who would have been hired in any case—in the early years of the Comprehensive Employment and Training Administration (CETA) programs. Fechter's work led directly to the decision to restrict CETA program eligibility to low-income and disadvantaged workers. The Institute's commitment to research on employment issues and the evaluation of employment and training programs has continued ever since. Recent Institute work includes contributions to the literature on wage discrimination, the labor market problems of youth, and the evaluation of new state work-welfare initiatives.

This volume is an effort to stand back from the details of labor market scholarship and take a hard look at what we know and do not know about how to solve the issues—domestic and international—that will face the U.S. labor market as we enter the 1990s. In addition to the human suffering occasioned by unemployment, the toll it takes in terms of lost productive potential is great. With the aging of our population and the increasing intensity of foreign competition, the loss becomes ever more costly.

Intended as a nontechnical discussion for the public policy student, interested lay reader, and government official, this volume makes a valuable contribution to the debate we all should be engaging in about what the appropriate role of government should be in helping people help themselves through work, and how that role can most effectively be carried out.

William Gorham
President

INTRODUCTION

D. Lee Bawden

This book makes a modest attempt to rethink both the goals of employment policy and the means to achieve those goals in the future. Some of the goals relate to reducing unemployment, others to increasing labor market efficiency and reducing inequities, still others to meeting the challenge of rising international competition.

Two primary themes run through the volume: (1) employment policy in this country has failed to reach the employment goals taken for granted in the early 1960s as achievable; and (2) while much remains unknown, enough has been learned from past successes and failures to shape a more effective employment policy in the future.

THE POLICY CONTENT

After the Great Depression until the late 1950s unemployment was regarded primarily as a cyclical problem. Keynesian economics dominated employment policy; unemployment was to be kept low by keeping aggregate demand high via monetary and fiscal policy. Despite the lofty language of the Employment Act of 1946, this passive "demand management" approach remained the primary vehicle of employment policy until about 1960, when a more active policy began to take shape. The 1960s and early 1970s saw the promulgation of programs to train or retrain workers, expand unemployment benefits, create public service jobs for the unemployed, and provide equal opportunity in employment for minorities, women, the aged, and the handicapped. These efforts, some of which were experimental in nature, were the result of both a change in policy—to recognize and address the problems of disadvantaged workers (the structurally unemployed) and those who were discriminated against in the labor market—and a fortuitous increase in tax revenues from increased productivity that provided funding for new programs.

1

The pendulum swung the other way in the 1980s. Because of increased defense spending and tax cuts, federal revenues available for domestic programs have declined. Training programs have been cut back, public service employment has been eliminated, equal opportunity and affirmative action initiatives have been curtailed, and unemployment benefits have been reduced.

Not all this retrenchment, however, can be attributed to a conservative president or to fiscal pressures to reduce budgets. Negative perceptions of the effectiveness of certain programs (perceptions based in part on program evaluations) and the possibly unintended consequences of others (for example, work disincentives of Unemployment Compensation, fiscal substitution in public service employment) also have diminished public support for an expansive employment policy in this country.

Yet the problems remain. Structural unemployment has become more concentrated, producing a growing underclass whose problems have not yet been seriously addressed. Underemployment—workers overqualified for low-wage jobs—has increased. Discrimination, while perhaps less overt, remains a serious problem.

In spite of these facts, the public is unlikely to support a more expansive and aggressive employment policy if it is simply a warmed-over version of the programs of the 1970s. Nor do they have to. The "social experimentation" of the 1960s and 1970s revealed a great deal about what programs are feasible, which ones work, and how to better structure programs to achieve their desired objectives. As important, the need for more effective initiatives will be exacerbated because the 1990s are not going to be the same as the last two decades. Important social, economic, and demographic changes are altering or will alter both the demand for and supply of labor, as well as the functioning of the labor market. For example:

□ Our economy is increasingly becoming internationalized through greater foreign competition, multinational industries, international cartels, and the interdependence of financial markets.

□ Partly because of a more international economy and partly because of technological change, greater numbers of middle-aged (dislocated) workers are having to change careers, as smokestack industries decline and high tech industries expand.

□ Labor markets are adjusting to a rising number of immigrants, both legal and illegal, affecting wages and job opportunities for U.S. citizens.

□ The composition of the work force is changing—there are more older workers and women in the labor force, requiring adjustments in retirement policies, wage structures, work hours, and auxiliary services (such as child care).

□ Equal opportunity and affirmative action policies are becoming less effective as racial and sexual discrimination are becoming less overt and more subtle.

□ Although the situation is improving, the inadequacy of private pensions over the last half century will place a greater burden on workers to provide for the economic well-being and medical needs of older citizens as their relative numbers increase.

□ Despite rising education levels, over a quarter of the adult population lacks a high school education, and many of those do not have the basic skills to be trained or retrained for the expanding high tech and service jobs of the future.

□ There is a growing underclass whose members have little expectation of getting jobs in the mainstream economy, exacerbating the already serious social problems of crime, drug use, and welfare dependency.

U.S. employment policy in the past has not been very successful, and the future will require more innovative policies to meet the challenges that lie ahead.

THE BOOK

The book is one of a series sponsored by the Project on the Federal Social Role, Alan Pifer, Chair, and Forrest Chisman, Project Director. Funded by a number of private foundations, the Project's objective was to stimulate a rethinking of major policy objectives, in light of the changes in policy directions under the Reagan administration and as we reach the final decade of this century.

The choice of topics for the essays was greatly aided by an eminent advisory committee: Ray Marshall (chair), Secretary of the U.S. Department of Labor under President Carter; Malcom Lovell, Assistant Secretary of the U.S. Department of Labor under President Nixon and Under Secretary under President Reagan; William Kohlberg, President and Chief Executive Officer, National Alliance of Business; and Howard Samuel, President, Industrial Union Department, AFL-CIO.

When the papers for this book were commissioned, the unemployment rate was relatively high. Consequently, several of the chapters focus on how to reduce unemployment. As we go to press, the unemployment rate is considerably lower, and attention has turned to concerns over inflation and how to increase the human capital of the unemployed to meet the rising labor demand projected for the next century. Yet the issues in this book remain as relevant as ever—for two reasons. First, those papers that address the unemployment problem are primarily concerned with the disadvantaged and how government policy can help them to enter the mainstream economy. This issue is as important in a tight labor market as it is when unemployment is high. Second, the inevitability of the business cycle will all too soon find the nation again grappling with the problem of reduced consumer demand and rising unemployment.

THE CHAPTERS

Isabel Sawhill (chapter 1) identifies the major employment problems and proposes four major objectives of employment policy: providing jobs (reducing unemployment, creating more good jobs, improving productivity and earnings), assisting the disadvantaged (making the poor self-sufficient), and improving the functioning of the labor markets to insure fair treatment for workers and increase economic efficiency. She notes that these four objectives are central "because unemployment both creates hardship and represents a waste of human resources." She stresses that achievement of each of the four requires more than a successful employment policy as commonly understood (i.e., programs to directly provide jobs, training, and other assistance to specific groups). She argues that macroeconomic policy, reform of the educational system, income transfers (even though there is concern about their work disincentives), and less adversarial top-down approaches to managing people are all needed.

The next four chapters focus on the efficacy of specific ways to reduce unemployment: namely, public service employment, private sector wage subsidies, improving the labor market exchange, and government training programs.

George Johnson (chapter 2) focuses on the thorny issue of whether, and to what extent, any direct labor market intervention can increase overall employment given that labor market institutions inevitably work within the context of the macroeconomic level of activity. He looks at the problem of cyclical (short-term) unemployment and the problem of structural (long-term) unemployment. He holds out little hope for solving the former through employment programs. In the latter case he focuses on various ways in which the so-called natural rate of unemployment might be reduced. His view is that we do not yet know enough about long-run dynamics to design effective programs, but there is some promise for the future.

Robert Eisner (chapter 3) takes a considerably more optimistic view of the potential for labor market policy. He takes as given the importance of aggregate economic activity in reducing unemployment. His chapter concentrates on another issue—that the economist's assumption that labor is viewed by employers as interchangeable is a drastic oversimplification that distorts our view of employment policy. "Millions are unemployed because they cannot find a job where employers consider them worth hiring; at the same time employers who might consider them worth hiring cannot find them." He sees one key to the puzzle in the divergence between a firm's narrow self-interest (to minimize investment in worker training/retraining because it loses the payoff if the worker leaves) and the interest of firms in general and society, which is to see people working productively in jobs they choose. To rectify this situation he argues for careful consideration of a well-designed, employer-focused jobs tax credit.

Johnson and Eisner address different solutions to essentially the same problem. In large part, this difference in views represents a difference in the implicit weighting of two competing objectives—efficiency versus equity. Johnson places more emphasis on efficiency; Eisner gives more emphasis to equity.

Marc Bendick (chapter 4) focuses, like Eisner, on the economic waste that exists when the labor market does not do an adequate job of matching people who want jobs with the employers who want workers. In Bendick's case, the program examined is the federal–state Employment Service, the controversy that surrounds it, and how it could be revitalized to be more effective in improving the labor exchange process. He concludes that the agency, even as currently operated, is modestly effective in reducing frictional unemployment, and that it could be even more effective with funding to initiate certain improvements in operations, including state-of-the-art automated data processing. The funding Bendick envisions is relatively modest compared with the potential economic gains of a more highly utilized work force.

Burt Barnow (chapter 5) looks at the effectiveness of government-sponsored training programs as a way of increasing employability, based on evaluation evidence on the Comprehensive Employment and Training Act (CETA) and the earlier Manpower Development and Training Act (MDTA) initiatives. He finds that there is still a wide range of uncertainty as to their effectiveness, but that on balance they seem to have modest beneficial effects on the employment prospects of the disadvantaged, particularly women. He notes, however, that the effects are not large in part because they are short-term programs and in part because government funding for employment and training programs is the lowest in 20 years. He also provides an overview of the successor to CETA—the Job Training Partnership Act (JTPA) programs—and a national evaluation of JTDA that is currently underway. Barnow concludes by arguing that more attention should be given than is currently the case to both basic skills training and longer-term vocational training as ways to reduce unemployment.

The next two chapters address employment policy related to workers' rights (chapter 6) and equal opportunity in employment (chapter 7).

Ronald Ehrenberg (chapter 6) observes that protective labor legislation in the United States is much less comprehensive than in many of the other western industrialized nations. He examines the pros and cons of expanded legislation in four areas—hours of work, unjust dismissals, comparable worth, and plant shutdowns. His conclusion is that more stringent legislation would benefit nonunion workers more than union workers and, on equity grounds, may be a good idea. However, he cautions against a rapid expansion of protective labor rights legislation until there is more evidence on the consequences of such actions, including the effects on economic efficiency.

From a researcher's perspective, Ehrenberg's caution is appropriate; however, policymakers often have to act on less than conclusive evidence, and they weigh their decisions on both equity and efficiency grounds. My reading of the evidence to date suggests that more legislation protecting workers can be justified on equity grounds without unduly compromising efficiency. Indeed, as Ehrenberg notes, there has been recent legislative progress on the plant closings issue.

Chapter 7, by Leroy Clark, like chapter 4, focuses on improving the efficiency of implementing existing policy rather than examining new policy. It takes a somewhat different perspective from that of previous chapters, however, in that the author is a lawyer rather than an economist. Clark argues that the avenues for redress for both racial and sexual discrimination in the labor market are overlapping and confusing. He proposes that Title VII of the 1964 Civil Rights Act (with some minor amendments, including the provision for punitive damages) "should be the sole basis for private causes of action involving race or sex discrimination," and that the Equal Opportunity Employment Commission (EEOC) should be the "central actor in the employment discrimination field"—authority which is currently dispersed among the EEOC, the Department of Justice, the Department of Labor, and several other federal agencies. Clark further proposes that a special board, much like the War Labor Board of World War II, be established to arbitrate claims of race or sex discrimination in high-level positions and sex discrimination in female-dominated jobs.

The next two chapters deal with the internationalization of the U.S. economy and its implications for labor market policy in the United States. One of the most important economic trends since World War II has been the internationalization of the U.S. economy. Ray Marshall (chapter 8) reviews the history of the "globalization of markets" and concludes that we are "clearly losing our ability to maintain real wages and living standards" because of declining productivity vis-à-vis other nations. He suggests that a solution to this declining competitiveness is more cooperation between, and more focus on productivity by, both workers and management—with an emphasis on involving workers in more corporate decisions and greater commitment by management to employment security.

Extending Marshall's line of reasoning, Daniel Burton (chapter 9) argues for a comprehensive "policy package" to solve the employment problems that result from international competition. With some reservations, he proposes the use of more temporary and part-time workers—a practice used by some of our industrial competitors. Like Marshall, he proposes greater cooperation between labor and management. Burton also advocates stricter control of illegal immigrants, efforts to open foreign trade markets, improved macroeconomic policies, and better coordination of macroeconomic policies with other industrialized nations.

The final chapter is written by the codirector of the larger project of which this volume is a part. The author's perspective is one of political and moral philosophy, rather than economic theory. Forrest Chisman (chapter 10) argues that a full employment policy is more an issue of political will than of economic means. In his view an aggressive employment policy—with more federal leadership and more federal funding—would be both politically acceptable and fiscally feasible. He then outlines a four-part proposal for the implementation of a full employment policy that would be more than a political gesture.

Chapter One

RETHINKING EMPLOYMENT POLICY

Isabel V. Sawhill

One of the goals of the United States, as of most modern democracies, is to provide full employment. It has been an elusive goal at best, achieved more in wartime than in peacetime, and more for some groups than for others. For the past ten years, the unemployment rate in the United States has averaged 7.4 percent. Among blacks, it has averaged 14.8 percent; among teenagers, 18.8 percent; and among women maintaining families, 9.7 percent. Such figures would seem to be a direct affront to American aspirations.

Unemployment is not the only problem affecting American workers. Even among those who are employed, compensation levels, adjusted for inflation, were little higher in the mid-1980s than they had been ten years earlier. And for some groups, employment opportunities or rates of pay remain at levels that make it impossible for them to support a family above the poverty level. Finally, almost no one is satisfied with the way labor markets operate. Some complain about the unfair treatment accorded many workers, calling for greater government to insure that employee rights are protected. Others believe such government intervention reduces labor mobility and productivity, undermining U.S. competitiveness in world markets and prospects for growth.

The issue is what, if anything, can be done about these problems. To what extent does the nation have a coordinated, or even an uncoordinated, set of employment policies for dealing with them? Does it need such policies, and if so, how should we think about their objectives and their relationship to other policies? And how is the debate likely to be affected by a new political and fiscal environment as well as by the changing nature of the work force and the economy?

This chapter addresses these questions. Its major purpose is to map the terrain—define the scope and content of the issues and establish a framework for the more detailed assessment of various policy options in subsequent chapters.

A BACKWARD LOOK

Virtually all public policies—whether in the area of taxes, regulation, or spending—have an impact on labor markets, and often these impacts are substantial. Yet what most people seem to mean by employment policy is a set of reasonably discrete programs designed to directly provide jobs, training, or other assistance to specific groups such as youth, dislocated workers, the disadvantaged, or the victims of recession.

United States employment policy in this discrete sense was born in the 1930s in response to the massive unemployment accompanying the Great Depression. The New Deal work relief programs, though temporary, enrolled about 6 percent of the labor force or the equivalent of 6.8 million people in today's terms (Mangum 1975, 35). More permanent New Deal legislation established the unemployment insurance and social security systems, wage and hours standards, workmen's compensation, and the framework for collective bargaining.

The so-called manpower agenda was extended in the early 1960s in response to concerns about pockets of "structural" unemployment among experienced male family heads (the dislocated workers of that era), leading to passage of the Area Redevelopment Act and the Manpower Development and Training Act. (Structural unemployment is the unemployment that exists—even when there is no shortage of jobs—because of a mismatch between the skills or location of workers and jobs.) By the mid-1960s the focus had shifted to serving the disadvantaged as the War on Poverty was launched and a new set of programs, such as the Job Corps, the Neighborhood Youth Corps, Work Experience and Training, and the Community Action Program were launched.

In 1973 most existing manpower programs were consolidated as part of the Comprehensive Employment and Training Act (CETA). CETA was used as a vehicle for mounting a large-scale public service jobs program in response to the 1974–75 recession, and then retargeted on employing the disadvantaged in 1978. In 1982, it was replaced by the Job Training Partnership Act (JTPA) which put much greater emphasis on training (as opposed to job creation) and was structured to provide a greater decision-making role for the states and the private sector.

Even this brief history makes it clear that policymakers have viewed employment and training programs as serving a multiplicity of purposes. These have included helping the structurally unemployed adjust to changes in the economy, providing short-term employment opportunities or income to the cyclically unemployed, and improving the long-term labor market prospects of individuals traditionally served by welfare programs.

Despite their broad objectives, employment and training programs have always been modest in scale. (The work relief programs of the depression are an exception.) Even at their peak funding levels in the late 1970s, total outlays never exceeded $12 billion or 2 percent of all federal outlays, with the programs serving about 4 million people or 4 percent of the labor force—many for very short periods of time.

The Reagan administration targeted these programs for deep budget cuts in its first term, proposing a reduction of 69 percent by fiscal year 1985 relative to what outlays would have been under pre-Reagan policies.[1] The administration's view was that economic recovery would reduce unemployment to 6 or 7 percent, at which point any remaining problem would have to be characterized as structural— an inability of the unemployed to qualify for existing jobs, or their unwillingness to take them, rather then any overall shortage of job opportunities. Key to reducing structural unemployment were reforms of the minimum wage laws and the unemployment insurance program that would permit markets to operate more efficiently (*Economic Report of the President* 1983, 29).

These views reflect, of course, the conservative leanings of the Reagan administration and the crimp that large budget deficits have placed on spending for social programs, including employment and training. But they also reflect—and have helped to create—a growing sense on the part of many policy analysts and the public that past efforts to reduce unemployment or to assist the unemployed have been ineffective or counterproductive; that fighting unemployment with monetary or fiscal stimulus is inflationary; that employment programs create few if any new jobs; that minimum wages and other labor market regulations reduce employment opportunities (especially for youth); that training programs for the disadvantaged have done little to reduce poverty or welfare dependency; and that unemployment insurance creates disincentives to work.

Whether or not one accepts this indictment in all its particulars, it remains an influential view which cannot be ignored in thinking about the future. Thus, one clear need is a careful look at what is known about the effectiveness of past efforts in achieving various objectives and where the political consensus for continuing such efforts can be maintained or rebuilt.

Even if we were to judge past efforts harshly, it is not clear that the best substitute would be a policy of benign neglect. The problems these efforts seek to ameliorate—unemployment and poverty—are continuing reminders of the shortcomings of our economic and social institutions; few would dismiss the accompanying hardships and inefficiencies as outcomes we are powerless to affect. Thus, if we have failed to make as much headway against these problems as we would like, it may be because we need to probe more deeply for new understanding. Out of such probing may come new, and more successful, approaches.

THE NEW POLICY ENVIRONMENT: SETTING THE STAGE

Policy goals are ultimately determined in the political arena and are shaped by a variety of factors, such as the perceived seriousness of various economic and social problems and the availability of resources to deal with them. The policy environment is clearly different now than a decade ago. The real income of the average family was no higher in the mid-1980s than it had been in the late 1960s, making citizens less willing to pay higher taxes. Enormous federal budget deficits stemming from tax cuts and a military build-up have created equally large pressures to curb social program spending. Less confidence in the U.S. economy's ability to continue growing and to compete in world markets has shifted concern from issues of equity to issues of efficiency. And a highly successful attack by conservative intellectuals and a conservative president on the premises of the traditional liberal agenda has put the proponents of an activist government on the defensive.

At the same time, demographic trends are focusing attention more on the elderly and less on youth. The labor force participation of women has continued to increase—from 43 percent in 1970 to 55 percent in 1987 to a projected 59 percent in 1995—at the same time that early retirement is gradually eroding the proportion of men at work (Statistical Abstract 1985, 392). These trends, together with higher birth rates for blacks and Hispanics, mean that both women and minorities will be a larger proportion of the work force in the future than they have been in the past. On the other hand, the feminist and civil rights revolutions appear to have peaked, although continued frustration by these groups at the slow progress they have made has heightened interest in new approaches such as comparable worth (see Ehrenberg's discussion in chapter 6). Finally, with an increasing proportion of all families having two wage earners, a profound shift is occurring in the relationship of work to family life—a shift that has produced multiple stresses and new ad hoc coping mechanisms. By 1984, only 11 percent of all families consisted of a husband and a wife who did not work outside the home (Sawhill, June 1985, table 2).

Concerns about the effects of trade and technology on employment and wages have moved to the center of the agenda. A near consensus exists that both trade and technology are good for the long-run health of the economy but that they impose serious short-run adjustment costs on workers and communities. These costs must be reduced or shared more equitably.

Estimates of the number of workers displaced annually from their jobs because of structural changes in the economy vary from 90,000 to over 2 million. Based on a special survey, the U.S. Labor Department estimates the number at about 1 million per year.[2]

As the result of trade and technology, it is argued that "good" jobs are being replaced by "bad" jobs, that we are becoming a nation of hamburger stands, and that the middle class is disappearing. There is little question that displaced workers suffer serious income losses and must often settle for lower-wage jobs; but the issue of whether the economy as a whole has become more bifurcated has not been settled. It is true that the share of income going to the middle class (middle-income quintile) declined from 17.6 percent in 1970 to 16.8 percent in 1986, making each middle-income family $1,397 poorer, on average, in 1986 than they would have been if they had received the same share of income as in 1970. But much of this shift appears to be related to demographic change (more younger people and female-headed families at the bottom of the income distribution and more two-earner families at the top) rather than to the changing structure of the economy.[3]

Unemployment in the early 1980s was high both in the United States and in Europe, but the U.S. government's more or less benign neglect of the issue led to little or no public outcry—much to the surprise of some politicians and academicians (see the Chisman discussion in chapter 10). This attitude could stem from the public's fear of inflation, from its perception that safety nets are available for the unemployed, and that jobs exist for those who really want to work. In any case, by mid-1988 unemployment had fallen to around 5.5 percent, leading to a renewed concern about the inflationary potential of tight labor markets.

Finally, the War on Poverty has not been won. At 13.5 percent in 1987, the poverty rate was almost as high as it had been when the war was initially launched in the mid-1960s and higher than the 11 to 12 percent achieved in the mid-1970s. In the academic community, some consensus seems to be emerging that income transfers have helped to reduce the incidence of poverty, especially among the elderly, but that we have been less successful in moving people out of poverty through work (Danziger and Weinberg 1986). The public has always preferred the latter approach. And the group that now dominates the poverty population (female-headed families) is the group that seems to benefit most from employment and training programs—making many people optimistic that much more could be accomplished here.

WHAT SHOULD WE BE TRYING TO ACHIEVE?

Our objectives should be consistent with, or responsive to, the constraints and opportunities imposed by this new policy environment. It would be foolish, for example, to make demands on the budget or taxpayers that they are clearly not able or willing to meet in the foreseeable future. But too-ready acceptance of current budgetary limits would also be unwise. As noted above, past investments in employment policies have been small relative to the size of the federal budget and are also smaller than those made in many other countries.[4] In many cases, the costs of these investments have proved small relative to their benefits. Where the payoff is large, these investments should be made even if taxes have to be raised or other expenditures curtailed—and even though, in the new environment of fiscal stringency, the case will have to be more carefully made.

To take another example, it would be unwise to seek equity in job opportunities, pay, or benefits at the expense of growth or international competitiveness, but it would be equally unwise to ignore the human costs of unregulated markets or the unfinished agenda of the War on Poverty. Programs will need to be designed in ways that strike a balance.

Finally, in our objectives we should not try to accomplish too much. Market solutions in some cases may be the best that can be achieved. Where they are, attempts to improve upon them may only serve to discredit, by association, other potentially successful interventions.

With these caveats in mind, this chapter argues that an overall employment policy should have four major objectives:

☐ providing jobs (reducing unemployment)
☐ creating more good jobs (improving productivity and earnings)
☐ assisting the disadvantaged (making the poor self-sufficient), and
☐ improving the functioning of labor markets in ways that insure both fair treatment for workers and economic efficiency.

These four objectives are central not only to human welfare but also to the long-term vitality of the economy. Unemployment both creates hardship and represents a waste of valuable resources. Higher productivity and wages not only contribute to higher family incomes but also maintain the economic strength of the United States compared with the rest of the world. Raising the incomes of the disadvantaged through work provides direct benefits to those at the bottom of the economic ladder and also reduces the costs of dependency to the taxpayer. Improving the functioning of labor markets can lead to greater fairness and greater efficiency if hiring, promotion, and pay are based on merit rather than on such factors as race, sex, and seniority.

Achieving each of these four objectives requires much more than a successful employment policy, as that term is commonly understood. In the case of providing jobs, primary reliance must be placed on macroeconomic policies. Direct job-creation policies (such as subsidized employment opportunities in the public or private sector) may help alleviate some forms of structural unemployment or may reduce the amount of inflation associated with a lowering of the unemployment rate. In the case of creating more good jobs through improved productivity, the preeminent policy lever has been and will remain the publicly funded education system—a system which dwarfs adult training programs in scope and impact. In the case of assisting the disadvantaged, income transfers are likely to remain of critical importance, even though there is increasing concern about the work disincentives and long-term dependency they may create. In the case of the final objective, improved functioning of labor markets, it should be understood that government regulation is a blunt instrument that cannot always improve upon market outcomes. Within these limits, employment policies designed to achieve the above four objectives can play a constructive role.

PROVIDING JOBS

At one level, our ability to provide jobs for a growing population has been extremely good. The number of people employed in the United States has increased by more than 20 million since the mid-1970s, and by 44 million since the mid-1950s. Since employment did not grow as fast as the labor force, however, the unemployment rate tended to rise at each succeeding cyclical peak.

Some blamed this upward creep on growing structural unemployment caused by the changing demographic composition of the labor force, the proliferation of income transfers, the increased importance of trade to the overall economy, faster technological change, or other factors. They argue that these factors have increased the structural–frictional component of the problem—the so-called natural unemployment rate—from around 5 percent in the mid-1950s to around 6 percent in the mid-1980s. (The natural rate of unemployment is simply the rate at which it is assumed there is no more slack in the labor market and at which inflation therefore begins to accelerate.)

There is some credibility to the argument that demographic factors—especially the large influx of youth and women into the labor market—have had an influence. But as the baby boomers age and as women become more permanently attached to the labor force, the natural unemployment rate should decline toward 5 percent by the end of the decade.[5]

There is little evidence that nondemographic factors (for example, income transfers, trade, technology) have contributed very significantly to the increase in the natural rate. Unemployment insurance increases the level of unemployment but has not contributed to its upward trend. Productivity growth—the best indicator we have of technological change—declined rather than accelerated during the 1970s; so if technological unemployment is a problem it is not a new one. Increased foreign competition was not the primary cause of declining employment in manufacturing over the past decade; the real culprits have been increased U.S. productivity in that sector (reducing the work force needed for a given output), slowly rising domestic demand for manufactured goods, and, most recently, an overvalued dollar (Lawrence 1983). Even the demographic explanation for increased unemployment is of diminishing importance. By 1990, the teenage share of the labor force will be back where it was in the 1950s. And while the female share continues to rise, adult women currently have unemployment rates that are little higher than those of adult men, so the number of them who choose to work does not affect the overall unemployment rate very much.[6]

If increasing structural unemployment was not the explanation for the upward trend in the unemployment rate during the 1970s and early 1980s, what was? The answer is the tendency of policymakers to rely on high unemployment as an antidote to inflation. Inflation, in turn, is often the result of external price shocks introduced into an economy where relative wages and prices are not very flexible, so that an increase in prices in one sector is not necessarily offset by price declines in other sectors (Johnson discusses this explanation in chapter 2). Back in the 1950s and 1960s we were able to reduce the unemployment rate to around 4 percent without causing undue inflation. But during these two decades, food and import prices were rising more slowly than the consumer price index, thus exerting a downward drag on the inflation rate that helped to compensate for any upward pressure generated by excess demand in the labor market. In retrospect, it is clear that without these favorable price trends, we could not have reduced the unemployment rate below about 5 percent without generating inflation. Similarly favorable price trends during the early 1980s were one reason the economy was able to expand so rapidly without any resurgence of inflation, but such good luck will not continue indefinitely. Conversely, the major factor responsible for the secular rise in the unemployment rate during the 1970s was the need to maintain some economic slack to offset large and unexpected increases in inflation associated with oil and food price shocks, and the declining value of the dollar.[7]

Faced with these price developments, the Federal Reserve had two choices. It could offset the drain of higher prices on people's purchasing power by expanding the money supply, and thereby preventing—with lower interest rates—a rise in unemployment; but such a policy also brings higher inflation. Alternatively, the Federal Reserve could allow unemployment to rise enough to offset the price shocks, in other words, enlisting American workers in the fight against oil price inflation. In fact, it chose to do some of both, which is why the 1970s were plagued by both high unemployment and high inflation, and why some analysts looking at the data from this period have concluded that the unemployment rate necessary to keep inflation in check was as high as 7 percent.[8]

In sum, we have not been suffering from large increases in structural unemployment. We have been suffering from intentional cyclical unemployment—a slowing of the economy with a resulting shortage of jobs—designed to discipline the inflation process. Macroeconomic policy is increasingly driven by a fear of inflation, a fear that has grown in the aftermath of the 1970s' experience with a price explosion that seemed to have gotten out of control. This inflation did not, by and large, have its origins in the labor market, but price inflation has had profound consequences for our willingness to produce enough jobs for all those who want to work.

Three observations flow from this macroeconomic view of unemployment. First, the early 1980s have been more like the 1950s than the 1970s in the sense that the prices of imports and basic commodities such as oil have been subtracting from rather than adding to the underlying inflation rate. With lower commodity or import prices, employment can be stimulated by the Federal Reserve or Congress with correspondingly less impact on inflation. Conversely, any new burst of inflation caused by excessive deficits, a decline in the value of the dollar, or a shortage of some basic commodity will require another recession—or a long period of higher unemployment—to contain it.

Second, employment and training programs are largely powerless to combat high levels of cyclical unemployment, although if properly designed and coordinated with macroeconomic policy they can reduce the natural unemployment rate a little and permit more overall stimulus to be applied. The theory here is that fiscal stimulus targeted on particular groups of unemployed or underemployed workers or sectors of the economy is less inflationary than across-the-board stimulus, because the latter tends to bid up wage levels among already employed workers whereas the former does not. Indeed, we have never fully tested the potential of appropriately targeted job creation programs (including employment tax credits aimed at inducing an expansion of jobs in the private sector) to work around or change the inflation constraint on macroeconomic policy. The New Jobs Tax Credit in effect in 1977–78 is an exception. It provided tax subsidies to private employers who expanded employment levels beyond a base level. As Eisner notes in chapter 3, evaluations of the program suggest that it was effective both in increasing employment and reducing inflation.

Third, the best employment policy (apart from benign neglect of inflation) may be an effective incomes (wage–price) policy or other measures that do not place the full burden of fighting inflation on macroeconomic restraint. However, past experiences with incomes policies—which tend to reduce inflation only temporarily—suggest they are no panacea.[9] Improving the functioning of labor markets could also help—a topic to which I return in the discussion of the fourth employment objective below.

Once macroeconomic policy has reduced unemployment to 5 or 6 percent, what should we do, if anything, for those who are still unemployed? A large portion of those out of work when the unemployment rate falls to this level are simply between jobs or between school and work, and thus experiencing only short, often voluntary, spells of "frictional" unemployment. During periods of general prosperity, the unemployment numbers at any point are dominated by the frictionally unemployed. In mid-1988 almost half of those unemployed in any month had been out of work less than 5 weeks and three-quarters for less than 15 weeks (Bureau of Labor Statistics). As Bendick notes in chapter 4, providing more labor market information and more job search assistance can presumably reduce such frictional unemployment, and a variety of ways of achieving this—such as replacing or improving the publicly operated Job Service—could be examined (Stevens 1984; National Council on Employment Policy 1985).

More pressing is the problem of longer-term structural unemployment. From an analytical perspective, structural unemployment (and its frictional and cyclical complements) is a mushy concept. Presumably it includes all those people who have a hard time finding a job even when the economy is operating at full employment. In a full-employment economy, there are about as many vacancies as there are people looking for work, but because these people have the wrong skills or are in the wrong place a match does not take place. If we use as a crude estimate of structural unemployment the 23 percent of those who sought jobs for 15 weeks or more in mid-1988, then 1 to 2 percentage points of total unemployment could be labeled as structural—more if discouraged workers were included. This group of long-term unemployed is disproportionately male, black, and between 25 and 64 years old.[10]

Structural unemployment is sometimes equated with being disadvantaged—that is, coming from a low-income family—but this is a looser definition of the term. Clarity calls for separating the two problems, especially since there is not necessarily a high correlation between them. For example, of the 23.8 million people who experienced some unemployment during 1983, only about 23 percent lived in families with incomes below the poverty level (Sehgal 1985). Probably the best example of structural unemployment is the group known as dislocated workers. They are not necessarily poor. They can be the victims of economic change even in an era of overall prosperity. And their problems are location, skills, and the wage levels they are accustomed to.

The issue of wages (and the other terms of employment, including location) is critical. Conservatives argue, with some merit, that there are always jobs available somewhere *at some wage*. It is this fact that makes the whole concept of involuntary structural unemployment both subjective and controversial. Customary and legal minimums may prevent workers from offering to work at low wages, and we know from experiments with 100 percent wage subsidies that some job seekers are denied work even at a zero wage. Other job seekers have clearly priced themselves out of the market by almost anyone's standards, or are unemployed because they are unwilling to move to a new location. In between are a much larger number who cannot find work—at least not quickly—at the prevailing or customary wage for their occupation.

When we count the unemployed we lump all these groups together. Yet the average citizen understands that not all are equally deserving or in need of assistance, and as a result the consensus for positive action tends to break down. If we could find a way to make finer distinctions, the consensus might be rebuilt.

Suppose, for example, that a program was designed that would offer all participants a fully or partially subsidized temporary apprenticeship (in either the public or the private sector) that paid the minimum wage or slightly less (see Sawhill 1985c). Such a program would have a number of distinct advantages. It would increase the political acceptability of the jobs program among voters who are concerned about government programs that entitle participants to benefits with no quid pro quo. (The quo here is acceptance of a low wage and willingness to be trained.) It would be anti-inflationary by helping to hold down labor costs and thereby consistent with additional macroeconomic stimulus. It would serve only those highly motivated to work and clearly in need of assistance. It would cost the taxpayers less than past programs and it would cost the economy nothing since people with other employment alternatives would not be attracted into the program. In other words, it would provide jobs only for the "truly unemployable," and any output they produced would be a net addition to the gross national product. There would, of course, be complaints about undercutting existing wage standards, but then we must decide whether we are more concerned about unemployment or the wages of the employed.[11] The program would not provide enough income to support a family, but it would be a start and could be supplemented by the earnings of a spouse or by income transfers, or by the Earned Income Tax Credit (a refundable tax credit available to working poor families with children).

If implemented on an experimental basis, such a program could help resolve the old debate about whether there are, or are not, enough jobs. A low take-up rate would tend to support the conservative view that involuntary unemployment is partly voluntary. But a high take-up rate—as happened in the Youth Incentive Entitlement Program, a 1970s demonstration jobs program for disadvantaged youth—would suggest the problem really is one of not enough jobs.

It is often argued that in addition to directly providing jobs for the structurally unemployed, we should educate, train, or retrain them so that they can fill existing vacancies. This strategy has proved reasonably successful with women on welfare and dislocated workers (see chapter 5 by Barnow). However, the evaluation literature suggests that where training programs have been effective in helping people obtain jobs, it has been because the programs have served more of a placement than skills-enhancing function (see Taggart 1981). The risk in this case is that unemployment will be reshuffled rather than reduced.

CREATING MORE GOOD JOBS

People want "good" jobs—well-paid, secure, and with adequate fringe benefits and working conditions. Historically, very bad jobs have been legislated out of existence through wage and hour laws and health and safety standards. Collective bargaining has secured still further benefits for many workers. Accounts of factory conditions around the turn of the century remind us of how much has been accomplished by such efforts—no more child labor, a lower rate of industrial accidents, a much shorter work week, and a variety of protections against arbitrary actions by employers (Lipson 1981).

But increases in productivity are what ultimately permit higher wages, more fringe benefits, or a shorter work week. Without increased productivity, higher wages for some workers can only generate lower wages for others or bring more inflation, thus eroding the purchasing power of any wage gains.

Productivity increases since the turn of the century have made possible a fourfold increase in real wages for skilled workers. Even since 1947, productivity and real hourly compensation have more than doubled.

By now it has become almost a cliché to note that investments in people improve productivity as much as investments in plant and equipment. Statistical studies indicate that education has been as important a source of productivity growth as increased capital formation over the past 35 years (Denison 1979).

At the beginning of the 1980s, the nation was spending about $120 billion for education and training. About half of these outlays were for elementary and secondary education and a little over a quarter was for higher education. Another big chunk was spent by private business and industry and by the federal government to train their own employees. Only about $14 billion, or 6 percent, went for other federal training and training-related programs (Sawhill 1983). These figures make it clear that it is our system of public and private education that will most likely determine future productivity. Federal training programs, as currently constituted, have a much more specialized role to play in providing second-chance opportunities for the disadvantaged, as discussed more fully below.

Now that about 86 percent of young people complete at least a high school education and over one-fifth graduate from college, attention has begun to shift from the amount of education we are providing to its content. The quality of public education in this country has been extensively criticized in a number of recent reports, and the states have begun to move aggressively to meet these criticisms.

There has been far less interest in investing more in the mid-career education and training of adults. The arguments for public investment in this area are threefold. First, employers tend to underinvest in training relative to what they invest in plant and equipment because workers—unlike machines—are mobile and employers cannot be sure of capturing the return on human resource investments. Second, in a global economy the quality of a nation's work force may become its major source of international competitiveness since capital and technology flow across national borders with relative ease. Finally, to the extent that the economy of the future is built on services and technology rather than on the mass production of goods, a skilled and educated labor force becomes the nation's most strategic resource.

Any number of mechanisms for encouraging more investment in mid-career education and training have been suggested, including Individual Training Accounts, requirements that industry invest a certain amount every year (as in France), and government-subsidized, in-firm retraining programs during recessions (as in Sweden)

(Bendick and Egan 1982). The major drawback of these plans is cost, especially in the light of some uncertainty about the productivity benefits. On the other hand, no such inhibition has prevented a sizable public investment in plant and equipment via accelerated depreciation, investment tax credits, and preferential treatment for capital gains in the tax code. If the above arguments about our current underinvestment in human resources are correct, these priorities may bear some rethinking.

In the meantime, attention has focused on one particular group of mainstream workers—those who lose their jobs because of international competition, technology, or other structural changes in the economy. Retraining is thought to be one solution to this problem, and several careful studies have shown that it can improve reemployment prospects for such workers. However, these studies also suggest that job search assistance and counseling provide more benefits per dollar of program expenditures than does training. Moreover, there is as yet no hard evidence that the benefits of training for program participants exceed the costs of that training, but this may simply reflect the lack of long-term follow-up in most evaluations.[12]

HELPING THE DISADVANTAGED

A third goal of employment policies is to assist the disadvantaged to move toward self-sufficiency and to acquire a more equitable share of available jobs—good and bad. Specific strategies could involve targeted jobs programs and affirmative action on the demand side or training and remedial education on the supply side.

Although employment and training programs have been increasingly targeted on the disadvantaged since the early 1960s, there is no clear evidence of their success in the aggregate data. The pretransfer poverty rate among the nonaged is higher than at any time since the War on Poverty began.[13] To the extent that poverty has been reduced, it is because of the increased availability of cash and in-kind transfers and not because people are more self-sufficient than in the past. In short while the War on Poverty has reduced the pain of being poor, it has not cured the disease.

In addition to their limited success in moving people toward self-sufficiency, the programs also appear to have failed to produce a more equitable sharing of good and bad jobs. The distribution of earnings and of income actually has become more unequal over the past 20 years. While earnings differentials for whites and blacks have narrowed, differences in the employment rates widened. Almost the reverse seems to be true for women versus men: the male–female employment gap has narrowed but the earnings gap has varied little. Taken at face value, these data suggest women and minorities cannot avoid discrimination; they can only choose what form it will take.

This lack of clear progress as measured by aggregate data needs to be reconciled with evidence that at least some programs targeted on the disadvantaged, or designed to provide more opportunities for women and minorities, have been effective:[14]

□ Women on welfare seem to benefit from work experience, training, and job search assistance. Some recent experiments with workfare have successfully moved public assistance recipients into the labor market and are viewed positively by the recipients.

□ Providing a combination of part-time and summer jobs to in-school youth from low-income families (on the condition that they remain in, or return to, school) increases their employment and earnings while they are enrolled in the program.

□ The Job Corps, an intensive program of remedial education, skills training, health care, and other supportive services for very disadvantaged youth, is frequently cited for its high benefit–cost ratio.

□ Statistical studies of the effects of Equal Employment Opportunity Commission enforcement of Title VII and Office of Federal Contract Compliance Programs enforcement of the executive orders requiring nondiscrimination among federal contractors suggest that these efforts have probably had a modest impact on the employment and earnings of blacks and women, although the effects are clearest in the case of black male employment.[15]

Why have these successes not translated into more observed progress for disadvantaged youth, welfare mothers, or women and minorities more generally? There are a number of possible explanations with quite different policy implications.

□ *The programs have been a drop in the bucket compared to the need.* Employment and training programs have never served more than 10 percent of the eligible population. We have relied instead on income transfers as our major weapon in the War on Poverty. Currently, the Job Training Partnership Act, which is almost exclusively targeted on the disadvantaged, is estimated to be serving only

3 to 4 percent of the eligible population.[16] What is needed is an expansion in scale.

□ *Many of the programs have been relatively ineffective.* Examples would include short-term work experience programs for youth, and some early workfare programs. What is needed is reform, involving a replacement of less with more effective program models and better management.

□ *Even seemingly successful programs provide only temporary gains in employment and earnings that fade after a few years—or gains for participants that are offset by losses for equally disadvantaged nonparticipants.* Even well-designed evaluations have not been able to demonstrate success on this more stringent set of criteria, so it is possible that expanding the scope of even "good" programs might not produce all of the desired results. What may be needed is new or more comprehensive approaches based on a more sophisticated diagnosis of the underlying problems. For example, employment programs do not necessarily reduce the incidence of drug abuse, crime, and adolescent pregnancies among disadvantaged youth; yet it is these that may most impair their life chances.

□ *Even the best and most generously funded programs can be swamped by a bad economy or adverse demographic trends.* A deteriorating economy since the late 1960s explains much of the rise in pretransfer poverty rates, increasing income inequality, and poorer labor market prospects for new entrants, especially young black males whose unemployment has always been highly sensitive to macroeconomic conditions. At the same time, the baby boom, the rising labor force participation of women, and a flood of new immigrants have increased competition for entry-level jobs and have depressed wages or increased unemployment for those seeking these jobs. And the growth of female-headed families contributed to the increase in poverty rates and to widening disparities in the incomes of black and white families, despite some narrowing of earnings differentials by race.

The above four explanations for why employment policies have not been more successful in addressing poverty, dependency, and inequality are not mutually exclusive and I suspect all have been at work.

IMPROVING THE FUNCTIONING OF LABOR MARKETS

The overwhelming economic and social dependence of most people on their jobs has given rise to demands for protective labor laws; job

security; anitdiscrimination measures; retirement, disability, and unemployment insurance; pension rights; and so on. Some of these
protections have been achieved through collective bargaining and
some through legislation. Interestingly, while union influence appears to be on the decline and the federal government is retreating
from its formerly activist role in these areas, state governments are
becoming an increasingly important actor (Beyond Unions 1985).
Most significant perhaps are new court rulings and state laws that
challenge an employer's right to dismiss an employee at will and
that establish instead the concept of an implicit employment contract
enforceable in the courts. Also significant are an expansion of laws
prohibiting mandatory retirement, specifying that employees be informed about hazardous substances, and requiring notice of plant
shutdowns as well as severance pay for laid-off workers.

There are no easy solution to this tension between equity and efficiency. While these protections are welcomed by most affected workers
and their advocates, others view them as a source of economic inefficiency. They worry that if the United States continues down this
road it will develop the kind of sclerosis found in many European
countries where advance notice for shutdowns, extensive paid leave,
and severance pay are commonplace (Magaziner and Reich 1983).
Laws or regulations that make dismissals or layoffs costly, for example, make it more difficult for employers to adjust to changing
market demand. The paperwork and other burdens often associated
with various regulations (affirmative action, ERISA, occupational
health and safety) increase the costs of doing business. And extensive
governmental safety nets for the unemployed, the disabled, and the
retired can clearly affect incentives to work for beneficiaries and
taxpayers alike.

There is no easy solution to this tension between equity and efficiency. Some balancing of costs and benefits in each case would
seem appropriate, but I have seen little research that evaluates what
kind of a balance we have struck with current policies in many of
these areas.[17] It is impossible to eliminate—by the clumsy tool of
law or regulation—all occupational hazards, all discrimination, and
all unfair dismissals without paying some economic price. The challenge would seem to be to find more flexible, less costly remedies
and to weigh more carefully the cost against the benefits. As for the
broad-based social insurance programs that currently loom so large
in the federal budget, there is an extensive body of literature on their
economic effects, and the way these effects depend on program design. A program-by-program, or regulation-by-regulation, examination of costs and benefits is beyond the scope of this chapter. What

may be more useful is to raise some broader questions about the industrial relations system that has, in a more fundamental sense, produced the conflict between equity and efficiency. Indeed, it can be argued that it is our labor market institutions that are at least partially responsible for many of the problems I have been discussing and that real progress will require systemic reform.

In a nonindustrialized economy of self-employed farmers and artisans, there would be no labor market and thus no need to worry about unemployment, rates of pay, terms of employment, and relationships between workers and managers. The current labor market and industrial relations system evolved as a requirement of a modern economy built on the principles of specialization and large-scale production. Under the banner of scientific management known as Taylorism that was in vogue around the turn of the century, these principles of specialization and large-scale production were pushed to their limits. They served to greatly increase productivity and standards of living at a time when most of the labor force was both poor and poorly educated by today's standards, and the cost-reducing benefits of large-scale industrial technology were enormous. But the system also treated workers like cogs in a machine and eventually gave rise to a powerful union movement and a wide range of demands for employee rights and protections.

This history has bequeathed us an industrial relations system far less democratic than the polity it inhabits, that pits management against labor, that treats individual workers as largely interchangeable units of production, and that assumes capital and technology are the engines of growth. As many have noted, it is a dysfunctional system in a world where the labor force is highly educated and seeking a variety of rewards in addition to a day's pay for a day's work; where the shift from producing standardized goods to unstandardized goods, services, and information makes it far harder to monitor performance and puts more of a premium on employee skills, motivation, and initiative; and where capital and technology are widely available and thus not the key to remaining competitive in world markets.

Realization of this fact has created, in recent years, a movement for workplace reform. Variously termed *the new industrial relations,* improving *the quality of working life,* or simply *productivity through people,* the concept encompasses a broad array of efforts to increase employee satisfaction and productivity through such mechanisms as incentive pay plans, quality circles, worker participation in corporate decision making, and new styles of corporate leadership. Some of which typically accounts for 5 percent to 10 percent of total compensation. Moreover, many of these plans are retirement-oriented, deferred profit-sharing schemes rather than immediate cash distribution plans (Weitzman 1984, 80–81).

In a recent book entitled *The Share Economy*, Martin Weitzman spells out the social and economic effects that would follow from the widespread use of such gain sharing. Productivity and standards of living would be higher (although earnings would be more variable). Involuntary unemployment would be virtually eliminated and inflation would be lower. Employers would take far more interest in their employees, and discrimination would tend to disappear.[19]

It would be surprising if these claims were not met with skepticism, especially since the mechanism which causes all these good things to occur is too esoteric for the average person to comprehend easily.[20] But the idea of a share economy deserves a serious hearing.

SUMMARY AND CONCLUSIONS

The objectives of employment policy include lowering unemployment, increasing productivity and wages, assisting the disadvantaged (reducing poverty), and making the operation of the labor market fairer and more efficient. These are ambitious objectives that involve difficult trade-offs. It would be relatively easy to increase employment if we did not have to worry about inflation, relatively easy to reduce poverty if we did not have to worry about the costs of dependency, and relatively easy to achieve greater labor market efficiency if we did not have to worry about the human costs.

Perhaps the most difficult trade-off is the one between employment and wages. We could undoubtedly create more jobs if Americans were willing to accept lower wages. Alternatively, we could push up wage levels at the risk of creating more unemployment. This choice becomes especially acute in an economy open to increased foreign competition. Our standard of living is threatened by the millions of people in the less-developed or newly industrialized parts of the world willing to do, for less pay, the same work that we do. Of course, higher wages would not necessarily lead to greater unemployment if they were accompanied by some combination of protectionism that shielded us from import competition, a stimulative fiscal and monetary policy that reemployed displaced workers, or a decline in the value of the dollar that made even seemingly high-priced goods competitive in foreign markets. But each of these responses would, for different reasons,[21] ultimately lead to an erosion of the purchasing power of those higher wages and thus a deterioration in real standards of living. They are temporary solutions at best.

In the long run, if we are to solve the employment problem we must first solve the inflation problem. As long as unemployment is the only antidote to inflation, it will be tolerated as a necessary evil. My view is that solving the inflation problem may require major reforms in our industrial relations system but that much more debate and discussion will be needed if we are to move in that direction. In the meantime, it is clear that the unemployment rate can be lowered to between 5 or 6 percent without worrying about the inflationary consequences. In addition, something could be achieved by improving the efficiency of the process by which workers and jobs are matched. And, as a matter of equity, we should provide jobs for the truly unemployed, and adjustment assistance for displaced workers.

Ultimately, people want not just jobs but higher real pay, better working conditions, and more job security. It will be difficult, if not impossible, to achieve any lasting gains on this front unless productivity continues to improve. This will require more investment in human resources through education and on-the-job training as well as better management or utilization of people, including additional experiments with various forms of industrial democracy. It will also require a careful balancing of the costs and benefits of various kinds of protective labor legislation.

Creating more jobs or better paying jobs would tend to benefit everyone, but special efforts are needed to assist the most disadvantaged. Many past efforts—though small in scale—have been quite successful in moving young people or welfare recipients into jobs. The fact that such problems as youth unemployment, poverty, and welfare dependency remain is related more to adverse economic and demographic developments than it is to the shortcomings of the programs themselves.

Finally, the limitations of a free-enterprise ideology are nowhere clearer than in the case of the labor market. Where market outcomes are not to people's liking, the political system will, and should, prevail. While all such political interventions are well-intended and many are, on balance, socially beneficial, some produce cures that are worse than the disease. Nevertheless, political give-and-take is the only way to resolve the difficult trade-offs, and an informed debate is the only protection against faulty remedies.

Notes

1. What Congress finally enacted was a cut of 61 percent relative to prior law. Excluding public service employment (PSE), the proposed and enacted reductions were 48 percent and 36 percent, respectively. See Palmer and Sawhill (1984, 185).

2. The low estimate is from Bendick and Devine (1981) and covers all able-bodied adult job losers unemployed for more than 26 weeks in 1980 whose previous job was in a declining industry. The higher estimate is from the Congressional Budget Office (1982), and covers job losers in January 1983 from declining industries, plus all other unemployed persons in the region if that region was in a decline. The middle estimate of 1 million is an annualized estimate from the Bureau of Labor Statistics' special study of displaced workers and covers all those who lost a job between January 1979 and January 1984 because of a plant closure or move, slack work, or abolishment of a shift or position—and whose tenure on their previous job was at least three years. Given that the economy was in recession over much of this period, the long-term structural problem could be smaller than this.

3. See Rosenthal (1985); and Levitan and Carlson (1984). For a different view, see Kuttner (1983).

4. For a comparative perspective, see Haveman and Saks (1985).

5. For a more detailed discussion, see Sawhill (March 1985). See also Baily (1984).

6. For more detail, see Sawhill (March 1985); and Sawhill (1981)

7. Some of the inflation of the 1970s did result from overly tight labor markets. President Nixon allowed the economy to overheat in the early 1970s and President Carter may have made the same mistake in the late 1970s.

8. Other analysis, such as Gordon (1984)—after adjusting for the influence of price shocks on inflation—estimate that the unemployment rate consistent with no acceleration of inflation was about 6 percent.

9. For a detailed review, see Sawhill (1981).

10. Many people think the level of structural unemployment is higher than this but they are usually confusing cyclical and structural unemployment— something that is easy to do since they are not totally distinct categories.

11. It would have to be available to all to prevent displacement of noneligible by eligible workers.

12. For a more complete review, see Stone and Sawhill (1986).

13. From a low of 13 percent in 1969, it was 19.3 percent in 1983 and 16.6 percent in 1984. See Danziger, et al. (1986).

14. For reviews of the literature, see Bassi and Ashenfelter (1986); Taggart (1981); National Council on Employment Policy (1984); Wiseman (1985); and Reskin and Hartmann (1985).

15. For reviews of the literature, see Reskin and Hartmann (1985).

16. These estimates are from the Congressional Research Service.

17. However, for an excellent review of three areas where protective labor legislation is now being proposed—employment at will, comparable worth, and plant closings— see Ehrenberg's discussion in chapter 6 of this volume.

18. O'Toole (1981); Goodman (1980); General Accounting Office (1981); Levitan and Werneke (1984); Levitan and Johnson (1982); New York Stock Exchange (1982); Work in America Institute (1982).

19. In Weitzman (1984): "The welfare of a firm's workers will vie with the quality of its products as an important goal. The worker's greatest protection is his power to get a job elsewhere—that threat can do more to improve working conditions than legislation, standards, or collective militancy . . . (and) permanent excess demand for labor can do more to reduce or eliminate nonfunctional discrimination in the job market than all of the regulations, quotas, and affirmative action programs currently in existence" (121–22).

20. The essence is that the extra cost of hiring an additional worker is always less than the extra revenue the worker produces, leading to unlimited demand for labor.

21. Protectionism saves some jobs but increases the prices that consumers must pay for both domestic and imported goods. More stimulative fiscal and monetary policy can be used to create any number of jobs but, in the absence of productivity improvements or existing economic slack, will be inflationary. A large enough decline in the value of the dollar would enable us to undersell all of our foreign competitors, but would also lower the returns we received for our exports while raising the prices of things we import.

References

Baily, Martin N. May 1984. The Problem of Unemployment in the United States. In *Alternatives for the 1980's: Jobs for the Future: Strategies in a New Framework* 13. Washington: Center for National Policy.

Barnow, Burt S. June 1985. The Education, Training, and Work Experience of the Adults Labor Force from 1984 to 1995. Washington: National Commission for Employment Policy, Research Report Series 85–10.

———. September 1985. Government Training as a Means of Reducing Unemployment. Paper presented at Rethinking Employment Policy, a conference sponsored by The Project on the Federal Social Role and held at The Urban Institute, Washington.

Bassi, Laurie J., and Orley Ashenfelter. 1986. The Effect of Direct Job Creation and Training Programs on Low-Skilled Workers. In *Fighting Poverty: What Works and What Doesn't*, edited by Sheldon Danziger and Daniel Weinberg. Cambridge, Mass.: Harvard University Press.

Bendick, Jr., Marc. September 1985. Matching Workers and Job Opportunities: What Should Be the Federal Role? Paper presented at Rethinking Employment Policy, a conference sponsored by The Project the ideas have been borrowed from Japan and some from successful American companies such as IBM, Proctor and Gamble, and Hewlett-Packard.

Because of the amorphous nature of these experiments, it is hard to say what they have accomplished. Although there appears to be a correlation between corporate performance and innovative human resource programs, it is not clear which is cause and which is effect (Kanter 1983). Experts in the field point out that there have been many failures as well as successes and that much depends on how such efforts are conceived and implemented.[18] Some union leaders worry that they are a new and more subtle strategy for exploiting workers, while others have endorsed the concept.

In principle, these new approaches to managing people have the potential to fundamentally alter the functioning of the labor market and the economy. In a total workplace democracy where responsibilities and rewards were fully shared, distinctions between employers and employees would become blurred and the interests of firms and their workers would coincide. Then, just as in the economy of self-employed farmers, there would presumably be no involuntary unemployment (though incomes would fall if there were no market for the product), no shirking of responsibility, no failure to apply new insights to the production process, no exploitation of workers by managers, and no need for government to regulate the terms and conditions of employment.

Is this a utopia? Yes, but it provides a glimpse of how we might move beyond patchwork solutions to many of our current problems. Moreover, some movement in this direction is evident in the new arrangements being worked out between labor and management in General Motors' Saturn project—a project, which if successful, may be widely copied (Edid 1985).

Most significantly, interest has focused recently on gain-sharing systems that provide financial incentives to employees based on some measure of firm or group performance. In Japan, for example, industrial workers receive semiannual bonuses that average one-quarter of their total pay and can go as high as one-half of total pay. Many believe that this system, together with other much-discussed features of the Japanese industrial relations system, such as lifetime employment and a relatively egalitarian and employee-oriented workplace, are partially responsible for Japan's economic success (Marshall 1984; Weitzman 1984, 76).

In the United States, group incentive schemes are less extensively used. Perhaps 15 percent of firms use some form of incentive pay on the Federal Social Role and held at The Urban Institute, Washington. (Revised version is chapter 4 of this volume.)

Bendick, Jr., Marc, and Mary Lou Egan. 1982. Recycling America's Workers: Public and Private Approaches to MidCareer Retraining. Washington: Urban Institute Press.

Bendick, Jr., Marc, and Judith Radlinski Devine. October 1981. Workers Dislocated by Economic Change: Do They Need Federal Employment and Training Assistance? *Seventh Annual Report: The Federal Interest in Employment and Training.* Washington: National Commission for Employment Policy.

Beyond Unions: A Revolution in Employee Rights is in the Making. 8 July 1985. *Business Week.*

Brown, Charles, Curtis Gilroy, and Andrew Kohen. June 1982. The Effect of the Minimum Wage on Employment and Unemployment. *The Journal of Economic Literature* 20(2).

Burck, Charles G. 15 June 1981. Working Smarter. *Fortune.*

Carnevale, Anthony P. 1985. *Jobs for the Nation: Challenges for a Society Based on Work.* Alexandria, Va.: American Society for Training and Development.

Clark, Peter K. 1984. Productivity and Profits in the 1980s: Are They Really Improving. *Brookings Papers on Economic Activity* 1984:1. Washington: Brookings Institution.

Congressional Budget Office. July 1982. *Dislocated Workers: Issues and Federal Options.* Washington.

Danziger, Sheldon, Robert Haveman, and Robert Plotnick. 1986. AntiPoverty Policy: Effects on the Poor and the Nonpoor. In *Fighting Poverty: What Works and What Doesn't,* edited by Sheldon Danziger and Daniel Weinberg. Cambridge, Mass.: Harvard University Press.

Danziger, Sheldon, and Daniel Weinberg, eds. 1986. *Fighting Poverty: What Works and What Doesn't.* Cambridge, Mass.: Harvard University Press.

Denison, Edward F. 1979. *Accounting for Slower Economic Growth: The United States in the 1970s.* Washington: Brookings Institution.

Economic Report of the President. 1983. Washington.

Edid, Maralyn. 5 August 1985. How Power Will Be Balanced on Saturn's Shop Floor. *Business Week.*

Ehrenberg, Ronald G. September 1985. Workers' Rights: Rethinking Protective Labor Legislation. Paper presented at Rethinking Employment Policy, a conference sponsored by The Project on the Federal Social Role and held at The Urban Institute, Washington.

Eisner, Robert. September 1985. Employer Approaches to Reducing Unemployment. Paper presented at a conference on Rethinking Employment Policy, sponsored by The Project on the Federal Social Role and held at The Urban Institute, Washington.

General Accounting Office. 3 March 1981. *Productivity Sharing Programs:*

Can They Contribute to Productivity Improvement. Gaithersburg, Md.: GAO, AFMD-81–22.

Goodman, Jr., John L. 1983. *Public Opinion during the Reagan Administration: National Issues, Private Concerns.* Washington: Urban Institute Press.

Goodman, Paul S. August 1980. Realities of Improving the Quality of Work Life: Quality of Work Life Projects in the 1980s. *Labor Law Journal.*

Gordon, Robert J. 1984. Unemployment and Potential Output in the 1980s. *Brookings Papers on Economic Activity* 1984:2. Washington: Brookings Institution.

Haveman, Robert H., and Daniel H. Saks. Winter 1985. Transatlantic Lessons for Employment and Training Policy. *Industrial Relations* 24(1).

Hovey, Harold A. January 1985. *The Role of Federal Tax Policy in Employment Policy.* Washington: Center for Policy Research, National Governors' Association.

Kanter, Rosabeth Moss. 1983. *The Change Masters: Innovation for Productivity in the American Corporation.* New York: Simon and Schuster.

Kuttner, Bob. July 1983. The Declining Middle. *Atlantic Monthly* 25(1).

Lawrence, Robert Z. 1983. Is Trade Deindustrializing America? A Medium-Term Prospective. *Brookings Papers on Economic Activity* 1983:1. Washington: Brookings Institution.

Levitan, Sar A., and Peter E. Carlson. 25 June 1984. The Eroding Middle Class: A New Idea. Washington: Center for Social Policy Studies.

Levitan, Sar A., and Clifford M. Johnson. 1982. *Second Thoughts on Work.* Kalamazoo, Mich.: W.E. Upjohn Institute for Employment Research.

Levitan, Sar A., and Diane Werneke. 1984. *Productivity: Problems, Prospects, and Policies.* Baltimore: Johns Hopkins University Press.

Lipson, Samuel. 1981. Bread and Water. In *Working Changes and Choices,* edited by James O'Toole, Jane L. Scheiber, and Linda C. Wood. New York: Human Sciences Press.

Magaziner, Ira C., and Robert B. Reich. 1983. *Minding America's Business: The Decline and Rise of the American Economy.* New York: Vintage Books.

Mangum, Garth L. 1976. *Employability, Employment, and Income: A Reassessment of Manpower Policy.* Salt Lake City, Utah: Olympus Publishing Company.

Marshall, Ray. 15 November 1984. Employment and Industrial Relations Systems. Paper for The Economic Policy Council of the United Nations Association Jobs Panel.

Minimum Wage Study Commission. June 1981. *Report of the Minimum Wage Study Commission* 6. Washington.

National Commission for Manpower Policy. October 1978. *Work Time and Employment.* Special Report no. 28. Washington.

National Council on Employment Policy. May 1985. *Policy Statement on* the United States Employment Service. Washington: National Council on Employment Policy.

————. August 1984. *Investing in America's Future*, Washington: National Council on Employment Policy.

————. 11 May 1981. The New Industrial Relations. *Business Week*.

New York Stock Exchange, Office of Economic Research. 1982. *People and Productivity: A Challenge to Corporate America*. New York.

Office of Technology Assessment. April 1985. Preventing Illness and Injury in the Workplace. *OTA Report Brief*. Washington.

O'Toole, James. 10 August 1981. How Management Hinders Productivity. *Industry Week*.

Palmer, John L., and Isabel V. Sawhill, eds. 1984. *The Reagan Record: An Assessment of America's Changing Domestic Priorities*. Cambridge, Mass.: Ballinger Publishing Company.

Public Agenda Foundation. Fall 1983. *Putting the Work Ethic to Work: The Public Agenda Foundation*. New York.

Reskin, Barbara F., and Heidi I. Hartmann, eds. 1985. *Women's Work, Men's Work: Sex Segregation on the Jobs*. Washington: National Academy of Sciences Press.

Rosenthal, Neal H. March 1985. The Shrinking Middle Class: Myth or Reality? *Monthly Labor Review*.

Samuelson, Robert J. 1 March 1983. Change to Refashion or Doom Unionism. *Washington Post*.

————. 3 July 1985. Labor's Bleak Outlook. *Washington Post*.

Sawhill, Isabel V. September 1981a. The Full Employment Unemployment Rate. Washington: Urban Institute.

————. September 1981b. Incomes Policies. Washington: Urban Institute.

————. 1983. Human Resource Policies for the 1980s. In *The Regrowing of the American Economy*, edited by G. William Miller. Englewood Cliffs, N.J.: Prentice Hall.

————. 19 March 1985. Unemployment and Poverty: Can We Do Better? Testimony before the U.S. Congress, House Subcommittee on Banking, Finance, and Urban Affairs.

————. 20 June 1985. The President's Tax Proposals: Impacts on Fairness, Families, Federalism, and Future Growth. Testimony before the U.S. Congress, House Ways and Means Committee.

————. July 1985. Jobs for the Truly Unemployed. Washington: Urban Institute.

Sehgal, Ellen. August 1985. Employment Problems and Their Effect on Family Income, 1979–83. *Monthly Labor Review*, Research Summaries.

Stevens, David W. September 1984. Public- and Private-Employment Agency Roles in Providing Labor Market Information and Job Search Assistance: Past, Present and Future. Columbia, Mo.: Human Resource Data Systems.

Stone, Charles F., and Isabel V. Sawhill. June 1986. *Labor Market Implication of the Growing Internationalization of the U.S. Economy.* National Commission for Employment Policy, Research Report Series, RR-86–20.

Survey Research Center. July 1985. *Surveys of Consumer Attitudes.* Ann Arbor: Survey Research Center.

Taggart, Robert. 1981. *A Fisherman's Guide: An Assessment of Training and Remediation Strategies.* Kalamazoo, Mich.: W.E. Upjohn Institute for Employment Research.

Thurow, Lester C. 1983. *Dangerous Currents: The State of Economics.* New York: Random House.

U.S. Department of Labor, Bureau of Labor Statistics. July 1985. *Displaced Workers, 1979–83,* Bulletin 2240. Washington.

U.S. Department of Labor. 1980. *Exchanging Earnings for Leisure: Findings of an Exploratory National Survey on Work Time Preferences,* R&D Monograph 79. Washington.

Weitzman, Martin L. 1984. *The Share Economy: Conquering Stagflation.* Cambridge, Mass.: Harvard University Press.

Wiseman, Michael. July 1985. Workfare. *California Journal.*

Work in America Institute. 1982. *Productivity through Work Innovations.* Elmsford, New York: Pergamon Press.

Chapter Two

DO WE KNOW ENOUGH ABOUT THE UNEMPLOYMENT PROBLEM TO KNOW WHAT, IF ANYTHING, WILL HELP?

George E. Johnson

The question of the merits of direct labor market intervention to alleviate unemployment, whether cyclical or structural, has not been one of the hot topics of the 1980s. After the very severe recession in the early part of the decade, the overall civilian unemployment rate has fallen very gradually to under 6 percent in 1988. This is about equal to the rate in 1979, the year of the previous peak of the business cycle. It is high by pre-1974 standards, but compared with most West European countries, it is quite remarkable (see table 2.1).

Part of the reason for the reduced emphasis on the unemployment problem is the fact that the political agenda in the United States during the 1980s was dominated by an extremely conservative government. One can, for example, contrast the labor market section of the *Economic Report of the President* for 1978 with that for 1985. The former contained an 18–page discussion of the causes of high unemployment and of the dozens of existing programs designed to do something to lower it. The equivalent section of the 1985 volume was two pages long and called for essentially two policies to reduce unemployment: a reduction in unemployment compensation and the establishment of a youth subminimum wage. Accordingly, real per capita funding of federal employment and training programs fell by approximately 80 percent between 1979 and 1985–86 (see table 2.2). In the space of these seven years, we moved from an optimistically interventionist labor market policy to what might be described as a token effort.

But things have a habit of changing in this country; and, as I argue below, there is a fairly high probability that a more serious labor market policy will be adopted within the next few years. What form this policy will take depends on a host of factors (for example, political power configurations) that are very difficult to predict. It will

Table 2.1 STANDARDIZED UNEMPLOYMENT RATES FOR OECD COUNTRIES, 1975–79 AND 1984

Country	1975–79	1984
Australia	5.5	8.9
Canada	7.5	11.2
France	4.9	9.7
Germany	3.5	8.6
Italy	6.8	10.2
Japan	2.0	2.7
Netherlands	5.3	14.0
Spain	5.8	20.1
Sweden	1.9	3.1
United Kingdom	5.8	13.2
United States	6.9	7.4

Source: Bean, Layard, and Nickell (1985), table 1.

also depend importantly on perceptions at the time the new policies are formulated of (a) what is wrong with labor market institutions, and (b) which programmatic approaches appear to work and which do not.

I should confess at the outset that my message is relatively pessimistic. First, if we do not have a firm answer to *a*, above, there is little chance that we can answer *b*. In other words, it is difficult to know, even with the best available evaluation knowledge, whether or not a particular programmatic approach works. Second, much of the political motivation for introducing and expanding labor market programs is the desire to appear to "do something" when unemployment is unusually high—that is, at or just before the occurrence

Table 2.2 REAL PER CAPITA FUNDING OF EMPLOYMENT AND TRAINING PROGRAMS, 1963 TO 1985–86 (1972 DOLLARS)

	Real $ per capita		Real $ per capita		Real $ per capita
1963	0.40	1971	7.50	1979	28.90
1964	1.00	1972	12.90	1980	21.60
1965	2.90	1973	12.30	1981	16.60
1966	4.20	1974	8.70	1982	9.70
1967	5.10	1975	15.50	1983	8.60
1968	4.80	1976	17.60	1984	6.40
1969	5.90	1977	30.09	1985–86	6.00
1970	7.69	1978	22.00		

Source: Bassi and Ashenfelter (1986). Data for 1985–86 from Office of Management and Budget, personal communication.

of cyclical troughs. In my judgment there is no effective potential role of employment policy in a countercyclical context. A somewhat more convincing case can be made for the use of employment policy to accomplish long-term goals, but it is very difficult to reconcile long-term goals with that of getting as many of the unemployed into jobs as quickly as possible. Moreover, there are many pitfalls associated with the various programmatic approaches to the achievement of long-term objectives, and any rational future labor market policy must address these problems.

THE PROBLEM OF UNEMPLOYMENT

The crux of the problem, as I define it in this chapter, is the issue of whether any direct labor market intervention can increase aggregate employment given the macroeconomic context. (By "labor market intervention" I mean the set of governmental policies including the provision of training, public job provision, and employee and employer incentives.) It is one thing to get someone a job that someone else would have held. Indeed, there may be good reasons to redistribute jobs among the population; but that is not the focus in this chapter. It is quite another thing to get an additional member of the population employed.

Economic theory suggests that in a more or less competitive economy there is a particular rate of unemployment—termed the natural rate of unemployment (NRU)—at which the economy is in equilibrium. In other words, there is an unemployment rate at which all jobs at current wage rates are employed and all people willing to take them at those wage rates are employed (except for the inevitable temporary gaps as available jobs and workers are matched to one another). The supply of jobs, in the parlance of economics, equals the demand for jobs at going wages. If the unemployment rate is reduced below the NRU, inflation is stimulated and the above-normal level of unemployment cannot be sustained. The level of the NRU depends on factors such as size, type, and mobility of the labor force and the presence of any institutional factors that set (and keep) wages higher than a smoothly functioning labor market would set them.

The NRU, also known as the equilibrium rate of unemployment, is a long-run concept. There are, thus, two types of unemployment that labor market policies could, in principle, reduce: cyclical unemployment (by reducing unemployment rates during a recession) and long-term unemployment (by reducing the NRU).

There is an increasing amount of controversy concerning how stable the NRU is over time. By the conventional approach of the 1970s, the NRU is the weighted average of the equilibrium rates of each of the various demographic–occupational groups in the labor force, the value of each of which is determined in large part by the rates of turnover of both workers and jobs. Younger workers tend to have a relatively weak degree of labor market attachment, and, accordingly, the NRU rose through the 1970s as the labor force grew younger and has been falling since the late 1970s as the baby boomers have matured (see Perloff and Wachter 1979). In addition, most indicators of labor market "rigidity"—such as the proportion of workers represented by collective bargaining agreements or in government as opposed to private employment—have fallen, some rather precipitously, during the 1980s. Thus, it is not surprising in light of the received view of labor market behavior that the unemployment rate has returned in 1988 to its 1979 level.

An interesting new approach to the analysis of equilibrium unemployment is based on the hypothesis that behavior and habits prevalent this year may influence those next year. For example, if there is a serious recession that forces a large number of workers into a long spell of inactivity, their skills may deteriorate to the extent that many of them will have severe difficulty obtaining employment during the next recovery. This would imply that the value of the NRU in the current period will not depend simply on structural factors, but also on the previous path of the unemployment rate or, in other words, that unemployment is subect to a hysteresis effect. The evidence on hysteresis is, however, somewhat mixed; it seems to be important in explaining the persistence of high unemployment in Western Europe (and in the United States during the 1930s) but is probably not a very important factor in explaining the U.S. labor market situation at the present time.

There has been an apparent worsening of the NRU in the United States over the past 20 years, although the evidence for the value of the overall unemployment near the peak of the long expansion of the 1980s suggests that the secular worsening may have ended. The severity of unemployment in the trough of the last recession (a high of 10.7 percent at the trough in the fourth quarter of 1982) was higher than at any time since the Great Depression.

Why, then, does the unemployment problem seem to command so little public attention? It may be that the unemployment problem is dwarfed in people's minds by another problem, the productivity slowdown and its depressing effect on real wage growth. As of 1973 the average annual growth of real wages had been about 2 percent for a long time, certainly within the memory of every worker. After 1973 real wage growth virtually disappeared. The average annual rate of growth of real hourly compensation, in the nonfarm business sector from 1973 to 1980 was exactly zero, and from 1980 to 1987 it was 0.45 percent. By contrast, from 1947 to 1973 real wage growth averaged 2.63 percent per year. This implies that, because of *whatever* structural change(s) occurred after 1973, the average annual loss of real wage growth has been 2.4 percent over 14 years. This means that the average real wage in the economy would be 40 percent higher than it is now in the absence of this break in the rate of improvement, or, in other terms, about 28 percent less than it "should" be. Accordingly, a 1 percent rise in the NRU or even a deep recession that raises the overall unemployment rate by 3 to 5 percentage points for a year or two appears somewhat trivial in the face of the break in the trend of the real wage rate.

Even so, if, as is highly likely, there is a sharp rise in the overall unemployment rate at some point over the next few years, the public perception of the relative importance of the unemployment program will surely rise to the point where political promises to expand labor market programs will again be popular. It would seem prudent to prepare for such an eventuality by trying to understand which policies might work under which circumstances. The introduction and expansion of labor market programs have generally occurred in periods of high cyclical unemployment, to alleviate a particular bout of cyclical unemployment. But many programs have also been responsive to perceived long-run problems—low employment and earnings potential of particular groups, the very high unemployment rate of minority youth, the incentive problems of the population dependent on welfare benefits, and so forth. My discussion preserves the distinction between the short and the long run.

COUNTERRECESSIONARY POLICIES

One thing is clear about business cycles: they make the unemployment rate go up and down. But it is fair to say that there is little consensus among economists about just what *causes* business cycles and, accordingly, no consensus about how to avert them. Between the first quarter of 1948 and the first quarter of 1979 there were six episodes of a rise in the unemployment rate followed by a more gradual decline to a cyclical low. The average length of the full cycle in the unemployment rate (low to low) was 19.0 quarters—6.2 quarters of rise and 12.8 quarters of decline. The rise in the unemployment rate from the first quarter of 1979 to the fourth quarter of 1982 (which ignores a very brief, slight recovery in early 1980) was unusually long by postwar standards. The decline in unemployment since 1982 has also lasted an unusually long time (indeed, it threatens the record of the longest peacetime expansion, 1790–96). By historical standards we are therefore "due" for another recession, in fact, long overdue.

If we are going to experience a recession in, say, 1989 and we are going to attempt to use employment policy to alleviate it, now (fall 1988) would be the time to undertake the appropriate planning. The first problem with this is, of course, that the political–budgetary climate of the country has changed during the past decade such that it is highly unlikely that any politicians would find it advantageous to be "out in front" on such programs, but I will ignore this and stick to the economic issues.

The second problem is that we cannot be sure at any time that there will be a recession within any particular point in the future. For example, immediately after the stock market crash of October 1987 the fraction of forecasters who predicted the occurrence of a recession in 1988 rose sharply. Stock market prices are an important component of the Index of Leading Indicators and, based on historical experience, the probability of a downturn by the end of 1988 was over 90 percent. If this were an era of activist labor market policy, a rational administrator would surely have pressed the "on" button for the countercyclical unemployment program. That was the right thing to do *ex ante*; *ex post* it would have been a mistake. For whatever set of reasons, the economy shrugged off the stock market crash and the economic expansion continued for another year. I believe that the odds in favor of a recession in the following year are currently very high—historically, the duration of an expansion has increased the transitional probability of its death. But I would not bet the mortgage money on a recession occurring next year, and I would not advise the above-mentioned imaginary button pusher to set in motion a program that would be very costly if the recession did not in fact occur.

Suppose, however, we are able to know now what the unemployment rate will be—in the absence of a significant countercyclical employment policy—over the next few years. What are the arguments for and against "doing something" in response to a perfectly foreseen bout of unemployment?

To put this question in perspective, suppose that the United States had pursued a very active employment policy in 1982, a year in which the overall unemployment rate reached 9.6 percent. In particular, assume that the government had run a Temporary Public Employment Program (TPEP, pronounced tee-pep) in 1982, which provided jobs to unemployed persons and whose purpose was to reduce the unemployment rate to its value at the peak of the previous business cycle, 5.8 percent (the 1979 rate). Accordingly, a sufficient number of jobs would, by this obviously mythical program, bring the unemployment rates of adult men, adult women, and teenagers down to their 1979 values. Given the assumption that the measured labor force group was an accurate reflection of its true labor force, this would require that 2.319 million year-round jobs be provided for adult (age 20+) men, 1.136 million for adult women, and .341 million for teenagers. This yields a total of 3.796 million jobs which, at a per participant cost of $15,000 in 1982 terms, would have cost about $57 billion.

It has often been argued that the net social cost of employing large numbers of people in a recessionary environment like that in 1982 is zero. It is better, by this argument, to put the unemployed to work on socially useful projects and/or to place them in a training situation that would improve their future productivity, than to leave them to search for jobs that do not exist and to oversupply household services. A number of simple macroeconomic models can be constructed that will, indeed, generate this conclusion. One such model is based on the assumption that the average nominal wage level is set one period in advance in such a way as to clear the labor market (that is, to make unemployment equal to the NRU) on the basis of the expected values of the exogenous macroeconomic variables affecting the overall rate of economic activity (like the money supply). If the actual values of these exogenous variables turn out to equal their forecasted values (i.e., the various economic agents made correct predictions), everything is fine; the unemployment rate will equal the NRU. If the exogenous macroeconomic variables produce less economic activity than predicted, real wages will be too high to permit full employment, and "abnormally" high unemployment will prevail for at least a year, until new wage contracts are struck. (If wage contracts tend to last for more than a year, the recession caused by the unexpectedly low growth of the relevant exogenous variables could last for more than a year.)

Suppose that the recessionary conditions of 1982 were generated by a process consistent with the story in the preceding paragraph and that, as an anti-unemployment measure, 3.8 jobs were provided under TPEP. Suppose also that TPEP participants were engaged in the provision of many services—like weatherization of low-income housing and expanded day-care facilities—that most of the public felt was useful if not, like safety and educational service, essential. What would the unemployment rate in 1982 have been if TPEP had existed: 9.6 percent (the actual rate), 5.8 percent (the 1979 rate), or somewhere in between? In terms of the above model, there would have been no net social costs in 1982, for it would have had no impact on the average level of nominal wages and thus have no effect on the level of private sector employment. Further, on the assumption that TPEP was not financed by an increase in taxes, the program would have had the same effect on aggregate demand as a tax cut equal to the cost of TPEP. Given the openness of the U.S. economy and the international mobility of financial capital, this increase in aggregate demand could plausibily have resulted in a strengthening of the dollar and a concomitant reduction in net exports rather than an increase in the demand for private sector output.

Now we have to ask: if we had pursued this TPEP program, what would have happened to the economy in 1983? Under this simple (and simple-minded) model, wage rates would have adjusted at the end of 1982, so that the economy would have, subject to the absence of a further set of shocks, moved toward full employment in 1983. Assume, however, that many people expected TPEP to continue in 1983. To the extent that the program paid prevailing wages, wage rates in the private sector would be set higher than those consistent with full employment. If the program were discontinued, its 3.8 million participants would be unemployed (or part of them would displace nonparticipants in private sector jobs). If TPEP were continued, full employment would continue, but this full employment, like that in Sweden today, would not reflect an efficient long-run allocation of resources. This argument could be extended for several years, so that in 1988 we could have a 5.8 percent unemployment rate with, as a result of the continuation of TPEP, 3.8 million workers (adjusted for population growth) performing temporary public services rather than working in the private sector. Thus, by this scenario, there is a long-run social cost associated with a temporary employment program, and it is roughly equal to the discounted value of the difference between the wages of workers in private sector jobs and the value of their output in their temporary public jobs. Under some specifications of the macroeconomic adjustment process, a program that is of absolutely limited duration may not slow down the recovery in the private sector. This, however, would require a political discipline that is probably outside of the range ever observed in the United States. (Even the TPEP-like program of the depression—the Work Progress Administration [WPA]—survived into 1943, a year in which cyclical unemployment was not a big problem.) In our example, TPEP would have to have been set up so that it absolutely disappeared in 1983. This would have involved the delivery of pink slips to 3.8 million program participants at a time when there was no excess demand for labor (that is, job openings in the private sector were not abundant). There would obviously have been opposition to this and, at the very least, some doubt about whether TPEP would be terminated on schedule.

A slightly stronger case can be made concerning the expansion of training programs in times of severe recession and their subsequent contraction during the ensuing economic recovery. If the program is limited to periods of high unemployment, the net social cost of the trainees' time spent in that activity is in general much less than if they took their training during the boom phase of the cycle. Given that the effect on the participants' human capital is the same in both situations, the social benefit–cost ratio of training programs is greater, possibly much greater, than in times of full employment. Further, a training program, unlike a job, has a "natural" termination point, so there is less uncertainty about the program being continued beyond the duration of the recession.

There is, however, a major practical problem with a policy of expanding employment and training programs during recessions and contracting them during booms: the lack of continuity may reduce their effectiveness. This is perhaps more true of training than employment programs. Training is no better than the quality of supervision, and this simply cannot be very good if instructors are hired on a part-time basis. Indeed, it would be a cruel hoax played on program participants to raise expectations concerning future occupational advancement and then provide worthless instruction.

Most employment and training programs in the United States over the past two decades have been financed by the federal government but have been operated at various levels of state and local government or, more recently, by private employers. This is quite justifiable on the grounds that the civilian functions of the federal government are both quite limited and highly technical. It does, however, raise the further problem of possible use of these federal funds intended for the expansion of employment and/or training by lower levels of government or private firms to finance activities that would have occurred anyway. Thus the fiscal substitution effect was a major problem with the countercyclical jobs programs of the 1970s under the Comprehensive Employment and Training Act (CETA) (see Bassi and Ashenfelter 1986 for a recent summary of the evidence on this issue). CETA's replacement, the Job Training Partnership Act (JTPA), provides funds to private employers to train disadvantaged workers. Although I am not aware of any studies of this, JTPA must surely be subject to a similar substitution phenomenon. It would be a relatively easy matter for business firms to hire the same people they would have hired in the absence of the program and still receive government subsidies. To the extent that this is true, the only thing that would mitigate it is a desire on the part of individual business to "do good"; JTPA is a transfer program—albeit, a relatively small one—involving transfers from taxpayers to the owners of firms.

To summarize the discussion thus far: it is not at all clear that employment policies geared to the business cycle are justified. It makes intuitive sense—and is probably good politics—to make sure of the unemployed in periods of slack economic activity. It is, however, very difficult to recognize when an economy is entering a recession, still more difficult to predict future turning points in advance. Even if such predictions were possible, the net social cost of putting unemployed labor to work on some productive task is not as small as would be suggested by naive textbook models. Moreover, there are serious programmatic issues associated with the expansion and contraction of employment and training programs over the business cycle.

These points may seem fairly obvious to the reader. The problem, however, is that historically the push for expansion of labor market programs has been entirely a reaction to business cycles—the obvious desire of politicians to (appear to) "do something" about the terrible problem of unemployment. The time series of per capita spending on employment and training programs (see Bassi and Ashenfelter 1986) shows that their major expansion has followed increases in the unemployment by one to two years (the 1980s, of course, are an exception to this rule). Given the pattern of business cycles, this means that the "countercyclical" programs come on line just as the economy has recovered and they are no longer needed.

In the remainder of this paper I argue that a somewhat better case can be made for an employment policy based on long-term rather than short-term goals. The fact that most programs have been set up with the short term in mind is a serious obstacle to their success.

LONG-TERM POLICIES

It can be argued—and has, even by free market champion Milton Friedman—that the unemployment rate associated with normal periods is unnecessarily high; moreover, as noted earlier, it seems to have increased over the past two decades. In other terms, the NRU may reflect market imperfections, and the effect of these may be mitigated to some extent by various forms of long-term employment policy. In this section I discuss four types of imperfections that can cause abnormally high long-term unemployment and how certain kinds of labor market policies can reduce the excess unemployment associated with the NRU.

Minimum Wages and Youth Unemployment

The existence of minimum wage regulations provides an extremely straightforward example. Suppose as most economists believed until recently, that, because of legal requirement that firms pay at least the minimum wage, the wage rate in the youth labor market is set above its market-clearing value. If this is true there will be more job applicants than jobs at the minimum wage, and consequent job rationing as a normal feature of the youth labor market. The resultant unemployment for this sector of the labor market will be in excess of that consistent with normal job and worker turnover.

I have argued elsewhere that the case for the provision of employment programs or government-financed training in this situation is theoretically compelling (see Johnson 1980). Indeed, the notion that this sort of structural unemployment was the cause of the very high relative unemployment rates of teenagers during the 1970s was the intellectual foundation of the Targeted Jobs Tax Credit that was introduced into the tax system in 1978, and it underlay much of the support for the myriad of youth programs introduced in the mid-1970s.

If minimum wages were the cause of the high youth unemployment rates, one form of employment policy would be to eliminate that provision of the Fair Labor Standards Act (or, which is much the same thing, exempt youth from its coverage). Prior to the 1980s (and,

Table 2.3 FEDERAL MINIMUM WAGE IN REAL AND RELATIVE TERMS,
1979–87

	1979	1981	1987
(1) Minimum Wage	$2.90	$3.35	$3.35
(2) GNP deflator	1.00	1.20	1.49
(3) Manufacturing wage	6.70	7.99	9.91
(4) Real minimum (1)/(2)	2.90	2.80	2.25
(5) Relative minimum (1)/(3)	.433	.419	.338

Source: Author's calculations.

apparently, once again), however, this was considered simply out of the question from a political point of view. The reason we had a minimum wage law in the first place was the notion that without such a regulation cheap teenage workers would be substitutes for more expensive (unionized) adult workers and cause either a more severe adult unemployment problem or lower wage rates among low- and semi-skilled adults. Thus, the lobbyists for the AFL-CIO were able to keep effective minimum wage laws on the books through the 1970s and into the early 1980s.

If one applies a simple fixed-wage, single-market model to the labor market for youth (and very low-skilled adults), the theoretical benefits of the provision of public jobs and/or skills training to its members have very large net social benefits. For example, a program that hires youth to work on public projects does not cause any short- or long-run displacement of equivalent jobs in the private sector, because the prevailing wage in that market is the minimum wage, which is, by presumption, well above the market-clearing wage. The public provision of training to those adults with very low skills also has no opportunity cost, for there is sufficient unemployed labor in the market to replace them. Thus, granted this conceptual approach, only a political neanderthal would oppose these sorts of programs.

The problem with this is that the evidence in favor of such a model is rather thin. Since 1981 the minimum wage has been fixed in nominal terms at $3.35 per hour, but both the price level and the general wage level have increased substantially (see table 2.3). In many parts of the country, especially along the coasts, the prevailing wage for teenage labor is well in excess of $3.35; so the minimum wage is at the present time simply irrelevant in much of the country. The relative labor market situation of teenagers, however, did not improve markedly from 1979 to 1987. Their average unemployment rate fell from 16.1 percent to 15.4 percent, but their employment-population ratio fell from 48.5 percent to 45.5 percent. These developments are complicated by other factors—the elimination of youth employment programs and the decline of the relative population of teenagers—but it is clear that the reason for the very high unemployment rates of youth is not accounted for solely by the existence of minimum wages. (The best evidence prior to the post-1981 "experiment" was, as summarized by Brown, Gilroy, and Kohen [1982], that minimum wages had a very small negative effect on teenage unemployment, but this conclusion would probably be different in light of the new evidence.) Accordingly, with or without a reinstatement of effective minimum wages in the 1990s, labor market programs targeted toward those at the low end of the wage distribution do not seem to have as much potential to lower the NRU as was once thought.

Induced Unemployment

A second source of permanent abnormal unemployment (or nonemployment) is that caused by the availability of income-dependent transfer programs—such as Aid to Families with Dependent Children, food stamps, and unemployment compensation. This is not structural unemployment in the sense that the minimum wage rate may (theoretically, at times) prevent the youth labor market from clearing. It is, rather, a situation in which the availability of the transfer income imposes a cost of working on the transfer income recipient. This has the effect of lowering the effective labor supply of potential workers in relevant labor markets, raising the wage levels in these markets and, to the extent that individuals are counted as in the labor force while receiving transfer income, also the NRU.

The major groups for which this type of unemployment is relevant include the large number of adults who, for a variety of reasons, have relatively low labor market skills. Many of these people—because of the presence of young children or of physical and emotional handicaps—cannot work; but many others take low-skilled jobs and would, in the absence of transfer programs, have fairly high participation rates and relatively low unemployment rates.

A general policy that offers public jobs, private employment subsidies, or training opportunities to participants in income transfer programs makes a great deal of sense—from both a benefit–cost and income-distribution point of view. The first and third of these approaches drive up the wage rate for low-skilled labor and increase total employment. (The effects of the second policy, wage subsidies to private employers, is somewhat problematical.) A program like the welfare program proposed by the Carter administration in 1977 —the Program for Better Jobs and Income (PBJI)—was designed to accomplish these ends (although there was considerable question about how many public service jobs would actually have been allocated to welfare recipients rather than to normal state and local government workers). In theory, much of the cost of such a program would be offset by the reduced costs of the transfer programs.

Current discussions of welfare reform have moved somewhat to the right of the proposals of the 1970s, with mandatory participation in employment and training programs a condition for continued participation in the transfer program. Many of the workfare proposals I have seen—such as limiting eligibility for Medicaid for former welfare recipients—appear as thinly disguised cuts in welfare benefits. This may or may not be desirable—a political question that is outside the scope of this essay.

Until recently I believed that the available evidence was strongly in favor of the hypothesis that the net wage elasticity of labor supply of the population of income transfer recipients was both positive and large, the necessary condition for a PBJI-type program to be successful. Recent studies, however, have concluded that the labor supply elasticity is quite small (see, in particular, Bassi 1986). If this new conclusion is correct, subsidies and other programs to shift the labor demand curve for the low-skilled to the right—although arguably justifiable on income distribution grounds—will not be as socially cost effective as was previously believed. In other words, it is not clear, empirically, how induced is the "induced unemployment" phenomenon. One way to resolve this uncertainty is to do in the welfare area what was done after 1981 to the minimum wage: let the benefits get very small and then observe whether there are large increases in labor force participation on the part of those who would have been transfer program recipients. I, personally, would vote against this experiment, but it would resolve the scientific issues.

Shock and Transitional Unemployment

A much publicized form of long-run unemployment is that caused by shifts in demand among industries, occupations, and regions. The best known economic model of this phenomenon is that of Lilien (1982). The idea behind it is that major changes or shocks in the structure of the demand for labor across the above characteristics

Table 2.4 INDICES OF INTERSTATE DISPERSION OF EMPLOYMENT GROWTH
OVER POSTWAR BUSINESS CYCLES

Business cycle	% Dispersion of employment growth
1953–1957	1.33
1957–1969	0.45
1969–1973	0.71
1973–1979	0.60
1979–1987	0.57

Source: Author's calculations.
Note: % dispersion of employment growth refers to the percentage of the labor force that would have to change states during the average year of that business cycle in order for the structure of state employment rates to remain constant.

require various amounts of time for workers to adjust to the new circumstances. Business cycles, by Lilien's argument, are caused by real shocks in the composition of demand, and the NRU fluctuates as the size of the shock changes.

There is a great deal of question about whether the empirical results in the Lilien model are as supportive of his theory as he claims (see Abraham and Katz 1986; and Johnson and Layard 1986). Specifically, it is more likely that declines in the rate of economic activity cause variation in employment growth by industry (Lilien's shock variable) rather than vice versa. Further, there is no evidence that a secular increase in the variation in employment growth across industries has caused the increase in the NRU.

Despite the lack of convincing macroeconomic evidence in support of the shock–unemployment hypothesis, however, there is abundant casual evidence that labor market adjustment problems have been rather severe during the 1980s. In particular, there has been a dramatic shift of economic activity in the United States away from the Rust Belt toward the Sun Belt. To check on the possibility that this phenomenon—the sharp employment declines incurred by the Allentowns and Flints—is responsible for the upward trend in the NRU, I calculated an index of the annualized dispersion in employment growth between states over the course of each business cycle since 1953. This index (see table 2.4) is the weighted sum of the absolute value of the difference between the percentage rate of growth of employment in each state and in the aggregate economy over the course of each business cycle, divided by two times the number of years in the cycle. The resultant number is equal to the percentage of the labor force that would have to change states during the average year of that business cycle in order for the structure of state unemployment rates to remain constant from the first to the second cyclical peak. To the extent that increases in the frequency of shocks has been a causative factor in the secular rise in the NRU, this index should have risen since the 1960s. As table 2.4 reveals, this is not the case; the degree of demand shifting during the current business cycle is approximately equal to its average value over business cycles of the postwar period. Accordingly, there is little support—at least from this admittedly simple test—for the set of policies (such as migration allowances or the targeting of employment and training programs toward declining areas) based on the presumption of increasing regional imbalance.

A different conclusion might result from a test of this form that took account of industry and occupational as well as regional demand; but I suspect that this would not be the case.

Structural Unemployment

A final form of long-run unemployment that is useful to discuss is structural unemployment. By this I mean large-scale unemployment of duration greater than a single business cycle that is caused by the inability of the average real wage level to adjust so that the unemployment equals its frictional rate in normal times. The hypothesis discussed above, that youth unemployment is (or was) above its frictional value because of minimum wage legislation, is an example of structural unemployment applying to a specific group of workers. The more general form of structural unemployment occurs when the entire labor market is subject to above-equilibrium wages.

I should note that this form of unemployment does not seem to be very relevant for the United States in the postwar period. There is no institutional mechanism that would force the general level of real wage rates above its market-clearing value. Indeed, as discussed above, real wages have been stagnant in the United States since 1973 in response to a decline in the underlying rate of productivity growth. If the level of real wages had continued after 1973 at the historical 2 percent per annum rate, our unemployment rate would be at values rivaling those in the depression rather than in the neighborhood of 6 percent. There is some evidence that in the first several years following the initial oil price shock the real wage rate in part of the unionized sector (motor vehicles, steel, airlines, and other such industries) continued to rise in real terms at pre-1973 rates. These increases, however, did not spill over to other industries and, for a variety of reasons, the abnormally high wages in these industries declined after 1978 ("givebacks" and all that).

This form of structural unemployment has been taken by many economists as the principal cause of the dramatic increase in most West European countries indicated in table 2.2. Real wage growth, by and large, has continued in these countries; and it is not surprising that their performance with respect to employment is inferior to that of the United States. It is also interesting to note that real wages in the United States grew at a very rapid rate during the depression of the 1930s. The fact that the annual rate of growth of nominal wages exceeded the rate of price inflation from 1929 to 1934 is not very surprising, for the rate of inflation was – 4.8 percent in the face of the collapse of the banking system, and nominal wages fell only by 1 percent per annum. During the next seven years, however, manufacturing wage rates grew by 3.2 percent per year faster than the price level, even though the rate of price inflation averaged a positive 1 percent. This rise in the real wage can be attributed to unionism and to various New Deal policies (such as the Fair Labor Standards Act) whose purpose was to restore purchasing power to workers and end the depression. Again, if the United States had an institutional climate more similar to that of the 1930s (and Western European countries today), the current unemployment situation would be calamitous.

But suppose that we were experiencing massive unemployment caused by a real wage level that is, say, 35 percent higher than it actually is. (Put differently, suppose we are talking about the Netherlands today or the United States in 1936.) What would be the potential of various labor market policies? First, in such a situation— whatever the underlying macroeconomic model of the economy— neither monetary nor fiscal policy can have any impact on employment. If, for example, the money supply were increased by 10 percent, both wages and prices would rise by 10 percent and employment would be unaffected. Second, in an economy with institutionally fixed real wages and substantial unemployment, training the low-skilled population for better jobs would have no impact on employment and output; there are *no jobs* available for the training program graduates.

A massive public works program (such as the WPA) would seem the only option for reducing unemployment in such a situation. The only potential drawback to this is the possibility that the reduction in unemployment could cause the real wage in the private sector to be increased (by union militancy) further, thus implying a simple substitution of public works employment for private sector employment with no change in aggregate unemployment.

It should be reemphasized that the labor market in the United States is not currently characterized by this type of economywide structural unemployment. Moreover, given the nature of our institutions, we are not likely to face this kind of massive unemployment in the foreseeable future. There is, therefore, no need to consider such policies as union-busting, profit-sharing, or governmental interference in the wage-setting process in order to attack the unemployment problem.

THE LIMITATIONS OF AN ACTIVE LABOR MARKET POLICY

Let me return to the original set of questions concerning the potential efficacy of labor market policy that I posed at the outset: what is wrong with the labor market and which programmatic approaches would be most likely to have a favorable outcome?

First, although unemployment (and perhaps more important in the present context, underemployment) is a fairly severe problem even at the peak of the business cycle, most of the attention to the problem—and consequently the initiation of funding of labor market program—arises during economic downswings. Even an ardent viewer of C-SPAN (round-the-clock public affairs television) hears virtually nothing about the need to "do something" about unemployment when the economy is at what now passes for full employment. Thus, most policy proposals over the course of time are focused on the reduction of cyclical unemployment rather than taking a long-term view. Unfortunately, it is this kind of unemployment about which we know the least—although we know enough to conclude that countercyclical employment and training policy is neither helpful nor feasible.

It is important to stress once again, however, that the next round of labor market programs will be introduced during the next economic downturn. The problem is that we can only hope that some of the programs turn out to be effective long-term measures. The component of these programs that is a reaction to the high unemployment rate of 1990 (or whenever) cannot be expected to be any more beneficial than, say, the Emergency Jobs Appropriation Act of 1983.

Second, in principle, a much stronger case can be made for long-term training programs, such as those designed to improve the distribution of income to alleviate unemployment. There is abundant direct evidence that a significant fraction of adults in the United States have low labor market skills and could benefit from a government-subsidized augmentation of their human capital. Further, after 25 years of evaluative research, there is now reasonably firm evidence that these programs are modestly effective (see, for example, Bassi 1983; Heckman and Robb 1986; LaLonde 1986; Card and Sullivan 1988; and Farkas, Smith, and Stromsdorfer 1983).

One disturbing aspect of the question of the desirability of doing something positive for the unemployed and underemployed in the United States concerns the extent to which the domestic labor market has become integrated into the world economy. In conventional labor market models, the aggregate population of the country and its innate distribution ability are treated as independent of labor market conditions, and the distribution of skills is assumed to adjust to the relative wage structure (net of taxes and transfers) in the long run. A perhaps more relevant way to represent the labor market in the United States now is to assume, instead, that the adult population at the low end of the skill distribution is subject to an infinite elasticity of supply at what would be considered by our standards an extremely low net real wage rate. Justification of this alternative assumption is the realization (as reflected in the Immigration Reform and Control Act of 1986) that, for whatever political or strategic reasons, the United States may not have much ability to control the inflow of illegal immigrants from Latin America (see Burton's discussion in chapter 9 for amplification).

If this depiction of the nature of the U.S. labor market is correct, it implies that many direct labor market policies can have only a limited impact on the long-run welfare of the domestic low-skilled population. For example, in the absence of additional immigration, a program to train some low-skilled adults for higher skilled employment will increase both the successful trainees' earnings and the average earnings of those low-skilled workers who are not trained because of the diminution of competition in that market. With relatively unrestricted immigration, however, the increase in the net real wages of the low-skilled population will attract additional immigration until the relative attractiveness of the U.S. and relevant Latin American low-skilled labor markets are brought back to equilibrium. In this case the benefits to the training program are restricted to the trainees rather than to both the trainees and nonparticipants in the program. The same argument applies, unfortunately, to public jobs or wage (or employment) subsidy programs.

This "open borders" consideration does not imply that we should do nothing about the problems of high unemployment and low earnings among the low-skilled members of our society. It does, however, suggest that the task is more difficult than it was 25 years ago when the United States first got into the business of direct labor market policies.

Great care must be taken in the formulation of a new set of labor market policies if they are to have a chance of working well. Many of the past (and current) programs were set up without, it seems, a great deal of attention to their operational feasibility. The CETA procedure of turning federal funds over to state and local governments, on the assumption that those closest to the problem know the most about it, was an open invitation for the use of these funds for purposes other than the provision of employment and training services. Similarly, I would be very surprised if the current JTPA, which gives funds to firms to train workers, were not subject to the same problem— probably, given the profit motive, on a larger scale. The provision of employment subsidies targeted toward particular groups of workers appears to make a lot of sense on both efficiency and equity grounds; but, alas (I am party responsible for this mistake), the experience of the TJTC suggests that the official labeling of a job applicant as a "problem case" does not, even with a large subsidy, increase the demand for that person.

The problems are difficult: programs are set up in response to one problem, they are not necessarily effective in regard to another; we do not fully understand the nature of the unemployment problem; the motivation of many of the agents who must administer programs is inconsistent with the national objective of reducing unemployment and poverty; the supply of low-skilled labor is, due to immigration, unlimited; and so on. Does this mean that we should, as we have essentially done in the 1980s, give up? My own view, which is a personal political opinion rather than a conclusion following from economic analysis, is no. That the problem is very difficult does not mean that we should ignore it.

I hope, however, that those who set up the next round of employment policy will adhere to the following two principles:

□ do not oversell what your programs can accomplish, and
□ make sure that each new program has a strong evaluation component so that future policy designers can learn from your mistakes.

References

Abraham, Katherine, and Lawrence Katz. June 1986. Cyclical Unemployment: Sectoral Shifts or Aggregate Disturbances? *Journal of Political Economy.*

Bassi, Laurie J. August 1986. The U.S. Welfare System: Poverty Trap or Safety Net? Unpublished paper.

Bassi, Laurie J., and Orley Ashenfelter. 1986. The Effect of Direct Job Creation and Training Programs on Low-Skilled Workers. In *Fighting Poverty: What Works and What Doesn't,* edited by S. Danziger and D. Weinberger. Cambridge, Mass.: Harvard University Press.

Bean, C.R., P.R.G. Layard, and S.J. Nickell, 1986. The Rise in Unemployment: A Multicountry Study. *Economica.*

Farkas, George, D. Alton Smith, and Ernst W. Stromsdorfer. Fall 1986. The Youth Entitlement Demonstration: Subsidized Employment with a Schooling Requirement. *Journal of Human Resources.*

Heckman, J., and R. Rubb. 1986. Alternative Methods for Solving the Problem of Section Bias in Evaluating the Impact of Treatments on Outcomes. *Drawing Inferences from Self Selected Samples,* edited by Wainter. New York: Springer Verlag.

Johnson, George E. July 1980. The Theory of Labour Market Intervention. *Economica.*

Johnson, George E., and Richard Layard. 1986. The Natural Rate of Unemployment: Explanation and Policy. In *Handbook of Labor Economics,* edited by O. Ashenfelter and R. Layardo. Amsterdam: North-Holland Publishing.

Lalonde, Robert. September 1986. Evaluating the Econometric Evaluations of Training Programs with Experimental Data. *American Economic Review.*

Lerman, Robert I. 1982. A Comparison of Worker and Wage Subsidies. In *Jobs for Disadvantaged Workers,* edited by R. Haveman and J. Palmer. Washington: Brookings Institution.

Lilien, David. August 1982. Sectoral Shifts and Cyclical Unemployment. *Journal of Political Economy.*

Perloff, Jeffrey, and Michael Wachter. 1979. A Production Function Non-Accelerating Inflation Approach to Potential Unemployment. *Journal of Monetary Economics.* Supplement.

Chapter Three

EMPLOYER APPROACHES TO REDUCING UNEMPLOYMENT

Robert Eisner

"If it ain't broke, don't fix it!" Unfortunately, labor markets in a more or less competitive, profit-oriented economy such as ours do need some fixing.

The most obvious failing is to be seen in unemployment rates, which have ranged between a recession peak of 10.7 percent and 5.3 percent after five and one-half years of recovery. These figures, of course, include only those in the labor force who are not working at all. Discouraged workers who have dropped out of the labor force, those who have not entered because of presumed inability to find satisfactory employment, and those part-time for economic reasons would add at least several percentage points to these figures. For the first quarter of 1988, when the "official" rate was 5.7 percent, the Bureau of Labor Statistics' full-time equivalent measure of total unemployment amounted to 10 million people, a full 8.8 percent of the labor force.

Of some 115 million in civilian employment in the United States, 98 million are in private employment. The determinants of aggregate employment and any substantial solution to the problem of unemployment are to be found in the workings of the private sector.

The infatuation in some quarters with assumptions of market clearing and the "natural" rate of unemployment has, I believe, been cooled or at least isolated. There should again be widespread recognition that a major portion of unemployment has frequently stemmed from inadequate aggregate demand. We need not dwell here on the well-known remedies for this "Keynesian" underemployment: cutting taxes, increasing government spending, and increasing the supply of money and credit. I should stress, though, that inadequate demand not only contributes to cyclical unemployment; it exacerbates the problems of frictional and structural unemployment on which I focus in this chapter.

59

For even aside from the issue of adequate aggregate demand, our economy cannot be expected, without appropriate policy action, to reach an optimal level of employment. The problem, I suggest, relates to the fact that our system is characterized by neither socialism nor slavery. If it were, the costs of unemployment would be internalized to the decisionmakers. Under socialism the state planners would aim to train and utilize all of their human resources. Under slavery, the private entrepreneur would wish to maximize the value of his investment in human capital. Under free, private capitalism the costs of unemployment are not the proper concern of the employer. And because we are not prepared generally to let the unemployed starve in the street, the costs of unemployment are not even met entirely by the unemployed. We have a clear instance of negative externalities in labor markets.

If labor markets were all perfect in the sense that labor were viewed by employers as interchangeable (homogeneous), we could imagine one supply curve for all labor in which the supply of labor was a function of the real wage and the demand for workers a function of the labor cost of producing an additional unit of output. There would be no involuntarily unemployed in that those not working would consist exclusively of individuals who, in view of their own personal preferences and the general productivity of labor which determined the real wage, chose not to work.

In actuality, labor is heterogeneous and quite imperfectly interchangeable. Individuals of different ages, sexes, races, education, training, and experience, as well as different location and selling power, appear to employers to have different potential values and find different and variable prospects for employment. Many individuals, indeed millions, do not appear to potential employers to promise sufficient return to warrant payment of wages as high as customary rates of pay, minimum wage rates, alternatives available through welfare or in the form of unemployment benefits, or whatever would be necessary to induce potential workers to give up their alternatives to employment.

Millions are unemployed because they cannot find a job where employers consider them worth hiring; at the same time, employers who might consider them worth hiring cannot find them. Much of the problem relates to risk and uncertainty. A prospective employee might turn out to be worth hiring, but the potential employer cannot be sure.

Further, if an employee—frequently a youngster with no significant experience—once trained, proves to be worthwhile, there is nothing to stop the employee from taking that new experience to another employer. The first employer meets the break-in costs but, if the gamble pays off, does not secure the benefits. Thus we have a clear divergence between the self-interest that must guide a competitive firm and the interests of firms in general, or of society, which is to see people in productive labor of their choice rather than idle and dependent upon public support.

SOME GENERAL ANALYTICAL CONSIDERATIONS

Much has been made of the need to subsidize business investment in physical capital. Our tax system has in fact, contrary to some loudly proclaimed beliefs, been heavily biased in the direction of such investment. The Office of Management and Budget's estimate of revenue losses due to tax expenditures for fiscal year 1986 included $25.9 billion for the investment tax credit (now repealed), $33.4 billion for accelerated depreciation, and $31.2 billion for the capital gains exclusions. These sum to the substantial figure of $90.5 billion. The one tax expenditure listed to subsidize employment, the Targeted Jobs Tax Credit, was expected to lose the Treasury about $.4 billion (OMB 1986, G43–44).

Yet there is every reason to believe that business investment in physical capital is one activity that can most safely be left to a free market. Presuming adequate aggregate demand and a monetary and credit regime that permits a free flow of capital, one should expect that when business invests in what is profitable it will be investing in what is productive. Tax incentives for investment, to the extent that they are effective, bring about investment that would not otherwise have seemed sufficiently profitable or productive. The $100 machine, offering real economic returns with a present value of only $90, is purchased because the tax subsidies raise the present value of total returns to $115. The massive tax expenditures for investment, further swollen by inflation-boosted, interest-deductible borrowing to finance unrealized as well as realized capital gains, have subsidized largely unproductive investment, which has in some cases induced substitution of physical capital for labor.

Unlike its treatment of business capital, government policy largely discourages the employment of labor. Much is made, by some, of the restrictive effect of the minimum wage, where it applies, currently at $3.35 per hour—no higher in real terms than it was years ago. But direct taxes on labor are much more pervasive and have been rising repeatedly. In 1988, they were 15.02 percent on the bulk of wages and salaries (up to $45,000 for each employee) for social security (FICA) and another some 6 percent for the first $7,000 of wages for unemployment insurance (FUTA). Employers must recognize these as added costs of employing workers, while unemployment insurance, paradoxically, lowers the cost of firing. It should be added, though, that the expected eventual returns from social security and unemployment benefits may make employees more willing to take jobs, perhaps at lower pay, to the extent that they are taken into account but not (as I would expect they are) heavily discounted.

Income maintenance without work generally has the effect of discouraging labor. Put technically, the income elasticity of demand for leisure is certainly positive. Our social insurance system, however desirable, and analogous private insurance that offers income in case of disability or retirement, reduce the incentive or pressure to stay in a job. Provisions in welfare systems or in social security (for those between the ages of 65 and 70) that dictate loss of benefits in connection with work may particularly sharply reduce employment.

Government discouragement of employment is superimposed on a system where, unlike the case of business capital, there is reason to expect, in free markets, critical underemployment. This relates to endemic externalities in the fact that labor services and the payment for them involve human capital. As indicated above, because we are not a slave economy, while firms can expect to realize the value of their investment in physical capital (which they can own), it may not pay them to invest in the human capital of workers who may not stay with them once they become more valuable. And workers may be unwilling or unable to pay their own training costs in the form of sharply lower or even negative wages.

Adoption and implementation of policies to reduce unemployment have frequently been impeded by fears of inflation. Constraints on aggregate demand have been imposed without determining whether inflationary pressures stemmed from excess demand or reduced supply. Shortages of demand have then increased cyclical unemployment, which has interacted with and magnified structural and frictional unemployment.

At the firm level, the increases in demand that might raise output and employment are thought to cause movements up rising marginal cost curves. Increases in employment also move labor up rising supply curves. Both factors then contribute to higher prices and, as the process continues, to inflation.

Concern for inflationary consequences has probably unduly inhibited demand-stimulating measures to increase employment. First, it is not clear that the U.S. economy has ever suffered much demand-induced inflation except as a consequence of the huge increases in government spending associated with wars or in the release of pent-up purchasing power in their aftermath. Second, it is doubtful that policymakers have properly evaluated the relative social costs of unemployment and the essentially moderate peace-time inflation we have generally experienced.

But given this concern for inflation, misguided or not, policy measures that can contribute to both higher employment and lower inflation are in order. We look for instruments that will lower firms' marginal cost curves and increase the effective supply of labor. Recognizing the heterogeneities of labor supply and labor demand, we seek to generate jobs for those unemployed and out of the labor force; the goal is to do so without increasing the demand for those types of labor that are in short supply, and perhaps even easing tight labor markets.

We may begin by reminding ourselves of some of the government interventions that have tended to reduce employment and aggravate the problem of reducing unemployment. High on the list must be increasing direct taxes on labor, to which we have already referred. Only in the implausible case of a perfectly elastic supply of labor and perfectly price-elastic demand for market output could one argue that increasing payroll taxes does not decrease the quantity of labor employed. The exact amounts of the effect will of course depend upon the elasticity of substitution of labor for other factors of production, the elasticity of labor supply, and the price elasticities of demand for output. To the extent that the supply of labor is elastic, firms will find themselves endeavoring to substitute other factors for labor and raise prices. If changes in other taxes, transfers, government expenditures, and the money supply do not offer compensating sources of increased demand, there would be both substitution and output effects against market employment.

Also to be noted are various governmental restrictions on employment. Some are directed against women, as in the armed forces and state and local police and fire departments. Some are directed against youth, in unnecessary age requirements for employment. These restrictions in some cases apply to activities licensed and controlled by government, such as taxi services. With regard to this last, government is often used to limit entry and thus directly reduce total employment.

The minimum wage has frequently been cited as a cause of unemployment, especially for youth. The argument on theoretical grounds is that, by raising (presumably) marginal labor cost above the net marginal revenue product for certain types of potential employees, it prevents their employment. This would apply to those with few skills or marketable abilities and to those who might be willing to accept initially low wages in return for the training and job experience which would permit them to earn more later.

There is indeed a theoretical problem with the argument. If a firm faces a rising supply curve for the type of labor involved, its marginal labor cost will be above the wage it pays. It is possible that the imposed minimum wage, which would be the new marginal labor cost, would be below the old marginal labor cost and thus generate an increased demand for labor, as pointed out many years ago by George Stigler (1946).

Whether this theoretical possibility is relevant in most labor markets is unclear, but the empirical evidence that the minimum wage is substantially responsible for unemployment is doubtful. Brown, Gilroy, and Kohen (1982), after surveying a vast number of studies on the subject, suggest that the best estimates of the impact of a 10 percent increase in the minimum wage is a 1 percent decrease in employment among teenagers and a lesser effect, perhaps even positive, on employment of young adults. Much relevant employment is in fact not covered by the minimum wage and it is questionable whether it is now high enough, or under current legislative proposals will get high enough, to make much difference where it does apply.

CURRENT EMPLOYER JOBS SUBSIDIES

The one employer-focused governmental program to stimulate employment in the United States today is the Targeted Jobs Tax Credit (TJTC). It applies to nine groups of recipients of payments under means-tested transfer programs, economically disadvantaged (as measured by family income), or disabled. The categories include: economically disadvantaged youths ages 18 to 24, economically disadvantaged Vietnam-era veterans, economically disadvantaged former convicts, economically disadvantaged youths seeking summer employment, general assistance recipients, supplemental security income (SSI) recipients, recipients of Aid to Families with Dependent Children (AFDC) and Work Incentive (WIN) Program registrants, vocational rehabilitation referrals, and a small category of economically disadvantaged cooperative education students.

Until 1986, the program allowed a credit against income taxes equal to 50 percent of the first $6,000 of qualified first-year wages and 25 percent of the first $6,000 of second-year wages paid to a member of a targeted group. The maximum credit per employee was thus $3,000 the first year and $1,500 the second. For the summer program, however, the credit was equal to 85 percent of up to $3,000 of wages, for one summer only, for a maximum credit of $2,550. The employer's tax deduction for the cost of wages is reduced by the amount of the credit.

The TJTC actually lapsed on 31 December 1985. The current extension to 31 December 1988, was enacted, retroactive to its 1985 expiration, on 21 October 1986, and entailed a substantial curtailment of the credit. It is now 40 percent, not 50 percent, of the first $6,000 of earnings and applies to the first year only. There is also a new requirement that the employee be retained for a minimum period of 90 days, involving at least 120 hours of employment, and for the summer youth program a minimum of 20 hours over 14 days. The following discussion and evaluation, however, relate to experience prior to legislation of this current version.

Implementation of the program entails provision by designated local agencies of vouchers indicating eligibility. To receive credits, employers must request certificates confirming eligibility on or before the day the employee begins work, or within five days if a preliminary voucher had already been received. This provision was intended to prevent employers from merely collecting a windfall on workers who had been hired without thought of the credit.

The major groups in terms of participation up to 1985, by far, were the economically disadvantaged youths—defined as those in families with incomes equal to or less than 70 percent of the Bureau of Labor Statistics' lower living standard—and the AFDC recipients and WIN registrants. The youths accounted for 58.3 percent of a total of 563,381 certifications in fiscal year 1984, a figure which rose to 621,889 in 1985 (for all categories except the cooperative education students) while the AFDC–WIN group accounted for 15 percent. The total number of vouchers was considerably larger—1,337,637—and, of these, 46.8 percent were for youths and 23.4 percent were for individuals in the AFDC–WIN category. For 313,493 vouchers issued in the AFDC–WIN group, there were certifications of only 84,769, or 27 percent. Of the total of jobs credit vouchers issued in 1984, certifications came to 42 percent.

With all the vouchers and certifications, as reported by Christensen (1984) in a staff memorandum prepared for the Congressional Budget Office, "only about 10 percent of employers have used the credit, and employers have claimed the credit for fewer than 10 percent of the eligible workers they have hired" (Christensen 1984, 32–33). One obvious factor inhibiting employer participation was lack of tax liabilities against which the credit may be used. This accounts for some 30 percent of employers.

Many employers who could derive tax advantage from the program did not use it. This may be attributed to lack of knowledge, to the cost in time and effort of filling out applications and forms and setting up a system for identifying or recruiting eligible workers, and to a general reluctance to get involved with government programs. A major obstacle was, as John Bishop (1985) puts it, "the perception that the types of individuals for which subsidies are available are not the types of people they currently hire and would not perform adequately if they were hired" (5–55).

The credit has been used in relatively larger proportion by larger firms and by firms with larger numbers of workers who might be eligible. Bishop lists employers most likely to participate as those who: "had many employees; had high turnover and new hire rates; had an unskilled work force; paid below average wage rates; were parts of large multi-establishment corporations; were members of local business organizations, did not mind dealing with government officials; had a nonunion work force" (5–34).

Only 3 to 4 percent of employers accounting for 16 percent of the nation's jobs receive the TJTC, according to Bishop. Even more striking, as he also reports, citing the Congressional Budget Office, only 10 percent of the working disadvantaged youths who are eligible for TJTC are claimed by their employer (Bishop and Kang 1987). Eligible youths do not bother to get vouchers, and employers cannot tell or do not try to ascertain which of their job applicants are eligible. And widely cited experiments in which results were compared for job seekers who advertised their subsidy potential to employers, and those who did not, brought a startling conclusion. Those who reported their vouchers were less successful in securing jobs than those who offered employers no such benefit. The stigma attached to being in an identified disadvantaged group apparently outweighed the potential tax or subsidy benefits (see Burtless and Cheston 1981; Burtless 1984; Burtless and Haveman 1985).

Surveys and employment data indicate somewhat higher employment of youths by employers who participate in the TJTC program than by those who do not. Since there is no clear evidence that firms using the credit have increased their total employment more than other firms, it is possible that increased employment of youths, if it occurred, may have been at the expense of adult employment in these firms.

This does not rule out a possible net increase in employment, however. For displaced adult workers may have been more able to locate jobs elsewhere than the disadvantaged youths hired under the TJTC program. The argument has indeed been made by Baily and Tobin (1977 and 1978) and Nichols (1980) that an effective anti-inflationary way of stimulating employment may be precisely to increase the demand for low-skilled, hard-to-employ, or disadvantaged workers, while easing labor market pressures where workers usually in high demand are employed.

It is clear that the program has suffered from employer ignorance and antipathy, from the stigma attached to individuals labeled members of disadvantaged groups, and from real and perceived burdens of locating and securing certification of eligible workers. Administration of the program has been handicapped by lack of funds and motivated personnel. Wide variation among states in proportions of eligibles who are vouchered and certified testifies to the unevenness of administration. At best the program needs nurturing.

A number of useful suggestions for improving the cost-effectiveness of the TJTC were offered by Bishop (1985). These included: protecting employers from the danger of discrimination suits for giving preference to TJTC eligibles; reducing the first-year credit from 50 percent to 25 percent for major categories including that for disadvantaged youths; reducing the summer youth credit from 85 percent to 50 percent; adding a $4,000 training-cost subsidy; substituting a low-income unemployed senior citizen category for the more stigmatizing SSI class; and substituting a low-income, unemployed adult category (over age 25) for the AFDC, General Assistance, SSI, ex-convict, and Vietnam Veteran groups. He also had a number of important administrative recommendations to increase vouchering and certification, including incentive payments to local employment service offices and outreach programs targeted on firms that might hire large numbers of TJTC eligibles.

Testimony (March 1985) before the Subcommittee on Select Revenue Measures of the House Committee on Ways and Means indicated considerable support for TJTC among certain classes of employers. Fast food and hotel chains, in particular, seem to have made substantial use of the credit. In a number of instances, large employers made systematic efforts to obtain eligible workers and were often apparently encouraged to hire youths, without knowing their individual eligibility, in the expectation that substantial proportions of them would in fact prove eligible.

There were moves in Congress in 1985 to extend the TJTC for five years, increase the amount of wages eligible for the credit from $6,000 to $10,000 and liberalize the definition of an economically disadvantaged family by raising the income ceiling from 70 percent to 80 percent of the Bureau of Labor Statistics' lower living standard. The amendments seemed in order, partly as merely an adjustment to inflation, but partly, as well, to increase applicability and broaden the targeting. They might have complemented a general program to reduce the stigmatizing attached to designation as a member of a disadvantaged group. In fact, however, as noted above, these broadening changes were not adopted and the credit was curtailed.

THE OLD "NEW JOBS TAX CREDIT"

The major forerunner of the TJTC was the much broader New Jobs Tax Credit (NJTC) of 1977. This was not explicitly focused, thus creating no stigmatized groups. It was also marginal, applying to additional employment, and hence potentially more cost effective.

The NJTC offered a reduction in employer income taxes for increases in employment over 102 percent of that of the previous year. The base for the credit was increases in the amount of wages subject to FUTA contributions (for unemployment insurance) up to the (1977 statutory) amount of $4,200 per worker. The tax credit of 50 percent of such increases in wages thus came to a maximum of $2,100 per worker. As with the TJTC, however, since wage-cost tax deductions were reduced by the amount of the credit, actual tax reductions varied with the employer's marginal tax bracket.

The credit was limited to 50 percent of the increase in total wage and salary payments over 105 percent of those of the previous year. This was intended to discourage substitution of lower-paid or part-time workers for existing workers with higher annual earnings. Since wages per worker subject to the credit were limited to $4,200, though, the credit as a proportion of wages of additional workers was greater the less that their wages exceeded $4,200. Further, the employer could increase its credit by increasing wage payments to those who earned less than $4,200 in the previous year, increasing their hours or their rates of pay until their annual compensation reached that maximum.

The NJTC contained a limitation of $100,000 in tax credits per employer. This meant that the credit could be available only for increases of up to 48 employees (beyond 102 percent of previous employment) earning $4,200 or more. There was a further restriction that the credit could not be more than 25 percent of the total of current compensation of up to $4,200 per employee.

Individual employers could thus be categorized in three groups with reference to the NJTC: those who would not expand employment by more than 2 percent and hence would be unaffected by it; those who would expand employment by more than 2 percent and whose amounts (and composition) of expansion might be affected by the credit; and firms, essentially large ones, whose rate of expansion without the credit would be 48 employees or more, and hence would be offered no incentive to increase employment further.

There was no significant promotion of the NJTC and much of its potential incentive effect during 1977 was lost because of widespread ignorance of its existence among the small firms that it might have been expected to influence. A survey by the Bureau of the Census for the Department of Labor found only about one-third of respondents reporting awareness of the credit in February 1978. Of this third, less than 20 percent indicated that they qualified for the credit, some 30 percent reported insufficient growth in FUTA wages, 18 percent reported insufficient growth in total wages, and 27 percent of firms indicated that they did not know whether they qualified. A survey by the National Federation of Independent Business found only 50 percent of small-firm respondents knowing of the availability of the credit as late as April 1978, when 1977 tax returns were being prepared. It would appear that many firms learned of the credit from their accountants in time to claim its benefits but too late to have it affect their employment decisions.

Nevertheless, use of the New Jobs Tax Credit was enormous in comparison with the later Targeted Jobs Tax Credit. Bishop (1985) reports that 1.1 million firms, more than 30 percent of the total nationwide and more than half of eligible firms, received a new jobs tax credit in 1978 while, in 1979, fewer than 25,000 companies received a targeted jobs tax credit.

In its two years of operation, Bishop adds, the NJTC subsidized more than four million person-years of employment. And several studies found that it increased employment. The National Federation of Independent Business estimated 300,000 extra jobs by the summer of 1978 (McKevitt 1978). A study by Perloff and Wachter (1980), using ordinary least squares regressions and multinomial logit distributions of percentage growth in employment, offered evidence "that firms which knew about the credit increased employment by (over) 3 percent more than some of the firms who were ignorant of the program." There may have been some confounding of cause and effect but the Perloff and Wachter study may be taken to imply an increase of as many as 700,000 jobs in 1977. A study by Bishop (1981) estimated 150,000 to 670,000 extra jobs by the summer of 1978 in construction and distribution alone.

These substantial estimated effects of the NJTC are all the more remarkable in the light of its deficiencies. The high base of 102 percent of previous employment made many businesses, particularly in a recession period, immune to the incentives because they could have no reasonable hope of reaching the threshhold at which the credit would become effective. And the ceiling of $100,000 (or 48 additional full-credit employees) would appear to have eliminated the incentive to increase employment among the large, rapidly growing firms which experience with the TJTC suggests would be most likely to prove responsive.

A PROGRAM FOR THE FUTURE

What, if anything, to do in the way of encouraging private employment comes back to our perception of the problem. If we are content with the current employment situation there is nothing to do. That means accepting overall rates of unemployment of almost 6 percent and all the additional percentage points for discouraged workers and those only partially employed for economic reasons. It also means accepting disproportionate unemployment among certain categories of the population, in particular, blacks and some other minorities, youths, and black youths in particular.

If we believe that a free market "solution" is optimal, there is still need for new policies because current interferences with the free market in the form of payroll taxes, regulations, trade restrictions and the like are far from neutral in their effect upon labor markets. One might hence think first of removing government interferences with free market employment decisions. We might eliminate special taxes on labor such as payroll taxes, raising revenues instead from general income or consumption taxes. We might remove minimum wage and other restrictions upon wage payments. We might eliminate age and gender job restrictions and avoid government support in various discriminatory practices. We should eliminate such anti-employment provisions as the current reduction and cancellation of social security benefits for earned income of those between the ages of 65 and 70.

But with all of that, a free market solution may well leave us with suboptimal employment overall and with deep pockets of unemployment. These relate, as I have suggested, to the heterogeneity of labor; to serious information costs in matching jobs and workers, particularly for those without experience; to suboptimal investment in human capital; and to differences between individual and social risk.

To the extent that many of these difficulties focus more severely on those from low-skill categories whose productivity is viewed as below widely prevailing wage levels, wage subsidies to the individual would appear useful. If these were of a flat amount, say one dollar per hour, they would be relatively more valuable in employing low-wage labor. The subsidy could indeed be focused more sharply on low-wage individuals by setting it as a fraction (such as 50 percent) of the difference between a target wage (say, $6.00 per hour) and the actual wage paid. This latter formula, as suggested by Bishop (1985), would thus phase out as the individual obtained a higher wage. Bishop adds that eligibility could be limited to target groups and the level of the target wage could be related to geographical, demographic, or other characteristics.

A wage subsidy might be paid directly to workers rather than to employers. This might encourage employment and legal, as opposed to illegal or underground, activity. Many potential workers do not find employment at minimum wages worthwhile, given all of the associated costs as well as personal disutility. A subsidy to workers might significantly increase job search and employment for those not working because they cannot find decent jobs at decent pay.

If, contrary to the evidence offered and summarized by Brown, Gilroy, and Kohen (1982) and by Brown (1981), minimal wage law restrictions are having a significant impact on employment, wage subsidies to employers would seem a useful way of finessing the problem. The minimum wage requirements, with their appeals to our sense of justice and equity, could be retained, and wages could be offered sufficient to induce labor force participation and still not violate employers' need, in maximizing profits, to keep the net gain from an additional unit of product above the cost of producing that unit.

A variety of employment tax credits were suggested and analyzed in a series of papers by Fethke and Williamson (January, July, and November 1976); Kesselman, Williamson, and Berndt (1977); and Fethke, Policano, and Williamson (1978). They pointed to the possibilities of securing large employment effects with relatively small direct loss of tax revenues by utilizing a marginal credit, that is, a credit for employment over a certain base period. They also noted the possibilities of varying the base as part of countercyclical policy.

Revival of a marginal subsidy such as the NJTC on a longer-run or permanent basis raises questions as to how to define and vary the base over time. For one thing, if the base for an individual firm is high, such as the 102 percent of previous eligible wages in the NJTC, many firms are unable to receive the subsidy. This raises questions of equity but, perhaps more seriously, of potency in that the possibility of stimulating employment in many firms is ruled out.

Further, a high base may invite cycling, that is, reducing employment one year in order to be able to raise it enough the next to receive a subsidy, even though average employment is unchanged. On the other hand, a low base increases the likelihood that the subsidy will be used for employment that firms would generate anyway.

If the base for each firm is a fixed level of employment, the subsidy may be related directly to the extent that employment exceeds the base, and the effective rate of subsidy equals its nominal rate. If employment in a firm grows, however, it may eventually exceed the base considerably and hence produce a situation in which, again, massive subsidies are given for jobs that the firm would offer without the subsidy, and the incentive effects per dollar of subsidy will become small. If a firm's employment declines so far below the base that it can have no hope of reaching it, all incentive effects will be gone.

An obvious remedy for either of these difficulties might appear to be a firm-specific base which rises as the firm's employment increases and falls as its employment declines. A difficulty with this, as with the current marginal tax credit for research and development (see Eisner, Albert, and Sullivan 1984) is that the marginal effective credit may become substantially less than the nominal credit and, in conjunction with other restrictions, may actually become negative.

In general, firms with employment already beyond base, and anticipating that it would be beyond base in the future, must reckon that any further increase in current employment, which would be rewarded with an increased current subsidy, would result in a higher base and hence a lower subsidy in the future. Thus, viewed at the margin where an incentive would be effective, the value of the subsidy is reduced to the present value of the difference between having the subsidy now and having it later. If the base is the previous year's employment, for example, the value of a 50 percent wage subsidy or tax credit is reduced, for a discount or interest rate of 10 percent, to 4.55 percent (50 percent minus 50 percent/1.1).

To the extent that the cycling problem may prove relevant (which I find doubtful because of the various costs associated with altering employment and output), such a variable base would make the problem more serious. Any cycling problem can be reduced by lowering the base and by smoothing its variation in a moving average formulation. If the base is made an average of a number of years of previous employment, the present value of the loss of future subsidies as a consequence of increasing employment to enjoy a current subsidy is reduced. Thus, for example, for a base which is a moving average of the employment of the last three years, the present value of a 50 percent subsidy is $50\% - 50\% (1.1^{-1} + 1.1^{-2} + 1.1^{-3})/3$, which equals 8.55%.

There are some reasonably effective ways to achieve an essentially marginal credit that is tailored over time to the firm's particular situation, without allowing the feedback of the firm's own actions to vitiate the credit. The compromise solution consists of choosing a firm-specific base, but having it vary over time in a way that is not affected by the firm's own employment decisions. One might, for example, make the base 95 percent of average employment in some base period, say the years 1986, 1987, and 1988, which would be appropriate for calculation of the subsidy for 1989 employment. For 1990 employment, however, the base would be adjusted by the percentage by which employment in the entire industry changed from 1988 to 1989. Thus the firm's actions to increase employment in 1989 would at most trivially deprive it of credit in 1990 (or later years), and the effective rate of credit would be approximately equal to the nominal rate.

It would of course be important, for this solution to work, that the firm itself not account for such a large share of the employment of the "industry" that its base will vary significantly with its own employment decisions. Firms might be asked themselves to designate the one-digit, two-digit, or three-digit industry or industries in which they best fit, subject to the restriction that they designate an industry or set of industries such that their own employment is less than some specified percent of the aggregate. (The designation could of course be subject to regulatory check for reasonable plausibility.)

Ideally, we should aim at an appropriately neutral tax system and use direct subsidies as a means of encouraging employment where that is desired. If we are forced to a second-best solution of using the tax system, we would wish to supplement it by direct subsidies to firms without tax liabilities, either because they lack taxable income or because they are nonprofit or not-for-profit corporations which are not subject to taxes. In the case of taxable firms lacking taxable income (or with other tax credits or tax expenditures reducing taxable income to zero), we could offer tax credits against FUTA (unemployment taxes) and FICA (social security taxes). Since nonprofit and not-for-profit businesses usually do pay these taxes, such credits could be applicable to them as well.

If we accept the premise that involuntary unemployment or underemployment reflects wasteful market failure, measures to stimulate employment appear justified. Our measures, however, must avoid, as far as possible, inducing firms to hire workers whose net marginal social product is still negative. We do not want to encourage firms to hoard labor which is unproductive to them at the expense of productivity elsewhere.

We also must look for a system of subsidies which is reasonably cost-efficient in not necessitating undue increases in tax rates or distorting work-leisure choices. To the extent that subsidies are targeted to particular groups or categories of individuals, we must strive to minimize, if not eliminate, the cost to untargeted groups.

It would appear that if our ultimate target is unemployment itself, we should devise subsidies that, avoiding as far as possible the pitfalls of moral hazard, are directed at unemployment. We might then develop a system that combines subsidies targeted to those where intervention seems particularly called for, with general subsidies applicable to all other unemployed.

The TJTC has, with some exceptions, targeted groups that were frequently too narrow, too unappealing, or too difficult to reach to generate major employer recruitment. The narrow targeting runs some risk of causing employment in the targeted group to be substituted for employment of others. The extremely low family income criterion used for most of the groups, in addition to adding to losses from stigmatizing, may offer a further danger of lowering of household income. As with the notorious history of the program for Aid to Families with Dependent Children (AFDC), if subsidies are really effective, existing income earners may be encouraged to leave the household or to quit their jobs to permit subsidization of others in the household.

Strong economic arguments can be made for job subsidies broadly targeted at all of those who want jobs. This might have some special focus on youth, where unemployment is most widespread, and on others where special assistance seems warranted. I would suggest the following package, therefore, both to illustrate possible application of appropriate principles for a new employment subsidy program and as a base for discussion.

□ Set a base for each firm of average employment for the years 1986, 1987, and 1988. This base will be effective for 1989. For 1990 and subsequent years it will be adjusted by the percentage by which employment in the relevant industry increases over the previous year. (Appropriate adjustments may be made for new firms.)
□ For net additions to employment beyond 95 percent of base employment, a 50 percent wage subsidy up to the amount of allowable unemployment insurance benefits (recent maxima of which have varied by state between $120 and $330 per week; average weekly benefits nationwide for those totally unemployed were $140 in the first half of 1987) for:
—those unemployed five weeks or more
—those under the age of 20 without jobs and with less than one year of prior employment
—those seeking employment after being out of the labor market due to child-bearing
—those seeking civilian employment after being out of the civilian labor force due to military service, and
—all others in the targeted groups under the current TJTC.
□ For all other additions to employment, offer a similar credit which employers can use only for increases in employment beyond 100 percent of base.
□ Have the U.S. Treasury pay payroll taxes out of general revenues for those under the age of 20.
□ If a system of tax credits rather than direct subsidies is to be employed, offer a tax credit against payroll taxes for FICA and FUTA rather than against corporate or individual income taxes. Have the U.S. Treasury make corresponding contributions to the social security and unemployment insurance funds, directly.

The threshhold of 95 percent of base employment for individuals in the special categories should lead employers enjoying the subsidies to give those workers preference, for the subsidies can be enjoyed only on these workers for the 5 percent of employment below base. The general eligibility for subsidies pertaining to employment beyond 100 percent of base would mitigate the danger that increased employment within the special groups would be at the expense of others.

The targeting of those unemployed for five weeks or more has some special appeal as well as some obvious dangers. Focusing directly on those suffering significantly more than frictional unemployment, it offers a promise of a direct cure, similar to heat-seeking missiles or drugs designed to find and destroy cancer cells while leaving the rest of the body undamaged.

There is, however, a moral hazard problem. Workers may find it appealing to enjoy brief periods of unemployment that will make them more attractive to employers. Similarly, employers may contribute to short-term unemployment by spurning those unemployed less than five weeks. These difficulties should not, however, have to prove overwhelming. For most workers, unemployment benefits would not be a preferred substitute to available employment. Most employers would prefer the efficiency of having long-term employees as opposed to regularly substituting them with the short-term unemployed. And various administrative safeguards might be introduced to reduce any such churning activities.

Elimination of social security payroll taxes for teenagers may be justified on grounds of equity as well as the encouragement of youth employment. Disproportionately fewer numbers of those who will begin work at an early age live long enough to receive major portions of their benefits.

Tying the tax credit to the payroll tax would make it effective for the large numbers of small companies that do not have business income tax liabilities. It would also make it effective for nonprofit institutions and ideally, as well, state and local government bodies and school districts that participate in the social security system. Nonprofit institutions such as schools, colleges, universities and hospitals, as well as governmental units, can prove to be particularly flexible employers, less pressed by cyclical profit concerns. Generally, tying the tax credit to payroll taxes rather than to business income taxes will offer a better opportunity for the direct reduction of labor costs, which can make job tax credits a tool for combatting both unemployment and inflation.

QUALIFICATIONS AND CONCLUSIONS

Various side effects must be recognized in any consideration of subsidies to increase employment. First, if the subsidies are given to employers, gross wages of target groups may be expected to rise. This may be viewed as a desired boon to the predominantly lower-income individuals where the incidence of unemployment is greatest.

For those outside of a target group eligible for the credit, however, wages may fall. The demand for the services of nontargeted workers may be reduced as employers direct themselves to workers for whom they can receive the subsidies. The consequences may include reduced employment among nontarget groups.

It is then particularly important that any system of job subsidies be accompanied by a general policy of maintaining employment. Significant subsidies for target groups should be complemented with incentives to prevent nontarget groups from falling back.

Second, effective job subsidies may in part increase employment without decreasing unemployment. This is because the subsidies may induce some currently nonemployed to enter the labor force.

Third, effective job subsidies may increase employment and output but raise output less than employment, thereby reducing labor productivity, particularly at the margin. There is a presumption that workers hired because of the subsidy are less productive; otherwise they would have been hired without the subsidy. And generally, with higher labor-to-capital ratios, we may expect productivity per worker to be lower. The bottom line, however, should be recognized as output per capita and not output per worker. In that sense, despite the decline in measured productivity, society may generally be better off.

Fourth, longer-run consequences of employment subsidies must be considered. What happens to workers when and if their eligibility expires? If the base or threshhold for marginal credits is kept close to current employment, what happens when a firm reaches the limit of its expansion capabilities? If the base is kept relatively low, can we avoid significant costs of labor hoarding to take advantage of the subsidy, which may make it more difficult for new, expanding firms to find workers?

Fifth, any system of job subsidies, however well devised, must inevitably involve significant amounts of leakage and waste. Employers will take advantage of the subsidy to hire workers that they would have hired anyway. Workers will find themselves in greater demand and with higher wages as a result of the subsidy, for jobs that they would have been offered and would have accepted at lower wages without the credit. One may hope that the public will accept these distributional consequences and recognize the net benefit of increased employment and output.

While the possibility of devising and implementing effective employment subsidies is enormously appealing, it would be foolish to oversell them. They present a number of difficulties in implementation and administration. Much of the hard-core unemployment and nonparticipation of the labor force will require more far-reaching intervention. For many without jobs the lack of skills, ability, education and training, ambition, or motivation will be too much for subsidies of 100 percent and more. Employers will not wish to risk hiring them at any price.

Solutions in such cases will have to be found in terms of comprehensive training, counseling, family support, and provision of new living arrangements where households have essentially ceased to function, along with direct government responsibility for job placement.

If significant unemployment is to be recognized as the scourge it is, its elimination must be a joint undertaking of government and the private sector. In that undertaking, if well conceived, a far-reaching and ambitious program of employment subsidies can play a major role.

References

Baily, Martin N., and James Tobin. 1977. Macroeconomic Effects of Selective Public Employment and Wage Subsidies. *Brookings Papers on Economic Activity* 2:511–41. Washington: Brookings Institution.

———. 1978. Inflation-Unemployment Consequences of Job Creation Policies. In *Creating Jobs: Public Employment Programs and Wage Subsidies*, edited by John L. Palmer, 43–75.

Bishop, John H. 1981. Employment and Pricing in Construction and Distribution Industries: The Impacts of Tax Policy. In *Studies in Labor Markets*, edited by Sherwin Rosen. Chicago: University of Chicago Press.

———. 1984. Statement before the U.S. Congress, House Ways and Means Committee, 98th Cong. In *Targeted Jobs Tax Credit Extension*, 125–45. Washington.

————. 1985. Subsidizing the Training of the Disadvantaged. Kalamazoo, Mich.: W.E. Upjohn Institute for Employment Research.

Bishop, John H., and S. Kang. 4 August 1987. Applying for Entitlements: Employers and the Targeted Jobs Credit. Ithaca, N.Y.: Cornell University.

Brown, Charles. 1981. Estimating the Effects of a Youth Differential on Teenagers and Adults. In *Report of the Minimum Wage Study Commission*, 389–427. Washington.

Brown, Charles, Curtis Gilroy, and Andrew Kohen. June 1982. The Effect of the Minimum Wage on Employment and Unemployment. *Journal of Economic Literature* 20(2): 487–528.

Burtless, Gary. 1985. Are Targeted Wage Subsidies Harmless? Evidence from a Wage Voucher Experiment. *International Labor Relations Review* 39(1): 105–14.

Burtless, Gary, and John Cheston. 30 July 1981. The Montgomery County (Dayton) Ohio Wage-Subsidy Voucher Experiment: Initial Findings. U.S. Department of Labor: Assistant Secretary for Policy Evaluation and Research (ASPER).

Burtless, Gary, and Robert H. Haveman. 1985. Policy Lessons from Three Labor Market Experiments. *Brookings General Series Reprint 410.* Washington: Brookings Institution.

Christensen, Sandra. 1984. The Targeted Jobs Tax Credit. In *Targeted Jobs Tax Credit Extension*, U.S. Congress, House Ways and Means Committee, 98th Cong., 30–82. Washington.

Eisner, Robert. 1979. Employment Taxes and Subsidies. In *Work Time and Employment*, by National Commission for Manpower Policy, 275–310. Washington.

Eisner, Robert, Steven H. Albert, and Martin A. Sullivan. June 1984. The New Incremental Tax Credit for R&D: Incentive or Disincentive? *National Tax Journal* 37:171–83.

Fethke, Gary C., Andrew J. Policano, and Samuel H. Williamson. April 1978. Macroeconomic Implications of Employment Tax Credit Policy. Working Paper Series No. 78–4. University of Iowa, College of Business Administration, Bureau of Business and Economic Research.

————. August 1978. *An Investigation of the Conceptual and Qualitative Impact of Employment Tax Credits.* Kalamazoo, Mich.: W.E. Upjohn Institute for Employment Research.

Fethke, Gary C. and Samuel H. Williamson. January 1976. The Effects of Employment Tax Credits. Working Paper Series No. 76–3. University of Iowa, College of Business Administration, Bureau of Business and Economic Research.

————. 21 July 1976. Employment Tax Credits as a Fiscal Policy Tool. Study prepared for the U.S. Congress Joint Economic Committee, Subcommittee on Economic Growth.

————. November 1976. Fiscal Implications of a Variable Base Wage Credit.

Working Paper Series No. 76–26. University of Iowa, College of Business Administration, Bureau of Business and Economic Research.

Haveman, Robert H., and John L. Palmer, editors. 1982. *Jobs for Disadvantaged Workers.* Washington: Brookings Institution.

Kesselman, Jonathan, Samuel H. Williamson, and Ernest R. Berndt. June 1977. Tax Credits for Employment Rather than Investment. *American Economic Review* 67:339–49.

McKevitt, James D. 1978. Statement. In *Jobs Tax Credit,* Joint Hearings before the Senate Finance Subcommittee on Administration of the Internal Revenue Code and the Senate Select Committee on Small Business, 95th Cong., 2d sess., 179–96. Washington.

Nichols, Donald A. 1982. Effects on the Noninflationary Unemployment Rate. In *Jobs for Disadvantaged Workers,* edited by Haveman and Palmer, 131–58.

Office of Management and Budget, Executive Office of the President. 1986. *Special Analyses Budget of the United States Government, Fiscal Year 1987.* Washington.

Palmer, John L., editor. 1978. *Creating Jobs: Public Employment Programs and Wage Subsidies.* Washington: Brookings Institution.

Perloff, Jeffrey M., and Michael L. Wachter. May 1979. The New Jobs Tax Credit: An Evaluation of the 1977–78 Wage Subsidy Program. *American Economic Review* 69:173–79.

Stigler, George. June 1946. The Economics of Minimum Wage Legislation. *American Economic Review* 36:358–65.

Chapter Four

MATCHING WORKERS AND JOB OPPORTUNITIES: WHAT ROLE FOR THE FEDERAL–STATE EMPLOYMENT SERVICE?

Marc Bendick, Jr.

The labor exchange process brings together individuals seeking jobs and employers seeking workers. Much is at stake for American society in the labor exchange process. Not only is there the predominantly private matter of providing income for individuals and production inputs for firms—no small undertaking in a labor market of 117 million workers, 16 million employers, and 20,000 defined occupations. The process also affects central concerns of public policy, including controlling unemployment and inflation, ensuring equal employment opportunity, and utilizing national resources for maximum productivity and growth.

The federal government takes its most direct role in the labor exchange process through the federal state Employment Service (also called the Job Service).[1] Controversy and dissatisfaction have surrounded this agency for a number of years, publicly recorded as long ago as 1965 by a task force chaired by George Shultz. Some persons argue for profoundly curtailing the Employment Service's role; others advocate substantially expanding it; and many (in both of these camps) demand that its operations be more efficient and effective. Options for revitalizing the Employment Service—and the federal role in the labor exchange process more generally—are the subject of this chapter.

HOW THE LABOR EXCHANGE PROCESS WORKS

A very large number of job matching transactions are consummated in the American economy each year. This number reflects the size of the U.S. labor market, noted above. It also reflects the dynamic nature of employment in the United States, where relatively few jobs last a lifetime. One recent survey of employees found that close to 30 percent had been in their present job less than one year, and their median number of years with their present employer was 3.2 (Horvath 1982). A high volume of labor market activity is required to service the resultant volume of job turnover, as well as to accommodate new entrants to the labor market and newly created job slots.

Typically, about 5 million workers (5 percent of the labor force) and a corresponding number of job vacancies are in the market at any time (Holt, et al. 1971). During a one-month period in 1976, 9.6 million persons (both employed and unemployed) looked for a job (Rosenfeld 1977). Between 25 million and 50 million labor exchange transactions are completed in the American economy each year (Holt 1973).

Formal Job-Search Methods

The pluralistic system for mediating these transactions parallels many aspects of the American social and economic system. Many different institutions, under a variety of for-profit, nonprofit, or government sponsorship, provide labor market information and labor exchange services. Thus, when a worker seeks a job or an employer seeks an employee, multiple means of search are available; firms and job seekers commonly utilize more than one.

The following are the most common labor exchange institutions playing some intermediating role between potential employers and workers (Labor Market Intermediaries 1978):

□ *Help-wanted advertisements.* Extensive classified advertising indicating available vacancies appears in newspapers as well as in specialized trade publications.
□ *Private employment agencies.* As of 1980, there were 8,000 private employment agencies nationwide with 110,000 employees. They are characteristically small (half had fewer than five employees), individually owned, and specialized by occupation. These agencies charge fees for their services—sometimes as high as one month's wages. While there is considerable variation in payment arrangements, often these fees are paid by the employer in the case of white-collar workers and by the job seeker in the case of blue-collar or lower-skilled white-collar workers.
□ *Placement offices of educational and training institutions.* Many educational and training institutions regard initial placement of their

graduates as part of their job-preparation function. This form of assistance thus most commonly serves new labor market entrants.

☐ *Unions or professional associations.* In some occupations, such as the construction trades, unions routinely operate hiring halls and are a primary source of job referrals. In other situations, unions or professional associations offer less dominant but still active assistance, for example, by running job fairs at annual conferences.

☐ *Temporary-help agencies.* A rapidly growing segment of the market consists of firms that hire individuals for the purpose of renting them to other firms.

☐ *Social services agencies.* Unemployment is often one of a range of problems with which nonprofit or public social service agencies may seek to assist troubled or disadvantaged individuals. Job placement assistance is therefore a service in which these agencies sometimes engage.

☐ *Former employers.* In some circumstances—particularly those of plant closure or mass permanent layoff—employers provide outplacement assistance to workers.

☐ *The Employment Service.* Last but not least comes the Employment Service.

Most job matching does not involve any of these intermediary institutions but instead is achieved by job seekers applying directly to firms. This process is sometimes referred to as plant-gate hiring because in manufacturing it often occurs by workers literally walking up to plant gates to inquire about opportunities.

Personal Referrals

Often these direct applications are based on or coupled with a referral by a friend, relative, neighbor, colleague, or other person already at work at the hiring firm. There is a strong tendency for both employers and job seekers to prefer applications that arise via personal contacts. From the point of view of the job seeker, a personal source of information not only provides access to the large number of job opportunities that are never formally announced or widely advertised, but it also provides more detailed information about the characteristics of the job than would be obtained from impersonal sources. Analogous benefits accrue to the hiring company because a referral by someone the company already knows prescreens job candidates and provides information not obtainable in normal selection processes. Many employers rely on personal referrals as virtually their exclusive method of recruitment (Wegmann 1983; Bishop, Barron, and Hollenbeck 1983).

Which of these channels are most heavily utilized and most successful in leading to placement? These questions, particularly the latter one, are answered by accumulating the results of dozens of small-scale studies of placement patterns in particular localities or among particular groups of job seekers. The results of these studies are consistent. Generally, about one-third of job seekers find positions through direct application to employers. Another one-third find jobs through personal referrals. All forms of intermediated job seeking—including those utilizing published want ads and relying on employment agencies, either public or private—account for the final one-third (Wegmann 1983).[2]

IS A PRIVATE LABOR EXCHANGE SYSTEM INADEQUATE?

Given the flow of transactions successfully accomplished each year and the scale and diversity of nongovernmental institutions, we are led to ask: Is not the private system alone adequate? What justifies government involvement such as through the creation of a public employment service?

Basic to answering this question is the principle that in accomplishing a job placement transaction, the nongovernmental system is generally concerned only with the interests of the worker and the employer directly involved. It has no financial or other incentive to represent the interests of third parties. Thus, while labor exchange transactions exercise important effects on society at large, those societal interests are not represented in the transaction. In the language of economic theory, labor market transactions are public goods— goods whose consumption affects not only the party directly involved but others in the community as well (Olsen 1965).

This section will catalogue four ways in which private labor exchange transactions may be concluded satisfactorily from the point of view of the transacting parties and yet fail to achieve the outcome that is in society's best interest. In each of the four cases, the public interest calls for investing greater resources in the labor exchange process than would be invested by the employers and job candidates directly involved.

Improving the Inflation–Unemployment Trade-Off

The first way in which this occurs concerns government's responsibility for managing the national economy to achieve prosperity and growth. The primary tools for doing so are macroeconomic—fiscal, monetary, and exchange-rate policies. For unemployment in excess of, perhaps, 6 percent, economists generally agree that such tools of demand management are the appropriate ones, and activities to enhance the placement of workers (as well as efforts at worker training) are largely irrelevant. However, macroeconomic policies used to reduce unemployment through general stimulation of demand run the risk of overstimulating demand and thus triggering inflation. This possibility prevents macroeconomic means from being used as the primary approach to reducing unemployment much below the 6 percent level.

Six percent is a widely accepted cutoff because unemployment below that level is believed to be primarily structural or structural–frictional, reflecting more the mismatch between available workers and job opportunities than deficiencies in the total number of job opportunities (Abraham 1983). Increased investment in labor exchange activity is one way a further reduction can be sought. Wider dissemination of notices of job vacancies and of available workers, better procedures for matching the one with the other, or better information on which to base workers' relocation or training decisions might all accelerate the movement of job seekers into employment. A recent evaluation of the Canadian agency that is the general equivalent of the U.S. Employment Service estimated that the average worker receiving job referrals from the (Canadian) agency experienced three fewer days of unemployment during each spell of joblessness than did similar job seekers not assisted by the agency (Employment and Immigration Canada 1980).

No studies are available providing similar estimates for the Employment Service in the United States. However, if its impact is approximately the same as in the Canadian case, then the agency's contribution to national prosperity is substantial. Later in the discussion we will see that the Employment Service provides placement information to about 15 million workers in a typical year. If that assistance saves each of these job seekers three days of unemployment, then it reduces national unemployment rolls by about 200,000 full-time-equivalent workers, about 2 percent of all unemployment. This translates into a reduction of 0.2 percent in the national unemployment rate. A 1 percent reduction in unemployment adds about $85 billion per year to national production and income (Congressional Budget Office 1983).[3] The 0.2 percent reduction thus increases national income about $20 billion per year.

Equal Employment Opportunity

A second public goods aspect of labor exchange transactions arises from social concerns about equity and equal opportunity for minorities, the disadvantaged, and others experiencing special employment difficulties. Many workers in these groups cannot afford the fees charged by private placement agencies to purchase private labor exchange services. Unless publicly provided services are made available to them, they will be handicapped in the competition for jobs. This handicap contradicts the American social ideal that current circumstances should be no obstacle to advancement opportunities.

A free public labor exchange can promote equal employment opportunity also by combatting discriminatory practices that may limit the employment opportunities of minorities, youth, women, older workers, the handicapped, and other groups. This process can work in several ways, depending on the nature of the employment practices creating the problem. In circumstances of deliberate discrimination by employers, public listings of job opportunities would allow minorities to apply for positions about which they might not otherwise have known. If their applications are then denied, the groundwork has been prepared for legal actions to force the employer to comply with antidiscrimination laws. A more common circumstance is that of employers who do not deliberately discriminate but who have no motivation to go beyond the methods of generating job applicants that are cheapest and most expeditious from their point of view—methods that often utilize personal contacts to which minorities might have no access. A "free" public labor exchange might encourage such employers to advertise vacancies more broadly, since the costs of doing would be minimized.

Federal Cost Savings

Modern industrial societies such as the United States generally do not allow poor or unemployed people to starve. Unemployment insurance forms the first tier of a safety net providing income when employment is not available. Income-tested public assistance programs (such as Aid to Families with Dependent Children, food stamps, and Medicaid) provide further income transfers when this resource is exhausted. A variety of other public programs provides training, counseling, work experience, or other assistance to enhance employability.

If a public labor exchange accelerates the employment process for individuals receiving such forms of government-provided assistance, then it can substitute for some of these other public efforts. The costs of the labor exchange activity might be partially or totally recouped from reduced needs for other types of public expenditure. Each 1 percent reduction in the national unemployment rate has been estimated to generate $39 billion per year in increased tax yields and $28 billion per year in reduced public expenditures for unemployment compensation and public assistance payments (Congressional Budget Office 1985).[4] If we utilize the estimate presented earlier that the Employment Service currently reduces the national unemployment rate by 0.2 percent, then corresponding offsets (combined increase in revenues and reduction in outlays) within the federal budget would total approximately $13 billion per year.

Economics of Scale in the Production of Information

The final rationale for public involvement in the labor exchange process involves considerations of efficiency in producing labor market information and labor exchange services. Many types of information-gathering and exchange activities exhibit strong economies of scale in their production. This means that a single large firm could accomplish the task at a lower cost per unit than if the activity were undertaken by normal market processes involving a number of smaller, competing firms. Such is likely to be the case in a labor search process, where it might be highly efficient, for example, for job seekers to contact a single source that lists all vacancies available in a labor market.

A danger in such a situation, however, is that one or a small number of large private firms might successfully muster these economies of scale to lower prices, drive out competitors, and seize control of the entire market. These monopolists, thus freed from the discipline of competition, could then, with impunity, charge prices for their products above those justified by their production costs. The monopolists would then reap unusual profits; but more importantly, in response to the inappropriately high prices, the total quantity of labor exchange services produced would be smaller than the socially optimal one.

In such circumstances, one way to achieve the efficiency obtainable through monopoly production and yet prevent private exploitation is to make the sole source a public agency.

Federal versus State Roles

Calculations such as I have presented that quantify the rationale for public intervention into the labor exchange process are speculative at best. However, they indicate the possible magnitude of payoffs to society from investing in public labor exchange activities beyond those already purchased by employers and job seekers themselves. Enhanced national income totaling $20 billion per year, some of which also constituted federal cost savings, amounting to some $13 billion per year, were identified. Additional benefits accrue in terms of equal employment access and increased efficiency in the production of labor exchange services, although the magnitude of these benefits resist even rough estimation. When these benefits are compared to the annual budget of the Employment Service—about $800 million per year—they indicate that the investment is probably repaid many times over. Expansion of the Employment Service role— at least on a modest scale—is therefore likely also to be justified on a return-on-investment basis.

The next question is whether the public responsibility to obtain these societal benefits properly rests with the federal or the state and local levels of government. This issue can be examined separately for each of the four public goods rationales discussed earlier. Macroeconomic stabilization is a federal responsibility in the United States because the main policy instruments necessary to grapple with the problems—including control of the money supply, the ability to run countercyclical budgetary deficits, and control of international exchange rates—reside there (Musgrave and Musgrave 1973). Equal employment opportunity is primarily a federal responsibility as well, largely for constitutional and historical reasons. Savings to government agencies from reduced unemployment accrue to both the federal and state–local programs, but because federal expenditures predominate in many social programs, the majority of costs savings accrue at the national level.

That leaves only considerations of production efficiency to rationalize state and local involvement in public labor exchange activity. To the extent that a single nationwide job bank is the most efficient way to provide labor exchange services, then the federal government would be the logical operating agency. However, most job placements take place on a more local level, and most job candidates would not benefit substantially from knowing about vacancies located across the country. Furthermore, given the many millions of exchange transactions occurring each year, it is likely that state or local job banks in many localities could themselves achieve substantial economies of scale. Additionally, because of widely varying conditions among labor markets, it is often efficient to allow state and local systems to tailor themselves to their local circumstances. Thus, a system in which federal financing and coordination is combined with state operations—which is the current structure of the Employment Service—may well be ideal.

However, it must be emphasized that the federal role in this combination is indispensable. The system addresses essentially national problems. Responsibility for raising adequate revenues to provide the socially desirable level of services must rest with the federal government. Strong federal supervision is also required to ensure that state operations are conducted consistently with national goals and with systems and procedures compatible with interstate operations. A true federal–state partnership is called for, not simply an assignment of responsibility to either level of government alone.

THE ORIGIN AND CURRENT STATUS OF THE EMPLOYMENT SERVICE

Of course, when organized public concern about employment placement first emerged early in the nineteenth century, articulation of the theoretical rationale for public action was not the first step (Breul 1965). Instead, public concern about unemployment in the United States initially formed on an ad hoc basis around the objectives of relieving destitution and promoting political and social stability. The earliest activities were undertaken by private charities, such as those of the Humane Society in New York, as early as 1809. These efforts included job creation (relief works) as well as job placement, and peaked during the recessions which racked the country throughout the century.

By the late nineteenth century, local and state governments had joined in these efforts. The first municipal placement agency was created in New York City in 1834, followed by San Francisco (1868), and Los Angeles and Seattle (1893). State governments became active starting with Ohio (1890) and followed before 1900 by Montana, New York, Nebraska, Illinois, and Missouri. By 1923, 32 states operated agencies, while some municipal agencies also continued to exist.

The Evolution of Federal Involvement

Federal participation in these efforts began with the Immigration and Naturalization Service in 1907. A system of 50 local placement offices was eventually developed, as well as a procedure for employers to post notices of job vacancies at immigrant ports of entry. The operation was temporarily mobilized for general labor placement during World War I.

Throughout the first 30 years of the twentieth century, support gradually increased for a more permanent and dominant federal presence. The motivating forces cited in this drive included fraud and other abuses by private agencies; chronic unemployment of urban labor combined with chronic shortages of farm labor; and the generally mediocre performance of the state and municipal systems. A 1916 investigation by the U.S. Commission on Industrial Relations charged that state and local public agencies were sloppy in their record keeping; served mostly poor, unproductive workers; that offices were located in slum areas; failed to attract public support; enjoyed the confidence of neither workers nor employers; staffs were undertrained and underpaid; and often their primary purpose was to dispense political patronage (Haber and Kruger 1964).

Such pressure finally achieved its goal under the emergency conditions of the Great Depression. The Wagner-Peyser Act, forging the present federal–state Employment Service out of fragmentary state systems, was enacted as part of the New Deal's Hundred Days in 1933. Initially, its role was to screen and place millions of workers into federally funded public works and job creation schemes such as the Civilian Conservation Corps and Works Progress Administration. As the economy started to revive, the Employment Service shifted its efforts toward placement into private sector jobs. Mobilized and federalized once again during World War II to handle war labor needs, it returned to its civilian role and federal–state structure in the postwar years.

While one piece of New Deal legislation—the Wagner-Peyser Act—created the Employment Service, a different New Deal law played a crucial role in shaping its future. In 1935, the Social Security Act established the nation's system of unemployment insurance. The law then combined this new creation with the Employment Service in a system of State Employment Security Agencies and made registration with the Employment Service a condition for receiving unemployment benefits.

This pairing began the process, expanded over subsequent decades, of commissioning the Employment Service to function as an administrative and enforcement arm of various federal income-transfer programs. This role has blurred the agency's sense of mission and has distracted resources from its labor placement efforts. Additionally, the pairing began to focus agency attention on persons experiencing difficulty in the labor market rather than on the mainstream work force. This focus has proceeded to such an extent that many employers avoid utilizing the agency's services because of the low probability that referred job candidates will be attractive; and many mainstream workers avoid the agency because of the stigma attached to being referred by them.

The Employment Service at Age 50

What then is the shape of the Employment Service today, 50 years after its creation?

First, it is an organization of relatively modest scope. It operates through a nationwide system of 2500 offices and 25,000 employees. But that scale is dwarfed by other nationwide government agencies with direct client service responsibilities. For example, the Employment Service's annual administrative budget of $800 million is only one-fifth as large as that of the federal Social Security Administration. In fact, it is more reasonable to compare the Employment Service's scale to that of a large private firm. Were it a private business, the agency's annual budget of about $800 million would place it seventy-eighth on *Fortune* magazine's list of diversified service companies. This ranking is approximately the same as Kelly Services, the nation's largest temporary employment firm, and Electronic Data Systems Corporation, a software services firm which, among other roles, administers several public programs under federal contract (*Fortune* 1985).[5]

Still, the Employment Service is not a small-scale operation. In fiscal year 1979, 15.5 million job seekers registered with the Service; 9.5 million job vacancies were listed; and 4.5 million individuals were placed (*Employment and Training Report of the President* 1980). Due to federal funding cutbacks since that time, the volume of individuals placed annually has fallen. In fiscal year 1985, it stood at 3.3 million.

The Employment Service retains the federal–state structure with which it was created. In this system, the federal role is primarily a financial one. Funding for the operation of the Employment Service comes from a payroll tax, collected as part of the Federal Unemployment Tax Act (FUTA), which goes into a trust fund called the Employment Service Administration Account.[6] It is then allocated among states on the basis of their population and unemployment rate. With these federal resources, states are free to operate the system as they choose, within federal guidelines. Many, but not all states have implemented computerized data processing systems. One indication of the general permissiveness with which the federal government has exercised its powers to control state activities is that there are no requirements to standardize these systems to facilitate interstate data exchange.

The Employment Service accounts for only a small proportion of job placements. The proportion varies both by locality and type of job, but the average figure is about 7 percent (Stevens 1978).[7] Among labor market intermediary institutions, this makes it a less frequently utilized source of placements than either private employment agencies or newspaper want ads. And, as was discussed earlier in this paper, all intermediary institutions together only account for one-third of placements.

The limited market niche occupied by the Employment Service is further indicated by the characteristics of workers and job vacancies typically processed by it. The largest volume of vacancies listed with the service are for relatively poorly paid, entry-level positions in domestic service jobs, clerical occupations, and high-turnover, blue-collar jobs. Establishments using the Employment Service most frequently include bars and restaurants, hospitals, private households, gasoline stations, personal-services firms, hotels, insurance companies, and retailers. One study found that only 7.8 percent of Employment Service job openings were in professional, managerial, or technical occupations (and half of these came from firms—such as federal contractors—that are required to list all vacancies with the service). In 1981, when the average wage in all U.S. nonfarm private employment was $7.25 per hour, the average wage for jobs found through the Employment Service was $4.26 per hour. In one four-week period, 37.5 percent of new job orders received by the Employment Service were classified as low-pay and low-status, when such jobs accounted for no more than 15 percent of all U.S. employment (U.S. Department of Labor 1978).

In short, the role that the Employment Service predominantly fills is that of a central labor exchange for jobs that require little screening of applicants and a fast response. However, this limited role is a useful one. It organizes a segment of the labor market that otherwise might be even more fragmented and chaotic than it is;

and it provides services to meet at least some of the immediate placement needs of many lower-skilled, new, or ill-equipped members of the labor force.

EVALUATING THE SYSTEM'S CURRENT PERFORMANCE

Do the Employment Service's efforts represent a cost-effective use of public resources? Suggestions that it does were provided by earlier discussion of the substantial public benefits that accrue from public labor exchange activities. But only one study directly addresses the question of whether the Employment Service lives up to that potential (Johnson, et al. 1983). That study concluded that the agency's activities, studied in 1980 and 1981, returned to society $1.80 for each dollar expended. Expenditures consisted of the agency's operating costs for making referrals and placements, averaging $81 per referral and $144 per placement. Benefits consisted of increased earnings of persons employed more rapidly or in better jobs as a result of agency activities (estimated by comparing them to similar workers not receiving agency assistance). Virtually all returns accrued from services provided to female workers, with less favorable results obtained from services provided to male workers.

Such findings suggest that, at a minimum, preservation of the Employment Service at its present level and in its present form is in the public interest. However, merely doing well enough to justify not being abolished is a low standard of performance. There is broad consensus among observers of the Employment Service that the organization generally falls far short of its potential; that it is less well-managed, efficient, and effective than it could be; and that few forces are currently at work to make it function better (Stevens 1984; Holt 1973; Nightingale, et al. 1977).

There is an additional important reason to invest effort in preserving and improving the Employment Service. In the 1980s, societal consensus on federal social policy has, to some extent, broken down. Concerning the appropriate roles of government, liberals and conservatives have gravitated toward more irreconcilable positions than they had held over the previous 20 years. In these unsettled circumstances, the Employment Service may present an opportunity to rediscover common ground. By facilitating the improvement of private labor markets and by avoiding selection of narrow population groups eligible to receive its services, public labor exchange activities should be more acceptable to conservatives than alternative federal employment initiatives such as public-sector job creation or training programs explicitly reserved for the disadvantaged. Yet by actually providing services to the disadvantaged and by representing the public interest in private transactions, these same activities should appeal to liberals. The Employment Service may represent a type of federal social activism consistent with the antigovernment ideology that shapes much of current U.S. social policy.[8] In response to this sense of unfilled expectations and residual promise, many reforms have been proposed for the Employment Service.

REFORM OPTION ONE: INCREMENTAL REFORM

The first alternative encompasses various proposals which would not alter the basic structure or mission of the agency but instead concentrate on increasing its operational efficiency and effectiveness.

Implementing Cost-Effective Automation Technology

Almost every discussion of the efficiency of the Employment Service starts with the issue of automated data processing. The labor exchange function involves tasks ideally suited to the application of modern computer systems: storage and frequent revision of large data sets; rapid access to information by many simultaneous users; and searching and matching among large numbers of data items. Yet the current level of data processing technology in the Employment Service is surprisingly primitive. Most states have implemented some degree of computerization, leaving a handful (including California) still using clumsy microfiche and index card systems. Of the automated states, about 20 have on-line systems with constant updates; the rest require batch processing and hand delivery of computer tapes (usually overnight). As of 1984, more than half the computers used in state systems were more than five years old (Interstate Conference of Employment Security Agenices 1984). As of 1985 only 16 states had systems for automated matching of applicants and job vacancies (Legrande 1985). The situation has not improved much since then.

The system in the state of Missouri provides an example of the sophisticated operating systems which are technologically possible. In Missouri, the entire state Employment Service is operated on a paperless basis. Its computer system connects every placement technician at all offices in the state (as well as in counties of Kansas and Illinois adjacent to the Kansas City and St. Louis metropolitan areas). The data bank of workers in the system contains files for 600,000 workers—25 percent of the state's entire civilian labor force—and includes detailed testing data as well as standard work histories and demographic information. New job-vacancy orders are entered into the system immediately upon receipt, and each action on a vacancy (such as referral of a job candidate) is also immediately recorded. The system allows placement technicians to search for job candidates or available vacancies using a wide variety of criteria, singly or in combination, and at varying levels of qualifications. The system also automatically produces a variety of reports for monitoring the processing of job applicants and vacancies and for comparing and evaluating the performance of individual offices and employees.

Perhaps most crucially, according to officials in Missouri, the system has resulted in employee productivity gains that have repaid most of the costs of developing, installing, and operating the system. In 1984 it was estimated that to automate those states still utilizing manual systems and to modernize all state systems to a reasonable level of current technology would require an investment of $283 million over a five-year period (Interstate Conference of Employment Security Agencies 1984). These expenditures would represent about 7 percent of the total Employment Service operating budget nationwide over that five-year period. It thus appears not to be an inordinate level of investment, but it does not seem to be materializing.

If the claims of Missouri officials are correct and the results are replicable in other states, then additional investments in state-of-the-art data processing technology should be immediately undertaken. Even in a tight fiscal environment such as the federal government currently faces, expenditures can be justified which save as much as they cost. Indeed, the federal role required to support automation may consist primarily of lending states money from the Employment Service trust fund, rather than making grants to them, since these loans could be repaid out of future savings in operating costs.

Improving the Interstate Placement System

After improved data processing, the reform that most appeals to the imagination is expansion of the Employment Service's role in interstate job placement. Much has been written on shifting regional patterns of employment in the United States, including the decline of the Frost Belt and the expansion of the Sun Belt. Could not a nationwide job bank assist unemployed steel workers in Ohio to obtain jobs building aircraft in California?

For the past decade, a rudimentary form of interstate job bank has been operated by the federal government in Albany, New York, through a contract with the New York State employment service. Currently, this system lists about 44,000 vacancies each year, a fraction of 1 percent of the vacancy flow handled by state systems. A more major-scale interstate exchange system has been estimated to cost about $30 to $40 million for annual operations (U.S. House of Representatives 1983)—about 5 percent of the Employment Services's annual budget; no estimates of the costs of initial development and installation are readily available.

Part of the reason for the limited performance of the present interstate system is the limited automation in states' own placement operations already noted. Only five states send to, and receive data from, the interstate system by telecommunications. The rest mail data tapes or, in the case of seven states, paper records. The resultant turnaround of eight to ten days means that many of the interstate listings are not timely.

Even if more ideal technology were in place, caution should govern expectations concerning the extent to which interstate exchanges of job listings would significantly reduce geographical imbalances in the American labor market. Lack of information on available job opportunities is only one element in workers' immobility. Many workers are reluctant to move for a variety of social and psychological reasons. More important, few workers are willing to undertake the expense of relocation unless the financial returns of the available job are substantial (Bendick 1984b). So long as typical vacancies listed with the Employment Service remain low-pay, entry-level positions, little purpose is served by advertising them across the country.

In short, however appealing the concept of expanded interstate placement may be, it appears that its development should be postponed until prerequisite technological and performance improvements are achieved in intrastate operations.

Altering Mandates to Focus on the Hard-to-Employ

More basic to the future of the Employment Service than any technological issue is that of the agency's mission. As is clear from its history, the agency has been repeatedly diverted from its fundamental labor exchange role by requirements to monitor the work availability of unemployment insurance beneficiaries and recipients of other income support programs. Over time, the agency has been legally required to expend special efforts on behalf of an ever-lengthening list of special groups of workers, each time further identifying itself with the hard-to-employ and separating it from the mainstream labor market.

Some commentators have advocated that both these processes be reversed—that the agency be relieved of special administrative functions and that special mandates be swept aside in favor of facilitating labor placement equally for all who seek assistance. One proposal would separate the Employment Service administratively (and even physically, in terms of local offices) from the Unemployment Insurance Service. Another would abolish mandatory Employment Service registration as a condition for receiving unemployment benefits and other income support. A third, already implemented in the Job Training Partnership Act of 1982, amended the Wagner-Peyser Act to delete special financial incentives provided to states as a reward for successfully placing members of selected target groups.

The benefits of such changes are hard to measure, but they might be substantial, at least in the long run. Staff, management attention, and other resources could be reallocated toward the basic placement function, which might then be pursued with increased vigor. The image of the agency might slowly change so that employers might increase their listing of higher-quality job opportunities. The expanded access to vacancies, in the long run, would increase the ability of the agency to open labor market opportunities to the hard-to-employ themselves.

The disadvantage of such actions is an almost certain reduction in the assistance provided in the short run for the disadvantaged and other vulnerable groups in the labor market. Employment Service local offices are constantly tempted to cultivate good relations with employers by referring their best job candidates and blocking referrals to those more difficult to place. This tendency to cream in the interests of better serving employers has been observed throughout the federal employment and training system in the past five years (see Nightingale [1985] and Barnow's further discussion in chapter 5).

Cultivating Relationships with Employers

A reduction in focus on the hard-to-employ would begin to implement another proposal for improving Employment Service performance: to build better relationships with employers and thereby to increase the Employment Service's share of the labor exchange market. Changes in this area, however, risk competing with private employment agencies.

A broader range of job candidates available for referrals might induce a broader range of employers to list their vacancies with the service. Currently, the agency receives referrals from only about 3 percent of all employers; there is substantial opportunity for expansion, both among employers already dealing with the Employment Service and other industries as well.

Some actions to improve relationships with employers would not involve the same potentially adverse impacts on the disadvantaged as was discussed above, but instead would represent straightforward improvements in efficiency. One example is provided by the concept of reorganizing work tasks within a local office to create account executives who serve as the single point of contact for all agency dealings with an employer. By establishing an ongoing personal relationship and by making one staff member responsible for learning in detail about a company's needs, the account executive form of organization can enhance the agency's ability to serve an employer and thus increase that firm's utilization of the service. It also represents implementation in a public agency of management practices common in private business. A second possibility would have the Employment Service become more active in contacting employers to develop job opportunities, rather than passively waiting for employers to contact them; 40 percent of all placements by private employment agencies are achieved through such efforts. A number of such changes in operational policy might be implemented without large additional expenditures.

These possibilities raise important questions of the justification for a publicly financed employment service. Better service to employers by the Employment Service might increase the extent to which job searches currently not assisted by any placement intermediary would be assisted and thus speeded. In that case, additional public goods benefits would be generated, and U.S. economy and society would be better off. But if the Employment Service too closely matches the role played by private employment agencies, then the major effect would be displacement of private activity with public activity. This outcome would generate few net benefits; would represent a politically unpopular intrusion of government into activity considered, in the United States, the legitimate province of private enterprise; and would provide public subsidies, in the form of free services, to many large and prosperous corporations.[9]

In short, the challenge is to improve Employment Service operations by adopting some of the approaches associated with successful operation of private employment agencies and yet not to shift the market niche of the agency from that of supplementing private activity to one of substituting for it.

Expanding Client Services

Referrals to vacancies is the core activity of a labor exchange agency, but it need not be the only one. Career counseling, testing and evaluation, applicant screening, and training in job search techniques are among the services provided by the Employment Service at various times and locations. In fiscal year 1981, 7 percent of all agency clients received counseling, 5 percent received testing, 1 percent obtained training referrals, and 12 percent got special attention for active job development. The rest simply received the core service of access to lists of vacancies (*Employment and Training Report of the President* 1982). Various proposals to enhance the operations of the Employment Service have advocated expanding the range of services offered and the proportion of agency clients receiving them. None of this has happened to date.

The experience of employment and training agencies other than the Employment Service is that, appropriately targeted and delivered, many of these services can be useful and cost-effective means of enhancing the employability of many workers (Bendick 1985). The question remains, however, whether or not the Employment Service is the appropriate agency for delivering such services. An alternative would be for the Employment Service to refer job seekers desiring such additional assistance to some other public agency—for example, the local service delivery agency implementing the Job Training Partnership Act or the local vocational education system. Alternatively, the Employment Service itself could be vastly expanded to absorb these other agencies and become a broad, multi-product human resources development agency.

The main current federal legislation covering employment services, the Job Training Partnership Act of 1982, provides federal human resources funding to states in a block-grant form (see chapter 5 for full discussion). This allows states considerable flexibility in selecting organizational arrangements to implement program operations. Perhaps the wisest course would be to observe the experience of states electing different organizational approaches before launching a major-scale reorganization to expand the range of functions provided by the Employment Service itself.

REFORM OPTION TWO: PRIVATIZATION

An alternative approach, which would render all proposals for agency reform irrelevant, would be to abolish the Employment Service altogether and turn over all federal labor exchange activities to the private sector (Butler 1985).

The most extreme version of this approach would withdraw all federal funding for labor exchange activities, thereby leaving private employers and job seekers to determine the quantity of labor exchange activity and labor market information. The public-goods reasons why such a course would deprive American society and the American economy of substantial benefits—amounting to many millions of dollars each year—are enough to reject this approach.

A more viable version of privatization would have the federal government continue to finance labor exchange activities, but to contract with private firms to deliver services rather than operate a public agency for this purpose. After all, economic theory argues that only the financing of public goods must be public, because financing is what determines the quantity produced; it does not require that actual production be a public activity. Given the extensive, diverse set of private labor-market intermediaries already operating in the American labor market, there would be little problem in locating willing private contractors.

Conversion into a Nonprofit Institution

One form in which the contracting-out approach has been discussed in the context of the Employment Service is to turn the agency itself into a private nonprofit foundation receiving government funding through service contracts. This foundation would then compete against alternative suppliers—both for-profit and nonprofit—for a state or locality's business.

These competitive pressures might serve as a catalyst to reforms in agency operations such as were discussed under reform option one. These might, in turn, improve the efficiency and effectiveness with which labor exchange services are provided—a positive outcome. However, it is likely that a more common result would be the eventual disappearance of many of these newly privatized organizations. This is because, with the exception of a small number of state and local agencies whose performance is above average, many Employment Service operations would be ill-equipped to upgrade their performance rapidly enough to compete.

Experience with Contracting Out

Of course, to the extent that inefficient public agencies would disappear and their work be transferred to more competent suppliers, the objective of obtaining greater efficiency in the delivery of public services would have been met. However, the results of past experiments with contracting out employment placement services suggest that the performance advantage of private agencies over public ones is more apparent than real. Often it derives primarily from the private agencies selecting the clients that are easiest to serve, rather than from greater efficiency in servicing the entire population which the public agency is required to handle.

One experiment was conducted in the Detroit area, where private, for-profit employment agencies were given contracts to find jobs for welfare recipients (Caragno, Cecil, and Ohls 1982). The private agencies succeeded in obtaining placements for less than 4 percent of their assigned welfare clients. These placements were typically of short duration and the same sorts of entry-level, low-wage placements typical of the Employment Service itself.

A second trial of contracting out involved 104 private agencies in four counties in California. In this case, 30 percent of welfare recipients were placed, which was considered a favorable outcome. However, the group which was accepted by these private firms for placement, and for whom this impressive placement rate was obtained, was drawn from the more qualified portions of the welfare client population. The program was not noticeably more successful than the public agency in dealing with the most disadvantaged, difficult-to-place cases. Furthermore, the costs of placement were substantially higher through private agencies—averaging $700 per placement—than they were in the public system. Similar results in terms of success rates, client creaming, and costs were reported in a parallel trial in Pennsylvania (Stevens 1984).

A final demonstration of the contracting-out approach involved efforts to reemploy dislocated midcareer industrial workers in Buffalo. The private agency in this case virtually failed to perform at all. One difficulty was that the firm was unused to dealing with blue-collar workers. A more basic problem was that in the severely depressed Buffalo economy, employers felt no need to deal with any kind of intermediary when seeking employees (Jerrett, et al. 1983).

In short, there is little evidence that privatizing the operations of the Employment Service would lead to enhanced efficiency.

REFORM OPTION THREE: A UNIVERSAL LABOR EXCHANGE SYSTEM

A final option for the future of the Employment Service would proceed in a manner exactly opposite to privatization. It would entail a dramatic expansion of the public role, including at least some displacement of private employment intermediation activity. For example, we could consider developing a public role on the model of that in Sweden. There, employment intermediation is a state monopoly. Private employment placement agencies are (with only limited exceptions) illegal, and every job vacancy must be listed with the state system (Bendick 1984a).

Such a state monopoly would presumably generate all possible economies of scale in the production of labor exchange services. And it would have the greatest opportunities to generate the three other forms of public goods benefits from labor exchange services because it would be best positioned to expand public activities to whatever scale is socially desirable.

One key question about the experience of Sweden is whether development of the state system increased the total amount of labor exchange services or merely substituted public activity for private activity. Estimates of the proportion of placements accounted for by the state system range from 50 percent to 70 percent. Earlier in this chapter I reported that the proportion of job placements in the United States accounted for by all intermediated modes of placement did not exceed one-third. If the proportion in Sweden, in the absence of the state monopoly, would be at all similar to that in the United States, then it appears that development of the state system has substantially increased the proportion of labor exchange activities that is intermediated. Thus, at least one precondition for the development of an expanded public system to generate increased amounts of public goods benefits appears to be satisfied.

Adapting to the American Context

Assuming that such a system might be desirable in the United States, would it be politically feasible?

One important aspect of this question is whether it would be feasible to require employers to list all job vacancies. The political costs of seeking this requirement would be substantial, as employers are generally adamantly opposed to it. They fear the administrative costs of processing a large volume of applications for each job opening, and they resent the loss of discretion to manage their employee search processes as they see fit.

Difference in circumstances between the United States and Sweden are instructive on this point. Sweden is a smaller, highly homogeneous society with a long tradition of tripartite cooperation among labor, management, and government. Public listings of job vacancies was made mandatory in Sweden in 1970. But prior to that legal mandate, about 60 percent of all vacancies were already being voluntarily listed with the public labor exchange—many times the market penetration in the United States. Belief in the efficacy of the system or in the social desirability of supporting the public system preceded, rather than followed, the legal requirements.

Where mandatory job listings have been tried in the United States—such as for large federal contractors—the results have not generally been impressive. Many of these listings appear to represent pro forma efforts to comply with legal requirements rather than serious efforts to expand the range of job applications. The net effect is extra paperwork without improvements in labor market outcomes.

A second major characteristic of the Swedish model is that it is a state monopoly. Given the private-market orientation of the American economic system, it is virtually impossible to imagine adoption of such a law in the United States.

In addition to being unlikely, the award of monopoly rights would probably be undesirable. Substantial economies of scale can presumably be captured without unifying all labor exchange activities into a single system. Besides, development of a monopoly might well stifle innovation in what is a very dynamic component of the American economy. Private firms are presently experimenting with a number of revolutionary ways to search for employees. For example, some high-technology companies are listing vacancies directly on computer files accessible from job seekers' home computers. At the same time, private placement firms are responding flexibly and creatively to changes in the market. There is rapid growth in private employment agencies—an increase in total employment of 431 percent in this industry over the 1960–80 period (Stevens 1984). Among temporary employment agencies, the growth rate has been 123 percent in only a five-year period. Outlawing private employment placement would probably be counterproductive in stifling such developments.

The Role of a Dramatic Goal

The upshot of these considerations is that, realistically, the U.S. Employment Service must continue to generate its own market niche parallel to other intermediaries operating in a pluralistic market, and continue to earn its listings rather than having them mandated.

The agenda for doing so presumably includes as first steps some of the incremental reforms discussed under reform option one. Thus, one approach to the question of whether an expanded public labor exchange role should be sought would be to postpone a decision until more modest and basic reforms have been implemented.

The difficulty with this strategy is that little progress might be made on small-scale reform measures unless momentum is generated by announcement of a more visionary objective. An alternative approach might involve declaring the development of a very visible, high-technology labor exchange system a national objective—much as the declaration that a national effort would be made to place a man on the moon. A crash program like the Manhattan Project could then be established to carry out the effort. The eventual benefits of the effort might not justify such drama; but the drama itself may be necessary to achieve any progress.

CONCLUSIONS

Strict conservatives would limit the role of government in the United States to a narrow core of essential public functions such as maintaining the national defense and preserving law and order. Nothing in this chapter has supported the claim that public intermediation in the labor market meets that most stringent test of legitimacy. However, much in the chapter has supported this public role in relation to a more realistic standard: is the public function providing useful services, with the benefits outweighing the costs? American society and the American economy derive substantial benefits from the Employment Service. The agency's activities generate multiple billions of dollars of public goods—goods that are undersupplied by the private market alone. The agency gains its market niche largely by displacing nonintermediated job search rather than at the expense of privately funded employment placement activity. The Employment Service is a national resource and could not be eliminated without substantial loss.

The question, then, is how best to preserve and enhance the performance of an agency which, while turning in a cost-effective performance, offers substantial opportunities for improvement. Which of the three options for the future is most likely to develop the federal role in the labor exchange process in the most socially beneficial manner?

Among the three, the privatization approach seems the least likely to be productive, although it might lead to some improvements in the internal efficiency of the agency. However, its most likely result would be to accelerate the process of agency shrinkage and withdrawal of federal support, furthering the trend of the past eight years. Dramatic expansion of the agency and its role offers some possibilities but also embodies some dangers. Unrealistic expectations, as well as political opposition, could threaten both the success of an expansion effort and the survival of the agency itself.

The approach of incremental reform, while lacking the excitement associated with the other two approaches, probably offers the greatest possibilities for actual improvement. Steady attention to mundane operations is probably the key to generating surprising social benefits—for agency reform, just as for this underappreciated agency itself.

Notes

The author gratefully acknowledges the helpful comments of C. Bruce Cornett, Mary Lou Egan, and David W. Stevens.

1. Government influences this process in indirect ways as well, such as through laws forbidding discrimination in hiring, governing the compensation and conditions of employment, and licensing and regulating occupations. Also, government agencies other than the Employment Service undertake labor exchange activities, either in conjunction with their role as an employer or as part of other employment and training initiatives. These roles are largely beyond the scope of this chapter.

2. See also Stevens (1978); U.S. Department of Labor (1975); and U.S. Department of Labor (1976).

3. This assumes that the person becoming employed does not simply displace someone else onto the unemployment rolls, in which case the net savings may be zero.

4. The same caution stated in note 3 also applies here.

5. Federal budget numbers refer to fiscal year 1985 (*Federal Budget of the United States, Fiscal Year 1986*, I-05) and exclude funds for labor market information activities.

6. Currently, the level of this tax is .8 percent of the first $7,000 in wages earned by an employee each year (i.e., a maximum of $56 per employee).

7. These estimates refer to the proportion of successful placements. In surveys on use of the system (whether or not use led to placement and whether or not other job-seeking approaches were also utilized), about 25 percent of unemployed job seekers report using the Employment Service. In many cases, however, that use refers simply to registering with the Employment Service to establish eligibility for unemployment insurance benefits.

8. For more on what American ideology allows in terms of public social roles, see Bendick (forthcoming).

9. The services are not precisely free, of course, in the sense that employers have paid a $56 annual tax per employee to fund the Employment Service. But they are free in the sense that, once that tax has been paid, no additional charges are levied for services performed.

References

Abraham, Katherine G. September 1983. Structural/Frictional vs. Deficient Demand Unemployment: Some New Evidence. *American Economic Review* 73.

Bendick, Jr., Marc. 1984a. The Swedish Active Labor Market System for Reemploying Displaced Workers. *Journal of Health and Human Resources Administration* 6:209–24. February.

———. 1984b. Worker Mobility in Response to Plant Closure. In *Managing Plant Closures and Occupational Readjustment*, edited by Richard Swigart. Washington: National Center for Occupational Readjustment.

———. 1985. Employment and Training Programs to Reduce Structural Unemployment. In *Policy Studies Review Annual*, edited by Ray Rist, 7:359–78. New Brunswick, N.J.: Transaction Books.

———. Forthcoming. Privatization: An Idea To Be Taken Seriously. In *Privatization and the Welfare State*, edited by Sheila Kamerman and Alfred J. Kahn. Princeton: Princeton University Press.

Bishop, John, John Barron, and Kevin Hollenbeck. 1983. *Recruiting Workers: How Recruitment Policies Affect the Flow of Applicants and the Quality of New Workers*. Columbus, Ohio: National Center for Research in Vocational Education.

Breul, Frank. 1965. Early History of Aid to the Unemployed in the United States. In *In Aid of the Unemployed*, edited by Joseph R. Becker. Baltimore: Johns Hopkins University Press.

Butler, Stuart M. 1985. *Privatizing Federal Spending*. New York: Universe Books.

Carcagno, George, Robert Cecil, and James C. Ohls. Winter 1982. Using Private Employment Agencies to Place Public Assistance Clients in Jobs. *Journal of Human Resources* 17:132–43.

Economic and Budgetary Outlook, Fiscal Years 1986–1991. 1985. Washington: Congressional Budget Office.

Employment and Training Report of the President. 1980 and 1982. Washington.

Federal Budget of the United States, Fiscal Year 1986. Washington: Congressional Budget Office.

Haber, William, and Daniel H. Kruger. 1964. *The Role of the United States Employment Service in a Changing Economy*. Kalamazoo, Mich.: W.E. Upjohn Institute for Employment Research.

Holt, Charles C. 1973. *The Potential Impact of the Employment Service on the Economy*. Washington: Urban Institute.

Hold, Charles C., Duncan MacRae, Stuart O. Schweitzer, and Ralph E. Smith. 1971. *Manpower Programs to Reduce Inflation and Unemployment*. Washington: Urban Institute.

Horvath, Francis. September 1982. Job Tenure of Workers in January 1981. *Monthly Labor Review* 105.

The Impact of the Canadian Placement Service on the Labour Market. 1980. Ottawa: Employment and Immigration Canada.

Jerrett, Marcia, et al. 1983. *Serving the Dislocated Worker*. Cambridge, Mass.: Abt Associates.

Jobseeking Methods Used by American Workers. 1975. Washington: U.S. Department of Labor.

Johnson, Terry R., et al. 1983. *A National Evaluation of the Impact of the United States Employment Service*. Menlo Park, Calif.: SRI International.

Labor Market Intermediaries. 1978. Washington: National Commission for Employment Policy.

Legrande, Linda. 1985. *The National Job Bank System*. Washington: Congressional Research Service.

Musgrave, Richard A., and Peggy B. Musgrave. 1973. *Public Finance in Theory and Practice*. New York: McGraw Hill.

Nightingale, Demetra Smith. 1985. *Federal Employment and Training Policy Changes During the Reagan Administration: State and Local Responses*. Washington: Urban Institute Press.

Nightingale, Demetra, et al. 1977. *The Employment Service: An Institutional Analysis*. Washington: U.S. Department of Labor.

Olsen, Mancur. 1965. *The Logic of Collective Action.* Cambridge, Mass.: Harvard University Press.

The Outlook for Economic Recovery. 1983. Washington: Congressional Budget Office.

Recruitment, Job Search, and the United States Employment Service. 1976. Washington: U.S. Department of Labor.

A Report on the Data Processing Financing Needs of the Employment Security System. 1984. Washington: Interstate Conference of Employment Security Agencies.

Rosenfeld, Carl. March 1977. The Extent of Job Search by Employed Workers. *Monthly Labor Review* 100.

Stevens, David W. 1978. A Reexamination of What is Known about Job-seeking Behavior in the United States. In *Labor Market Intermediaries.* Washington: National Commission for Employment Policy.

———. 1984. *Public and Private Employment Agency Roles in Providing Labor Market Information and Job Search Assistance.* Columbia, Mo.: Human Resources Data Systems.

U.S. Department of Labor. 1977. *The Employment Service: An Institutional Analysis.* Washington.

———. 1973. *The Public Employment Service and Help Wanted Ads.* Washington: U.S. Department of Labor.

U.S. House of Representatives, Committee on Science and Technology. April 1983. *Hearings on Job Forecasting.*

Wegmann, Robert G. 1983. *Dealing with High Unemployment: Improving Job Search Strategies and Other Policy Options.* Houston, Tex.: University of Houston.

Chapter Five

GOVERNMENT TRAINING AS A MEANS OF REDUCING UNEMPLOYMENT

Burt S. Barnow

Since the early 1960s, government-sponsored training programs have been used as part of the nation's overall strategy for attempting to reduce unemployment and poverty. As defined in this paper, government training programs include classroom or on-the-job instruction in vocational skills, job search, and, in some cases, basic education. They do not include direct employment programs, such as public service employment and work experience, which are sometimes grouped with training programs.

Defining government training programs is not as simple a task as one might expect. Classroom training provided under government training programs sometimes focuses entirely, or in part, on basic education rather than vocational skills.[1] Vocational education, especially at the postsecondary level, provides instruction in a classroom setting that may be identical to the instruction provided in training programs. Finally, on-the-job training programs, where employers are reimbursed for up to 50 percent of wages, do not necessarily have formal training components and in some instances could be viewed more appropriately as wage subsidies than training. In reviewing the record of training programs, the reader should be aware that some of what has been characterized as training may not be what one would typically consider to be training.

Government training programs are only a small component of the gross national product and of government spending. One should not conclude, however, that training programs are therefore an unimportant or insignificant tool to be used in reducing unemployment. There is evidence, albeit tentative, that government training programs, on average, have had a positive impact on the employment and earnings of participants. In developing an overall employment policy for the nation, the successes of training programs should be kept in mind as well as the failures. Perhaps most important, even in this period of new federalism, where state and local governments are asked to assume increased responsibility for program content, an overall effort must be made to determine what works best and to concentrate on replicating the best features if training programs are to maximize effectiveness.

BACKGROUND ON GOVERNMENT TRAINING PROGRAMS

For the past two decades the federal government has been providing training to selected target groups through a series of laws. This section briefly reviews earlier programs and provides more detail about the Job Training Partnership Act (JTPA), which is currently the major training legislation in effect.

Prior Training Programs

The Manpower Development and Training Act (MDTA) of 1962 served as the nation's principal training program until 1973. The program's original premise was that automation in factories was likely to lead to substantial unemployment among experienced workers who would not be well prepared for the major changes that would occur.[2] Massive dislocation did not take place, so the program was amended in 1963 to enroll younger participants. At the same time that the anticipated automation crisis failed to materialize, the country began its War on Poverty, and MDTA became more oriented toward the economically disadvantaged. MDTA provided institutional and on-the-job training to participants through national contracts and agreements with state and local governments.

In 1973, MDTA was replaced by the Comprehensive Employment and Training Act (CETA). CETA consolidated a number of employment and training initiatives, and it assigned primary responsibility for administering programs to local units of government called prime sponsors. Public service employment and work experience programs were also included under CETA. CETA was amended several times over the decade it was in existence. The training programs were not affected greatly by the amendments, although the volume of public service employment grew rapidly, later was reduced, and finally was eliminated from the program. The training programs were oriented toward the economically disadvantaged, with some provision for upgrading and retraining; the public service employment programs served both countercyclical and structural purposes.

The Job Training Partnership Act

In October 1983, the Job Training Partnership Act replaced CETA as the major employment and training legislation in the United States. Programs supported under JTPA include training for economically disadvantaged youth and adults under Title IIA, a summer jobs program for disadvantaged youth under Title IIB, a training program for dislocated workers under Title III, and a series of national programs under Title IV.[3]

JTPA differs from CETA in several ways that have influenced who is served and how they are served; it is too soon to know if JTPA will differ in how well participants are served. The Title IIA program is the major training component for the economically disadvantaged, replacing Titles IIB and IIC of CETA. The major eligibility criteria for Title IIA are having a low family income or receiving welfare payments.[4] Ninety percent of the Title IIA participants must meet one of the criteria defining economically disadvantaged. The remaining 10 percent can have other barriers to employment. Interestingly, unemployment is not an eligibility criterion, and a full-time employed family head earning the minimum wage is likely to be eligible for the program under the criteria defining economically disadvantaged.

JTPA lists nearly 30 activities under Title IIA that can be classified under the broad categories of classroom training, on-the-job training, job search assistance, or work experience. As under CETA, participants in on-the-job training receive wages from their employer, which are typically subsidized at a rate of 50 percent. Those enrolled in classroom training are less likely to receive stipends than CETA enrollees, however, because JTPA places strict limits on the share of funds that can be used for paying stipends and other forms of financial support (e.g., allowances and needs-based payments).

Significant organizational differences also exist between JTPA and CETA training programs for the economically disadvantaged. JTPA programs are operated at the local level by what are called service delivery areas (SDAs), which report to the state government. Under CETA the prime sponsors, operating at the local level, reported instead to the federal government. Although the intent was to have fewer SDAs than the number of prime sponsors under CETA, there actually are more (almost 600 SDAs compared to about 450 CETA prime sponsors); this has occurred because there is no provision for a single entity—called a balance-of-state prime sponsor under CETA—to cover rural and small labor market areas. This means that what once was one CETA balance-of-state area may now be several SDAs.

Each SDA is required to have a private industry council (PIC), and a majority of the PIC members must be representatives of the private sector, selected from nominations by a general-purpose business organization. The PICs, which approve SDA policies and actions, can exercise a great deal of authority.

Another important feature of the Title IIA training program is that the governor of each state must issue performance standards for the SDAs in the state. The secretary of labor has issued four national standards for adults (the rate at which participants enter employment, cost per participant entering employment, average wage at placement, and the rate at which participants on welfare enter employment) and three national standards for youth under age 22 (the rate at which youth participants enter employment, positive termination rate, and cost per positive termination).[5] Governors may weight the secretary's standards, and they can add additional standards or delete one or more of the secretary's standards. They may also use a series of regression models developed by the Department of Labor to adjust the standards for local economic conditions and the demographic characteristics of participants in order to encourage services to individuals in groups that are harder to place. Governors may provide financial incentives to SDAs that exceed their standards and take sanctions against SDAs that fail to meet the standards two years in a row. Governors are also permitted to award extra funds to SDAs for including hard-to-serve individuals.

The provisions of JTPA noted above—restrictions on stipends, support services, and work experience; the strong role of the private sector through the private industry councils; and the emphasis on performance—led many observers to predict that JTPA would "cream" among the economically disadvantaged, that is, would serve those with the brightest employment prospects rather than those most in need. A study by Walker, Feldstein, and Solow (1985) covering the first nine months of the program bears out these predictions; they conclude that "most SDAs did not pay any attention to the statute's broad mandate to serve the most in need of and able to benefit from its services." However, this creaming phenomenon should be kept in perspective—94 percent of the participants during this period were classified as economically disadvantaged.

JTPA enrolled 586,000 individuals during the nine-month transition year from 1 October 1983 through 30 June 1984 in Title IIA

programs; during the first 12 months of operation the program enrolled 759,000 individuals.[6] For the most recently reported program
year, July 1986 through June 1987, slightly over 786,000 individuals
enrolled in the program. On average, there were about 350,000 participants in the program at any given time. Characteristics of the
enrollees for the most recent program year available, July 1986 through
June 1987, are shown in table 5.1. Nearly half (46 percent) were
members of a minority group, and 42 percent were receiving public
assistance at enrollment; these percentages have remained stable
over JTPA's existence. The only evidence of possible creaming from
the data available is the education level of the enrollees—56 percent
were high school graduates, including 17 percent who had some
education beyond high school. JTPA requires that at least 40 percent
of the expenditures be on youth, so it is not surprising that 42 percent
of the enrollees were youth under age 22.

Classroom training was the most common activity, with 36 percent
of the enrollees initially assigned in program year (PY) 1986. Another
22 percent were enrolled in on-the-job training, with 19 percent in
job search assistance, 9 percent in work experience, and 14 percent
in other activities. The Department of Labor has not published data
on what percent of classroom training is basic education rather than
vocational. Job search assistance was virtually unused under CETA.

There were some differences in enrollee characteristics among activities, as is shown in table 5.2. Men were overrepresented in on-
the-job training (56 percent), and underrepresented in classroom
training (39 percent). Youth under age 22 comprised 75 percent of
those enrolled in work experience but only 27 percent of the on-the-
job training enrollees. High school graduates comprised 72 percent
of on-the-job training enrollees, but only 27 percent of those in work
experience.

In summary, the JTPA Title IIA program is largely serving economically disadvantaged individuals, with a significant share of enrollees being members of minority groups and public assistance
recipients. However, many observers of the program believe that the
SDAs have made a deliberate effort to select the most employable
among the eligible population. Whether this is a wise policy will be
explored in the final section of the chapter.

The JTPA Title III program for dislocated workers differs substantially from the Title IIA program for the economically disadvantaged.
First, eligibility requirements are very broad and provide the states
great discretion in whom to serve; virtually any long-term unemployed worker could be considered eligible, as well as more obvious

Table 5.1 CHARACTERISTICS OF JTPA TITLE IIA ENROLLEES IN THE
TRANSITION YEAR (OCTOBER 1983–84) AND PROGRAM YEAR 1986
(JULY 1986–JUNE 1987)

Characteristics	Transition year (%)	Program year 1986 (%)
Sex		
Male	50	47
Female	50	53
Minority status		
White (excluding Hispanic)	54	54
Black (excluding Hispanic)	32	32
Hispanic	10	10
Other	4	4
Age at enrollment		
Less than 19	19	25
19–21	20	17
22–29	30	27
30–44	24	24
45–54	5	4
55 and older	2	3
Economically disadvantaged		
Yes	94	93
No	6	7
Receiving AFDC at application		
Yes	21	23
No	79	77
Receiving any public assistance at application		
Yes	41	42
No	59	58
Education status		
School dropout	24	26
Student (high school or less)	14	18
High school graduate (no postsecondary)	44	39
Post high school attendee	18	17

Sources: U.S. Department of Labor, Office of Strategic Planning and Policy
Development, Summary of JTLS Data for JTPA Title IIA Enrollments and
Terminations During the Transition Year, November 1984, table A-1; and U.S.
Department of Labor, Office of Strategic Planning and Policy Development,
Summary of JTQS Data for JTPA Title IIA and III Enrollments and Terminations
During PY 1986, December 1987, table C-1.

JTPA   Job Training Partnership Act.
AFDC   Aid to Families with Dependent Children.

Table 5.2 CHARACTERISTICS OF JTPA TITLE IIA ENROLLEES BY ACTIVITY,
PROGRAM YEAR 1986 (JULY 1986–JUNE 1987)

		Initial program activity				
Characteristics	Overall	Classroom training	On-the-job training	Job search assistance	Work experience	Other
Percent male	47	39	56	52	50	50
Percent minority	47	49	37	53	55	42
Percent under age 22	42	39	27	36	75	63
Percent economically disadvantaged	93	94	93	93	94	91
Percent receiving public assistance	42	49	33	37	45	42
Percent high school graduate	56	58	72	63	27	37

Source. U.S. Department of Labor, Office of Strategic Planning and Policy
Development, Summary of JTQS Data for JTPA Title IIA and III Enrollments and
Terminations During PY 1986, December 1987, 4.

groups such as those who lose their jobs through a plant closing or
mass layoff.[7] Second, the Title III program is a state program rather
than a local program, so not all areas within states necessarily receive
Title III funds. Third, the states are required to contribute to the
program, although the matching requirement is reduced for states
with above-average unemployment rates.

Data on Title III programs for dislocated workers are not likely
to be as accurate as the data for the Title IIA programs because the
original design of the data collection system did not cover Title
III programs administered directly by states. During PY 1986, 106,700
individuals enrolled in Title III programs.[8] Their characteristics
are presented in table 5.3. As would be expected, Title III participants differ significantly from Title IIA participants on a number
of characteristics. Nearly two-thirds of the participants are male,
and only 4 percent are under age 22. Over three-quarters of the
Title III enrollees are white. One-third of the participants are economically disadvantaged, and 6 percent received public assistance. Fewer than one in five of the Title III participants had less
than a high school education, and nearly one-third had some postsecondary education. Over half of the Title III participants were
collecting unemployment insurance at the time of enrollment, and
almost one-quarter had been out of work for at least 26 weeks prior
to enrollment.

The most common activity for Title III participants is job search

Table 5.3 CHARACTERISTICS OF JTPA TITLE III ENROLLEES, PROGRAM
YEAR 1986 (JULY 1986–JUNE 1987)

Characteristics	Percentage of enrollees
Sex	
Male	65
Female	35
Minority status	
White (excluding Hispanic)	77
Black (excluding Hispanic)	16
Hispanic	5
Other	2
Age at enrollment	1
19–21	3
22–29	21
30–44	48
45–54	18
55 and older	9
Economically disadvantaged	
Yes	32
No	68
Receiving AFDC at application	
Yes	1
No	99
Receiving any public assistance at application	
Yes	7
No	93
Education status	
School dropout	18
Student (high school or less)	1
High school graduate (no postsecondary)	52
Post high school attendee	30

Source: U.S. Department of Labor, Office of Strategic Planning and Policy
Development, Summary of JTQS Data for JTPA Title IIA and III Enrollments and
Terminations During PY 1986, table C-49.

assistance, with 50 percent of the enrollees in PY 1986. Twenty-six
percent of the enrollees were assigned to classroom training, 12 percent were assigned to on-the-job training, and 12 percent were assigned to other activities.

THE EFFECTIVENESS OF GOVERNMENT
TRAINING PROGRAMS

Before reviewing the findings from recent evaluations of training programs, it is worthwhile to put these studies in perspective. First, I review the criteria for success in a training program; then I discuss some of the technical problems that have made evaluating training programs so difficult.

Criteria for Success

Section 106 of JTPA puts the goals of government training programs in perspective by noting that "job training is an investment in human capital and not an expense." The return on the investment expected by Congress "is to be measured by the increased employment and earnings of participants and the reductions in welfare dependency."

Program benefits can be assessed either from the perspective of the participants or from society as a whole. If the programs do not yield expected net benefits to the participants, then no one will enroll. Because of the very limited stipends paid under JTPA, the participants must believe that the programs are likely to help them improve their employment and earnings prospects. There is no other reason to enroll.

The most comprehensive measure of benefits to the individual is the gain in earnings due to participation in the program. Note that we are considering earnings gains due to participation in the program—this is not necessarily the same as the difference between pre- and postprogram earnings, since some of the gross change in earnings might result from other factors. Because earnings are the product of hours worked and the wage rate, gains in earnings can result from an increase in either factor.

Earnings gains from a training program might not occur immediately after participation, and this is especially the case for youth. For example, youth participants might enter an advanced training program or continue their education as a result of participation. Thus, immediate earnings gains may serve as a poor proxy for the benefits to young participants. A program leading to an apprenticeship in a skilled trade may not have as large an immediate payoff as one leading to a job initia11y paying more but with no chance of advancement; but the preapprenticeship program might provide greater benefits in total.[9] Because job search assistance makes no attempt to provide work skills, its benefits might be of shorter duration than the earnings gains from vocational training programs.

A training program that produces gains in employment and earnings may be judged successful at the participant level, yet still fail to yield net benefits to society. In a traditional cost–benefit analysis, a training program would be considered of net benefit to society if the present value of the earnings gains to participants exceeds the costs of the program, including the opportunity costs of time spent in the program. Because the costs borne by workers in training programs generally consist primarily of the opportunity cost of their time, a training program can easily provide net benefits to participants yet fail to produce net benefits to society. Computing the net benefits of a government training program for society also requires taking into account other costs and benefits valued differently by individual participants and society as a whole. Four such factors are discussed below.

TRAINING AS A SCREENING DEVICE

Much of the training conducted under JTPA and its predecessors has been short-term in nature—frequently three months or less. Some observers have argued that such programs are unlikely to augment the participants' skills in so short a time, and that any earnings gains resulting from the program are merely a result of the program serving as a screening device or signal to employers of the participants' preexisting skills.[10] If this argument is correct, then the participants will be competing in the same low-skill labor market that exhibits high unemployment. The result is that the earnings gains to participants are at the expense of nonparticipants who could have filled the jobs as well as the participants; training programs simply rearrange the queue in the low-skill labor market (see Thurow 1975). In the extreme case, the earnings gains of the participants are fully offset by the losses to nonparticipants, and training programs are serving simply as expensive screening devices for employers.

How can one tell if training programs are actually adding to the participants' human capital? One way is to measure skill increases directly. Training programs sometimes include pretests and posttests for making assignments and determining if the participants have mastered the course's requirements; such competency-based training has become increasingly popular in recent years. JTPA encourages the measurement of skill gains by requiring performance standards for youth based on "the attainment of recognized employment competencies recognized by the private industry council" (section 106).

Even if skill gains do occur, this does not assure that the program is not serving primarily as a screening device. The tests could be poor measures of the skills, or the specific skills taught might not be needed by employers. If the wage rates of participants do not increase relative to nonparticipants, or if the participants do not gain employment in the occupations for which they were trained, this would provide evidence that the training is not providing additional *marketable* skills, at least in the short run.

THE TREATMENT OF REDUCTION IN WELFARE PAYMENTS

The traditional way of dealing with receipt of welfare payments at the participant level is to subtract any reduction in welfare payments from the increase in earnings to arrive at net income gains. For society, welfare payments are considered a transfer payment with offsetting gains and losses or some net gain if society places a positive value on income redistribution. Both perspectives need to be reconsidered. At the participant level, there is evidence that some welfare recipients prefer earned income to welfare—even if the amounts are equivalent—so simply subtracting welfare payments from earnings may not be the appropriate benefit measure. At the social level, large federal deficits in recent years have led to concern about reducing government expenditures in general and welfare programs in particular; JTPA specifically includes a reduction in welfare dependency as one of the three measures of return to the investment in training. Thus, in measuring society's costs and benefits from training programs, it might well be appropriate to reconsider how welfare payments are treated.

EMPLOYMENT AS A BENEFIT

Earnings gains do not necessarily reflect all of society's benefit from training programs. In the JTPA legislation, for example, employment is noted as an outcome in addition to earnings. Other legislation, such as the Full Employment Act and Humphrey-Hawkins Act, specifically denotes increased employment as a national priority. Because earnings gains result from wage increases for those with jobs as well as additional employment, it may be necessary to give extra weight to employment gains to properly reflect the nation's welfare.

REDISTRIBUTION OF EMPLOYMENT OPPORTUNITIES

Even if government training programs do not train participants for openings that would have remained vacant, they may enable the participants to compete for jobs that were inaccessible to them before the training. For example, there may not be a shortage of welders; but a training program in welding will offer new opportunities to the participants, even though it will be at the expense of those already in the field. Gottschalk (1983) notes that such an outcome is of benefit to society if it is desirable to spread the risk of unemployment more evenly across society, or if unemployment is considered more damaging for some groups than for other groups in society.

Problems in Estimating Program Impacts

The previous section discussed the outcomes of interest in assessing training programs. Unfortunately, it is easier to conceptualize such outcomes than to measure them.

Earnings gains are the most fundamental measure of program success, but there are a number of problems in determining the contribution of training programs to changes in earnings. It was noted above that simply subtracting the earnings of participants prior to the program from post-program earnings is unlikely to provide a good estimate, because the change may have resulted from other factors such as maturation (particularly for youth) or changes in economic conditions.

To avoid this problem, researchers sometimes compare the experience of participants with that of a group of similar nonparticipants and attribute the difference to the effects of the program. This general approach can be effective if the participants and nonparticipants are truly similar, as occurs in an experiment with random assignment to participant status, but it may lead to biased estimates if the two groups are not well matched.[11] For example, one is unlikely to obtain a good estimate of the effect of higher education on earnings by comparing the earnings of college graduates with the earnings of high school graduates. The latter group is likely to be less able on average and possibly less motivated. Statistical procedures have been developed to deal with the comparison difficulty, but they all rely upon particular assumptions. Moreover, the estimated impact is often quite sensitive to the assumptions made.

THE IMPACT OF GOVERNMENT TRAINING PROGRAMS ON EARNINGS

Evaluations of training programs under MDTA and CETA have generally found positive but moderately sized earnings impacts for adults.

Impact estimates from recent studies are presented in table 5.4.[12] Because the evaluations were not based on experiments, the researchers used somewhat different comparison groups and estimation techniques, resulting in a broad range of estimates.

The studies generally found positive annual earnings impacts, most of which ranged between $200 and $600, and a majority of the findings were statistically significant. Although there are several exceptions, these studies tended to find greater impacts for on-the-job training relative to classroom training, for women relative to men, and for minorities relative to whites. The study by Dickinson, Johnson, and West (1985) found no impact on earnings for women and a negative, statistically significant impact for men.

Because of the nonexperimental nature of the evaluations, it is not possible to identify one study as providing the best estimates. However, the general consensus in the evaluation community is that the impact of classroom training is about $500 per year, and the impact of on-the-job training is approximately $750, with some variation by sex and ethnic group.

The estimates discussed above are based on one or sometimes two years of postprogram experience. From a policy perspective, the extent to which the benefits persist is of critical importance. For example, if the first-year earnings gain is $500 and earnings then fall to the pretraining level, the value of the benefit of training is approximately $500. However, if the gains persist for 20 years and a 5 percent discount rate is used, the present value of the earnings gains is $6,200. If the earnings gain decreases by 20 percent annually, the present value of the benefits is $1,900.

For youth, the picture is considerably less clear. Although a large number of special demonstration projects were implemented in the 1970s to determine the impacts of a variety of programs for youth, little hard evidence emerged from the effort. A comprehensive review conducted by the National Academy of Sciences concluded that "not much was learned about how to reduce the long-term employment problems of American youth."[13]

Evidence on whether initial impacts are sustained over time is also limited. The Bloom and McLaughlin (1982) analysis of CETA, the Ashenfelter (1979) and Kiefer (1979) studies of MDTA, and the Mathematica Policy Research (1982) evaluation of the Job Corps all found evidence of sustained earnings gains beyond the first program year, especially for women. Because these training programs typically cost several thousand dollars per participant (and much more for the Job

Table 5.4 SUMMARY OF ESTIMATED CETA IMPACTS ON EARNINGS

	Westat (1981) FY 76	Westat (1984) FY 76	Westat (1984) FY 77	Bassi (1983)	Bassi et al. (1984) Nonwelfare disadvantaged adults	Bassi et al. (1984) Welfare	Bassi et al. (1984) Youth	Bloom and McLaughlin (1982)	DJW (1984) Adults	DJW (1984) Youth	Geraci (1984)
Overall											
White women	++	0	++	++	n.a.	++	n.a.	n.a.	n.a.	n.a.	n.a.
White men	++	+	++	++	++	++	0	n.a.	n.a.	n.a.	n.a.
Minority women	+	0	++	++	0	++	–	n.a.	n.a.	n.a.	n.a.
Minority men	++	+	++	0	++	++	0	n.a.	n.a.	n.a	n.a.
Women	n.a.	n.a.	n.a.	n.a.	n.a.	0	n.a.	n.a.	0	0	n.a.
Men	n.a.	n.a.	n.a.	n.a.	n.a.	n.a.	n.a.	n.a.	–	–	n.a.
PSE											
White women	+	0	++	++	n.a.	n.a.	n.a.	n.a.	n.a.	n.a.	n.a.
White men	++	n.a.	n.a.	++	+++	+++	++	n.a.	n.a.	n.a.	n.a.
Minority women	0	n.a.	n.a.	0	+	0	0	n.a.	n.a.	n.a.	n.a.
Minority men	++	n.a.	n.a.	0	0	0	–	n.a.	n.a.	n.a.	n.a.
Women	n.a.	n.a.	n.a.	n.a.	0	0	n.a.	n.a.	+	0	n.a.
Men	n.a.	n.a.	n.a.	n.a.	0	0	–	n.a.	n.a.	n.a.	+++
WE											
White women	0	–	+	n.a.	++	++	n.a.	n.a.	n.a.	n.a.	n.a.
White men	–	n.a.	n.a.	–	+	+	–	+++	n.a.	n.a.	n.a.
Minority women	+	n.a.	n.a.	+	+	++	–	–	n.a.	n.a.	n.a.
Minority men	0	n.a.	n.a.	–	+	0	–	++	n.a.	n.a.	n.a.
Women	0	n.a.	n.a.	n.a.	n.a.	n.a.	n.a.	+++	–	0	+
Men	n.a.	n.a.	n.a.	n.a.	n.a.	n.a.	n.a.	0	–	–	–

Program evaluation reports

	66–72							
CT								
White women	+	+	++	n.a.	n.a.	n.a.	n.a.	n.a.
White men	++	n.a.	n.a.	0	+	+	+	n.a.
Minority women	++	n.a.	n.a.	++	−	−	−	n.a.
Minority men	+++	n.a.	n.a.	++	+	+	+	n.a.
Women	n.a.	n.a.	n.a.	n.a.	0	n.a.	0	+++
Men	n.a.	n.a.	n.a.	n.a.	−	n.a.	−	+
OJT								
White women	++	++	+++	+	+	+	n.a.	n.a.
White men	++	n.a.	n.a.	+	+++	+++	0	+++
Minority women	+++	n.a.	n.a.	+++	++	++	+	+
Minority men	+++	n.a.	n.a.	+++	++	++	+	++
Women	n.a.	n.a.	n.a.	n.a.	+++	n.a.	+++	++
Men	n.a.	n.a.	n.a.	n.a.	+	n.a.	+	++
MUL								
White women	+	++	+++	++	++	+++	+	n.a.
White men	0	n.a.	n.a.	++	+++	+++	+	n.a.
Minority women	+++	+++	n.a.	+++	++	++	−	n.a.
Minority men	−	n.a.	n.a.	−−−	0	+++	−	n.a.
Women	n.a.	n.a.	n.a.	n.a.	n.a.	n.a.	n.a.	n.a.
Men	n.a.	n.a.	n.a.	n.a.	n.a.	n.a.	n.a.	n.a.

Source: Barnow (1987).

Coding scheme:

Earnings losses
−−− Greater than −$1,000
−− Between −$500 and −$999
− Between −$200 and −$499
0 Between −$199 and $199

Earnings gains
+++ Greater than $1,000
++ Between $500 and $999
+ Between $200 and $499

PSE = Public service employment, WE = Work experience, CT = Classroom training, OJT = On-the-job training, MUL = Multiple activities.

n.a. = Not available.

Corps), evidence of sustained gains is crucial to passing a cost–benefit test.

Are the evaluations of CETA and MDTA programs relevant to projecting the impact of JTPA? Although we will have to wait several years to answer that question, there are no strong reasons to anticipate greatly different results. JTPA on-the-job training programs are operating under similar conditions as did CETA, so their impact should not be dramatically different. For classroom training, some factors could be expected to increase the impact and other factors could be expected to reduce the impact. On the positive side, the limitations on stipends should eliminate participants who enrolled to collect the stipends. As a result, the average motivational level of JTPA participants should be higher. Also on the positive side, the performance standards for placement rates and wages at placement are likely to lead to more emphasis on placements. However, if the findings for CETA evaluations that those who are more disadvantaged gain the most are correct, the creaming that may be taking place under JTPA may reduce the impact. In addition, the cost performance standards may lead to shorter-term training, which past studies have found to have less impact.

The only data currently available on the success of JTPA are at termination. In the July–December 1986 period, 51 percent of the terminees in classroom training, 79 percent of those in on-the-job training, 75 percent of those in job search assistance, and 48 percent of those in work experience had jobs at termination (U.S. Department of Labor 1987). Average hourly wages for terminees who obtained employment were $5.03 for classroom training, $4.87 for on-the-job training, $4.63 for job search assistance, and $4.17 for work experience. Title III terminees, who are generally much less disadvantaged, tended to have more positive outcomes. In the July–December 1986 period, 70 percent of the terminees entered employment, and their average hourly wage rate was $7.29.

Training Programs and Skill Levels: Some Indirect Evidence on Impact

The point was made earlier that if training programs function as intended, by increasing skill levels, we would expect to find participants employed in the occupation for which they were trained, and we would expect wage rates to have increased as a result of the program. Although the evidence available cannot be considered definitive, it does not support the view that training achieves its impact through increasing skills.

Table 5.5 PROPORTION OF CETA PARTICIPANTS WHOSE POSTPROGRAM
OCCUPATIONAL FIELD MATCHED THE IN-PROGRAM
OCCUPATIONAL FIELD

Occupational area	Enrollees 12 months after terminations[a] July 1976–Sept 1977 (%)	Enrollees during second year after terminations[b] fiscal year 1979 (%)
Professional and technical	29	30
Clerical	41	42
Crafts	32	29
Operatives	39	38
Nonfarm labor	− 2	21
Service	[c]	33
Other	33	22

a. Based on data from table 5 in Westat, Continuous Longitudinal Manpower
Survey Follow-up Report no. 7: Postprogram Experience, with Pre/Post
Comparisons for Terminees Who Entered CETA During July 1976 through
September 1977, October 1982.
b. Based on data from table 30 in Westat, Continuous Longitudinal Manpower
Survey Follow-up Report No. 12: Postprogram Experience, with Pre/Post
Comparison, for Terminees Who Entered CETA during FY 1979, April 1984.
Percentages are for the longest (dominant) job held during the period.
c. Service jobs are included under *Other* in this report.

Table 5.5 presents evidence on how postprogram occupational
experience related to the in-program training field or employment
area for CETA participants. These data are not ideal for several reasons:

□ Public service employment and work experience are included in
the data, so the observed impacts are not due to training alone.
□ Youth who may have continued their education or enrolled in
advanced training are included, so the observed impacts are not
necessarily restricted to CETA alone.
□ Occupations are classified in broad categories, so even a person
whose occupation changed could remain in the same category, leading to a possible overestimate of occupational continuity.
□ Some movement out of the occupational categories may represent
promotions into better jobs, leading to a possible underestimate of
occupational continuity.

Even considering these data limitations, the results are not encouraging. The occupational retention rates 12 months after termi-

nation ranged from 22 percent for nonfarm labor to 41 percent for clerical workers for CETA enrollees from July 1976 through September 1977. The table also shows the proportion of enrollees during FY 1979 whose dominant job during the second year after termination was in the same occupational area as their in-program training or employment experience. These results are similar, ranging from 21 percent for nonfarm labor to 42 percent for clerical. CETA participants may have applied skills gained from their participation in other fields, but fewer than 50 percent made use of them in the same broad occupational field.

Several studies have examined the impact of training programs on wages; the messages are not consistent. The Bloom and McLaughlin study estimated that 22 percent of the impact of CETA training for women was on higher wage rates, but the report concludes that "only a small effect on wage rates was observed and thus it appears that there was probably little effect on job skills" (1982, 29). Westat did not directly estimate the impact of training on wage rates, but observed that "classroom training and on-the-job training terminees have particularly striking pre-to-post gains in average hourly wages, suggesting that these two program activities might be especially successful in inducing upward shifts in permanent earnings rates" (1982, 3–10). In trying to reconcile these conclusions, it should be noted that Westat's conclusions are based on gross-change data (and are, therefore, overestimates of program impact) and that the Bloom and McLaughin study did find that some of the impact of CETA training on earnings was due to increased wage rates.

To summarize, there is only weak evidence that CETA training programs increased the skill levels of participants. One and two years past termination, well under 50 percent of CETA participants were working in the broad occupational area of their in-program experience. Earnings gains appear to result more from increased employment than from increased wage rates, although there is some evidence of wage rate increases resulting from training.

THE ROLE OF GOVERNMENT TRAINING PROGRAMS

In trying to establish an appropriate role for government training programs, it should be reemphasized that their scale in the United States has never been very large, either in terms of resources allocated or in terms of possible need. Gottschalk (1983) points out that all employment and training programs together constituted a maximum of 2.5 percent of government outlays in the past 20 years, and most of the funding was for employment programs (public service employment and work experience) rather than training. By 1982, employment and training programs had fallen to .5 percent of outlays, the lowest figure since 1965. Training programs in this country also serve only a small portion of those eligible. Hunt and Rupp (1984) estimated that under 2 percent of the eligible population can be served annually by Title IIA of JTPA. Because the criteria for identifying dislocated workers eligible for Title III of JTPA are subjective in nature, estimates of the proportion of dislocated workers that are served are difficult to make; an analysis of a recent survey by Flaim and Sehgal (1985) estimated that 5.1 million workers were dislocated between 1979 and 1983.[14]

Training programs appear to be moderately successful in terms of increasing the earnings of disadvantaged participants, with the typical study finding a first-year impact of about $500.

Evidence on whether training programs have increased skill levels and led to wage rate increases and earnings increases that are sustained over time is mixed, but several studies have identified such gains. Training programs are clearly not going to end poverty in the United States—the average wage at placement of $4.53 per hour does not provide sufficient income from year-round full-time employment for a family of four to exceed the poverty level. Ironically, as noted, such a person would still be eligible for the program under the definition of economically disadvantaged.

But these average impacts can mask much of the success achieved by training programs. While it is unrealistic to expect that in the near future government training programs can be relied upon to play the major role in reducing unemployment and poverty, the government can take actions to both raise the average level of performance and reduce uncertainty about the programs' impact.

Both types of efforts call for additional research and experimentation. This does not mean a return to the days of a billion dollars per year in discretionary funds for demonstration projects, but rather a more modest increase from current levels of $38.9 million for projects and demonstrations and $18.3 million for research and evaluation. A special advisory panel established by the Department of Labor concluded that the traditional nonexperimental methods are not powerful enough to provide good estimates of the effectiveness of training programs, and the panel recommended that experiments be conducted to provide a more accurate assessment. In June 1986 the Department of Labor awarded two contracts to design and implement an experiment to determine the impact of training under JTPA. Although it will require several years to complete, the experiment is expected to provide a more accurate assessment of the effectiveness of training programs than has been previously possible.

The JTPA experiment should provide a good assessment of how effective training programs are on average, but it is unlikely to provide much guidance on how the programs can be improved. Other research is necessary. Currently, training programs teach vocational skills, job search skills, and basic education. Most evaluations of CETA programs have concentrated on evaluating the impact of vocational training, but we need to assess the utility of all three approaches.

Job search assistance programs have been used since the 1960s, but they have become increasingly popular under JTPA; perhaps because of pressure to keep costs low, about the same percentage of enrollees during PY 1986 receive job search assistance (19 percent) as receive on-the-job training (22 percent). If vocational training increases earnings primarily by providing a credential or simply through placement efforts, there may be less expensive activities that do as well. Job search assistance, for example, may produce a comparable impact at a lower cost per participant. Terminees from job search assistance have a higher entered employment—i.e., placement—rate than those from classroom training (77 percent compared to 52 percent in PY 1986), and the average wage at placement was only slightly lower—$4.68 per hour compared to $5.03 for classroom training graduates (see U.S. Department of Labor 1987). What we do not know, and will not know for several years, is how well earnings and employment gains are sustained from job search assistance relative to vocational training. Job search assistance should also be compared to the experience of the U.S. Employment Service, which also serves the economically disadvantaged but does not offer vocational training programs.

Training programs have typically lasted about three months. A subject that has not been thoroughly investigated is whether such a strategy is appropriate. Shorter programs mean that more participants can be served, but most evaluations have found greater returns for individuals who receive more than three months' training. For example, Westat (1982b) found that the impact on earnings from classroom training under CETA increased from $438 for those in the program 1 to 10 weeks, to $1,918 for those who received over 40 weeks of training. Part of the difference may be due to more able and motivated participants being assigned to longer programs, but it is likely that longer programs do have a greater impact on earnings. The only training program with a clear record of success is the Job Corps, which lasts substantially longer and is more intensive than typical JTPA programs. Performance standards under JTPA are likely to encourage short-term programs, as are the restrictions on stipends. There is not enough evidence to suggest that long-term training be strongly encouraged, but the available evidence suggests that current policy may overly encourage short-term training. Special experiments should be implemented to address this important issue.

The role of basic education in training programs has not been well addressed in the national evaluations of CETA. While there is little doubt that a great deal of basic education took place under CETA and is continuing to some extent under JTPA, the Department of Labor did not collect data on basic education in its primary evaluation data base on CETA. Berlin and Duhl (1984) argue compellingly that mastering basic educational skills can be an important factor in improving the employment and earnings of the economically disadvantaged. While some might claim that education is the responsibility of the educational system rather than the training system, Berlin and Duhl note that there is evidence that the two types of skills need to be addressed together, for both youth and adults. Careful evaluation of the role of basic education programs under JTPA is needed, and controlled experiments would be useful in assessing the importance of basic education in training programs.

Determining who should be served in government training programs is likely to remain controversial. There have been criticisms that JTPA has encouraged creaming at the local level but, as I have noted, 94 percent of the Title IIA participants have met what appear to be reasonably stringent eligibility criteria. Governors have the authority to use part of their funds to provide incentive grants to SDAs for "serving hard-to-serve individuals," and they can attempt to develop performance standards that do not discourage serving those with severe barriers to employment. Operationally, the problem is codifying the characteristics of the hard to serve. On measured characteristics, the JTPA participants do not appear to be the cream of the disadvantaged, so it is likely that any creaming that occurs is based on factors that are hard to measure. Trying to serve those most in need, as required by law, is likely to remain a difficult challenge so long as program performance remains an important goal of the program.

Training programs are not the only programs available to improve the employment and earnings of the economically disadvantaged. Other programs and policies that can affect unemployment include tax rates on earnings and transfer payments, employment tax credits, minimum wage and other labor law, and direct employment programs. These alternatives, however, also have limitations. Reducing labor costs to employers through tax credits or a reduced minimum wage cannot add skills to the work force, and targeted tax credits appear to have been ineffective.[15] Public service employment is relatively expensive; also, its impact is limited and total cost is increased if subsidized workers are substituted for regular employees. Most evaluations of work experience programs have found little, if any, impact on employment and earnings. The most promising possible alternatives to government training programs at this time are taking place in the welfare system, where some of the workfare programs and innovative Work Incentive Program (WIN) demonstrations appear successful. It should be noted, however, that most evaluations of training programs have found that those participants—single mothers on welfare—also benefit the most from traditional training programs.

Policymakers do not have the luxury of waiting for research and evaluation results to come in. A large economically disadvantaged population is in need of services today. Because the role of the federal government is much smaller under JTPA than it was under CETA or MDTA, the states and SDAs must play a larger role in assuring that effective training is provided. As noted above, the evidence so far indicates that strategies that warrant special attention include basic skills and longer-term training.

At the federal level, budget pressures have threatened the Job Corps program because of its high cost per participant. Efforts to reduce costs should be carried out cautiously, perhaps in the context of experiments, so that the features that led to the Job Corps' success are not lost. In addition, the Department of Labor can influence state and local programs through the performance standards set by the secretary of labor. The current standards are likely to discourage efforts with a long-term payoff in favor of those with small but immediate gains. Strong consideration should be given to assuring that the standards encourage or are at least neutral to basic education and long-term training.

The weight of the evidence available favors retention of the employment and training program offered under the Job Training Partnership Act. Major programmatic changes are probably not advisable at this time because of insufficient evidence and the major disruption to the provision of services that inevitably occurs when programs are modified too frequently. The Department of Labor, the states, the service delivery areas, and service providers should consider actions along the following lines:

☐ *Encouraging services to the most disadvantaged.* While it is very hard to document, there is widespread belief that the current JTPA system encourages creaming among the eligible population because of the emphasis on program performance as measured by status at placement. The Department of Labor has recognized this problem and has established a work group to assess the extent of the problem and recommend methods of modifying the performance standards system to provide more encouragement to service individuals with severe employment barriers. The most recent performance standards issued by the Department of Labor encourage more services to the severely disadvantaged.

☐ *Encouraging the provision of basic skills training.* Because educational skills are likely to pay off over the long run rather than the short run, there is a natural reluctance to emphasize basic skills training in JTPA. High school diplomas are no longer a clear indication of adequate job-related skills in reading and computation. Methods should be found to encourage provision of basic skills for both youth and adults.

☐ *Encouraging long-term training.* The evidence indicates that longer-term programs are more effective. In addition, the typical wages at placement are not high enough for many participants with families to escape poverty or earn their way off welfare. While JTPA cannot be expected to provide an adequate income for all participants, an effort to concentrate on longer, more intensive programs is likely to make a greater contribution toward self-sufficiency for the participants.

Notes

1. The U.S. Department of Labor does not maintain records on what proportion of participants receive basic education. Westat (1982) found that 38 percent of the FY 1979 enrollees in classroom training under the Comprehensive Employment and Training Act (CETA) reported no occupational area of training and noted that "many of these individuals received basic education rather than training for a specific occupation." Comparable data are not yet available for the Job Training Partnership Act (JTPA), but most observers believe that the proportion of participants enrolled in educational programs has declined significantly.

2. For detailed descriptions of employment and training programs from 1962 through 1973, see Perry, et al. (1975). Program descriptions and enrollment information can also be found in the annual *Manpower Report of the President*.

3. National programs authorized under Title IV of JTPA include Native American programs, migrant and seasonal farmworker programs, the Job Corps, veterans employment programs, and pilot programs. Title V of JTPA contains a series of amendments to the Wagner-Peyser Act regarding the U.S. Employment Service. Title IIB of JTPA authorizes the summer youth employment and training program, but it is primarily an employment program rather than a training program. Other federally sponsored training is provided to workers who lose their jobs due to foreign competition under the trade adjustment assistance program, and to recipients of Aid to Families with Dependent Children (AFDC) in the Work Incentive Program (WIN).

4. To be eligible for Title IIA of JTPA as economically disadvantaged, an individual must meet one of the following criteria: (1) receives, or is a member of a family that receives, cash welfare payments under a federal, state, or local welfare program; (2) has, or is a member of a family that has, received a total family income (exclusive of unemployment compensation, child support, and welfare) which, in relation to family size, does not exceed the higher of the poverty level or 70 percent of the lower living-standard income level; (3) is receiving food stamps; (4) is a state-supported foster child; or (5) is an adult, handicapped individual who receives welfare or meets the low-income criteria.

5. Positive terminations include enrollment in an educational program or another training program as well as obtaining employment.

6. Data on the Title IIA program are from U.S. Department of Labor (1984a). JTPA operates on a program-year (PY) basis from 1 July to 30 June; because the program started 1 October 1983, the first program year was nine months long.

7. The eligibility criteria for Title III of JTPA are: (1) have been terminated or laid off or have received a notice of termination or layoff from employment, are eligible for or have exhausted their entitlement to unemployment compensation, and are unlikely to return to their previous industry or occupation; (2) have been terminated, or have received a notice of termination of employment, as a result of any permanent closure of a plant or facility; or (3) are long-term unemployed and have limited opportunities for employment or reemployment in the same or a similar occupation in the area in which such individuals reside, including any older individuals who may have substantial barriers to employment by reason of age.

8. Information on Title III is from U.S. Department of Labor (1987). Only administrative data are available for the transition year.

9. The evaluation of the Job Corps by Mathematica Policy Research (1982) found that it took six months for Job Corps participants to earn as much as the comparison group, but their earnings gains remained for four years after leaving the program.

10. This reasoning has also been applied to higher education; see Taubman and Wales (1974).

11. This problem is generally referred to as selection bias. For a technical treatment of the issue, see, for example, Heckman (1979); Maddala and Lee (1976); Heckman and Robb (1982); and Barnow, Cain, and Goldberger (1980).

12. For a summary of the methods and findings from evaluations of CETA, see Barnow (1987).

13. This quotation is from a 13 November 1985 press release issued by the National Research Council. For a complete description of the Council's work, see Betsey, Hollister, and Papageorgiou (1985).

14. Other studies have estimated that there are fewer dislocated workers, but the JTPA eligibility criteria are very broad.

15. See Burtless (1964), who cites one study that concluded that targeted tax credits actually reduce earnings because of the stigma of being disadvantaged.

References

Abt Associates. September 1984. *The Downriver Community Conference Economic Readjustment Program: Final Evaluation Report*. Cambridge, Mass.

Ashenfelter, Orley. 1979. Estimating the Effect of Training Programs on Earnings with Longitudinal Data. In *Research in Labor Economics Supplement 1: Evaluating Manpower Training Programs*, edited by Farrell E. Bloch, 97–118. Greenwich, Conn.: JAI Press.

Barnow, Burt S. Spring 1987. The Impact of CETA Programs on Earnings: A Review of the Literature. *The Journal of Human Resources*, 157–93.

Barnow, Burt S., Glen G. Cain, and Arthur S. Goldberger. 1980. Issues in the Analysis of Selectivity Bias. In *Evaluation Studies Review Annual* Vol. 5, edited by Ernst W. Stromsdorfer and George Farka. Beverly Hills, Calif.: Sage Publications.

Bassi, Laurie J. February 1984. Estimating the Effect of Training Programs with Non-Random Selection. *Review of Economics and Statistics*, 36–42.

Berlin, Gordon, and Joanne Duhl. August 1984. Education, Equity, and Economic Excellence: The Critical Role of Second Chance Basic Skills and Job Training Programs. Mimeo.

Betsey, Charles L., Robinson G. Hollister, Jr., and Mary R. Papageorgiou. 1985. *Youth Employment and Training Programs: The YEDPA Years*. Washington: National Academy Press.

Bloom, Howard, and Maureen McLaughlin. July 1982. *CETA Training Programs—Do They Work For Adults?* Washington: Congressional Budget Office.

Dickinson, Katherine P., Terry R. Johnson, and Richard W. West. 1984. An Analysis of the Impact of CETA Programs on Participants' Earnings. Menlo Park, Calif.: SRI International.

Flaim, Paul O., and Ellen Sehgal. June 1985. Displaced Workers of 1979–1983: How Well Have They Fared? *Monthly Labor Review*, 3–16.

Geraci, Vincent J. 1984. Short-Term Indicators of Job Training Program Effects on Long-Term Participant Earnings. Austin, Tex.: University of Texas.

Gottschalk, Peter. 1983. U.S. Labor Market Policies Since the 1960s: A Survey of Programs and Their Effectiveness. Madison, Wisc.: Institute for Research on Poverty.

Heckman, James J. 1979. Sample Selection Bias as a Specification Error. *Econometrica* 47(1): 153–61.

Heckman, James J., and Richard Robb. 1982. The Longitudinal Analysis of Earnings. Mimeo.

Hunt, Allan H., and Kalman Rupp. n.d. The Implementation of Title IIA of JTPA in the States and Service Delivery Areas: The New Partnership and Program Directions. Paper presented at the 1984 winter meetings of the Industrial Relations Research Association.

Johnson, Terry R., Katherine P. Dickinson, and Richard W. West. Winter 1985. An Evaluation of the Impact of ES Referrals on Applicant Earnings. *Journal of Human Resources*, 117–37.

Kiefer, Nicholas M. 1979. The Economic Benefits from Four Government Training Programs. In *Research in Labor Economics Supplement 1: Evaluating Manpower Training Programs*, edited by Farrell E. Bloch, 154–86. Greenwich, Conn.: JAI Press.

Maddala, G.S., and L. Lee. 1976. Recursive Models with Qualitative Endogenous Variables. *Annals of Economic and Social Measurement* 5:525–45.

Mathematica Policy Research. 1982. *Evaluation of the Economic Impact of the Job Corps: Third Follow-up Report*. Princeton, N.J.: Mathematica Policy Research.

Perry, Charles R., et al. 1975. *The Impact of Government Manpower Programs*. Philadelphia: University of Pennsylvania.

Taubman, Paul, and Terence Wales. 1974. *Higher Education and Earnings: College as an Investment and a Screening Device*. New York: McGraw-Hill Book Company.

Thurow, Lester C. 1975. *Generating Inequality*. New York: Basic Books.

U.S. Department of Labor, Division of Performance Management and Evaluation. 1984a. Summary of JTLS Data for JTPA Title IIA Enrollments and Terminations During the Transition Year. Washington.

U.S. Department of Labor, Division of Performance Management and Evaluation. 1984b. Summary of JTPA Administrative Data from the JASR/JQSR Reporting System, for the Transition Year (October 1983–June 1984). Washington.

U.S. Department of Labor, Office of Strategic Planning and Policy Development. December 1987. Summary of JTQS for JTPA Title IIA and III Enrollments and Terminations During PY 1986. Washington.

Walker, Gary, Hilary Feldstein, and Katherine Solow. January 1985. *An Independent Sector Assessment of the Job Training Partnership Act*. New York: Grinker, Walker & Associates.

Westat. March 1981. *Continuous Longitudinal Manpower Survey Net Impact Report No. 1: Impact on 1977 Earnings of New FY 1976 CETA Enrollees in Selected Program Activities*. Washington.

———. October 1982. *Continuous Longitudinal Manpower Survey Follow-Up Report No. 7: Postprogram Experiences and Pre/Post Compar-*

isons for Terminees Who Entered CETA During July 1976 Through September 1977. Washington.

———. April 1984. *CLMS Follow-Up Report No. 12: Postprogram Experiences, with Pre/Post Comparisons for Terminees Who Entered CETA During FY 1979.* Washington.

Chapter Six

WORKERS' RIGHTS: RETHINKING PROTECTIVE LABOR LEGISLATION

Ronald G. Ehrenberg

The last 50 years have seen the federal government become involved with macroeconomic and labor market policies to stimulate increased employment; they also have seen the rapid growth of federal and state programs and legislation that seek to mandate conditions under which workers may be employed. These latter policies fall under the rubric of social insurance programs (such as workers' compensation; unemployment compensation; and the social security retirement, survivors', and disability programs) and protective legislation (such as minimum wage, maximum hours, child labor, occupational safety and health, private employees retirement income security, antidiscrimination, and mandatory retirement laws).

All these policies seek to mandate protection for workers in areas in which society perceives that workers have a right to be protected. Whether in areas of pecuniary compensation (insurance against unemployment, work injury, nonwork disability, or promised retirement benefits not being delivered) or nonpecuniary conditions of employment (occupational safety and health), in each case the implicit judgment was reached that private markets had in some sense failed and that government intervention was required. In each case the policies also led to market repercussions, as federally mandated changes in the employment relation invariably led employers to react to the changing constraints they faced. In some cases these responses resulted in increased employment; however, in other cases they resulted in a reduction in employment opportunities.[1]

This chapter focuses on directions in which protective labor legislation might be expanded in the United States over the next decade and the implications of expansion in each area for employment policy. Protective labor legislation is far less comprehensive in the United States than it is in many other western countries. While this may result from greater union strength in these countries and unions achieving through legislation many things that are left to the collective bargaining process in the United States, it does leave much room for expansion in protective labor legislation here.

For example, while for the most part in the United States employers can unilaterally terminate employees at will unless specific contract provisions protect the workers, in most European countries such dismissals are subject to various governmental review processes that may lead to reinstatement and/or severance pay if they are deemed unjust (National Board of Prices and Income 1970). To take another example, while in the United States we have an overtime pay premium to discourage employers' use of overtime hours and to encourage additional employment, several European countries have more stringent rules that require prior governmental or employee approval before any overtime can be worked (Stieber 1980b).

This chapter first provides a conceptual framework for analyzing proposed changes in protective labor legislation by considering hours-of-work legislation in the United States as attempting to correct for failures of private markets.[2] The discussion stresses the need to be explicit about how private markets have failed, the need for empirical evidence to test such market failure claims, the need for economic analysis of potential unintended side effects of proposed policy changes, and empirical estimates of the likely magnitudes of these effects.

This framework is then adapted to address three areas of proposed forms of protective labor legislation that have begun to receive public attention and that have considerable implications for employment policy: employment at will, comparable worth, and plant closings.

HOURS-OF-WORK LEGISLATION IN THE UNITED STATES

The earliest forms of hours-of-work legislation in the United States were initiated at the state level, applied to women and children, and had the aim of reducing fatigue and exhaustion (Commons and Andrews 1920; Paulsen 1959; and Phelps 1939). For example, in 1879, legislation regulating maximum hours of work was introduced in Massachusetts, where its supporters claimed that long workweeks were exhausting and caused women to age prematurely (Cahill 1932, 106–7). The first hours laws covering men in the private sector were also at the state level and covered occupations in which long workweeks adversely affected third parties or employees themselves. An

1890 Ohio law limited hours of workers who operated trains in the hope that this would reduce railroad accident rates and protect the traveling public. This law was quickly followed by state laws limiting workweeks in mining to protect miners, who were subject to unhealthy and unsafe working conditions (Paulsen 1959, 114).

In each of these cases an economic rationale for the protective labor legislation can be found in the fact that the marginal social cost of longer workweeks exceeded the marginal private cost to employers. In the absence of government intervention these divergencies persisted because low family income levels did not permit many women and children the luxury of turning down low-wage, long-hours jobs, because no good alternatives to the railroads existed for long-range travel and railroad passengers were not always accurately informed about railroad employees' workweeks, and because the limited alternate employment opportunities in mining communities often restricted the occupational choice of individuals in those areas. In each case, then, markets failed in the sense that wage or price differentials did not arise to compensate employees or third parties for the full risks they incurred because of long hours of work. The case for government intervention was strong; the only real question is why the legislation took the form of outright restrictions on hours rather than the use of tax or penalty schemes to increase employers' marginal private cost of longer hours.[3]

At the federal level throughout the early 1930s, bills were repeatedly introduced into Congress to limit the length of the workweek. While the goal of protecting existing employees from the ills associated with excessive fatigue remained, a second explicit purpose of such legislation was to increase employment by spreading the available work. Ultimately the Fair Labor Standards Act (FLSA), with its overtime provisions, was enacted on 25 June 1938.

Once again, the provisions of the act can be rationalized in terms of the divergence between private and social costs. Even if employers and their employees in the 1930s were satisfied with long workweeks, their private calculations ignored the social costs borne by the unemployed. The time and a half rate for overtime can be thought of as a tax to make employers bear the full marginal social costs of their hours decisions; it was meant to reduce the use of overtime hours and, to the extent that the increased costs do not substantially reduce total hours demanded, stimulate employment.[4] Furthermore, if employees were not satisfied with long workweeks during the 1930s but, because of market imperfections, did not have the freedom to choose employment with employers who offered shorter workweeks, the direct payment of the tax to the employees who worked longer workweeks can be understood as an attempt to remedy this imperfection.[5]

Although coverage under the overtime pay provisions of the FLSA has increased substantially over the last half century, the premium itself has remained constant at time and a half. Periodically proposals have been introduced in Congress to raise the premium to double time. A bill to amend the FLSA introduced into Congress in 1979 by Representative John Conyers of Michigan, for example, would have done this. It would also have prohibited mandatory assignment of overtime, and required premium pay after 35 rather than 40 hours.[6]

The underlying argument made to support such an increase in the overtime premium is that, although unemployment remains a pressing national problem, the use of overtime hours has increased in recent years. Moreover, continues the argument, since the enactment of the FLSA the deterrent effect of the overtime premium on the use of overtime has been weakened by the growing share of hiring and training costs, fringe benefits, and government-mandated insurance premiums in total compensation. Many of these costs are quasi-fixed or employee-related (for example, vacation pay, holiday pay, sick leave, hiring costs), rather than hours-related, in the sense that they do not vary with overtime hours. An increase in these quasi-fixed costs reduces employers' marginal costs of working their employees overtime relative to their costs of hiring additional employees. The growth of these costs, it is claimed, has been at least partially responsible for the increase in overtime and, therefore, an increase in the overtime premium paid by employers is required to offset this adverse effect.

A complete analysis of the desirability of raising the overtime premium requires answers to a number of empirical questions. Would higher overtime pay rates relative to the quasi-fixed costs of employment induce employers to reduce their usage of overtime hours? Would reductions in overtime hours be converted to full-time jobs or lost to capital substitution or output reductions? Would employers comply with the legislation? Would workers who previously worked overtime now moonlight at a second job and reduce the employment opportunities for unemployed individuals? Would the unemployed have the skills necessary to fill any new jobs that potentially might be created? Finally, what would be the income distribution consequences of the proposed policy change? Empirical analyses directed at answering all of these questions have led to the conclusion that raising the overtime premium would not be an effective way of stimulating employment growth, even though it would lead to a reduction in overtime hours, and that it would not have desirable income distribution consequences either (Ehrenberg and Schuman 1982).

Unless it can be demonstrated that market imperfections prevent currently employed workers from freely choosing the length of their workweeks, and that the existing overtime premium does not fully compensate these workers for the disutility associated with long workweeks, then no increase in the premium paid to *employees* is justified. But raising the overtime premium paid by employers might make sense for another reason. The revenue accruing from such an increase need not be distributed to employees in the form of higher premium pay received by them for overtime but, instead, go directly to aid the unemployed. For example, it could be contributed to the unemployment insurance fund or to employment and training program budgets. One can thus logically be in favor of raising the tax paid by employers when they use overtime hours but not in favor of raising the overtime premium paid to employees.

What about the Conyers proposal to legislate the prohibition of mandatory overtime, as is done in several European countries? Presumably such a proposal is based upon the belief that market imperfections persist in the labor market and that the overtime premium does not fully compensate employees for the disutility associated with mandatory overtime. One may question, however, if markets have failed here. A variety of overtime hours provisions appear to be offered in the labor market; for example, only 16 percent of the individuals in the 1977 *Michigan Quality of Employment Survey* who reported working overtime also reported that the overtime hours decision was made unilaterally by their employer and that overtime was mandatory in the sense that employees who refused it suffered a penalty (Quinn and Staines 1979, 90–91). In addition, roughly 20 percent of employees covered by major collective bargaining agreements in 1976 had explicit provisions in their contracts that gave them the right to refuse overtime (U.S. Bureau of Labor Statistics 1979).

To the extent that labor markets are competitive and establishments do offer differing overtime hours provisions (for example, employer determines, employee determines, penalty for refusal), compensating wage differentials should arise. To attract labor, establishments that offered distasteful mandatory overtime provisions would have to pay higher straight-time wages, higher overtime premiums, or higher fringe benefits than establishments in which such provisions did not occur. If fully compensating wage differentials exist, there is no case for legislative prohibitions against mandatory overtime. Evidence on the extent to which such compensating wage differentials currently do exist, therefore, is of importance to policymakers.

In fact, the only empirical study done on the topic found that, on average, such compensating differentials did not exist (Ehrenberg and Schumann 1984). This provides some support for a prohibition of mandatory overtime, although the benefits from such legislation would have to be weighed against the potential costs; the latter include reduced employer flexibility in scheduling production, and thus increased production costs, which would lead in turn to lower employment levels. The study also found, however, that compensating differentials did exist for employees who were union members. That is, unions were able to win for their members through the collective bargaining process what the market on average did not produce.[7] The workers most in need of the prohibition on mandatory overtime then are nonunion workers.

EMPLOYMENT AT WILL

Judging by the spate of articles in both academic journals and the popular press, reform of the employment-at-will doctrine to provide nonunion workers with protection against unjust dismissal appears to be one of the most pressing labor issues of the decade.[8] Put in simplest terms, the doctrine of employment at will asserts that both employers and employees have the right to terminate an employment relationship at any time. Of concern to workers is that under such a system they have no statutory protection against arbitrary decisions by employers to dismiss them.

Unlike virtually all European nations, which have specific legislation that prohibits unjust dismissals and that often mandates the use of labor courts or industrial tribunals to resolve disputes, for the most part in the United States the doctrine continues to prevail.[9] Unionized workers with specific contract provisions that govern discharges, as well as tenured teachers and workers under some civil service system, are not subject to this doctrine; and all workers receive some protection if they are dismissed for reasons that are prohibited under other federal statutes (such as race, sex, or age) since they may file suit for remedy under those statutes. Estimates are, however, that over 60 million workers in the United States have virtually no protection against unjust dismissal (Stieber 1984).

Concern over the issue arises because it is also estimated that each year around 4 to 5 percent of the labor force is discharged from their jobs (Stieber 1985; Block, Stieber, and Pincus 1983). Some of these discharges may be justified, due to willful and deliberate misconduct. But some may be unrelated to a worker's productivity on the job, and/or the penalty of dismissal may seem excessive relative to the worker's actions.

In the union sector, where contract language often protects workers from arbitrary dismissals, discharge rates tend to be lower.[10] Moreover, approximately half of the unionized workers who are discharged and who appeal these discharges through an arbitration process, as specified in their contracts, are reinstated (Stieber 1984). One researcher has estimated that if nonunion workers had similar rights to appeal their dismissals to impartial arbitrators and did so at the same rate that dismissed union workers did, approximately 150,000 discharged nonunion workers would be reinstated each year (Stieber 1985). To the extent that these workers suffer serious economic losses, employers are not bearing the full marginal social cost of unjustly dismissing workers, and a case for government intervention may exist.

In recent years, public policy in the United States relating to the employment-at-will issue has proceeded primarily through state judiciary systems. As of 1984, more than 20 state courts had adopted public policy or whistle-blowing exceptions to the doctrine. In these states workers cannot be discharged for actions that are consistent with public policy (for example, refusing an employer's request to commit perjury, refusing an employer's request not to serve on a jury, reporting a violation of an OSHA standard). Similarly, 13 state courts had adopted "implicit contract" exceptions. In these states, some of which also have public policy exceptions, workers cannot be dismissed without cause if actions taken by the employer (for example, oral statements, established past practices, statements in personnel manuals) implicitly promise such protection.[11]

These exceptions, however, appear to apply primarily to those dismissed executive and managerial employees who have the financial resources necessary to pursue redress through the courts. The majority of discharged workers are lower-level, blue-collar workers whose reasons for dismissal typically do not fall under the exceptions (Stieber 1984). While several state legislatures have introduced bills requiring "just cause" for dismissal and mediation and/or arbitration of disputes, no state bill has come to vote since 1975, and the only federal attempt at such legislation similarly failed to come to vote.[12]

Some observers have argued that a federal statute is required and pressure for such legislation may continue to build (Stieber and Murray 1983).

To understand the potential rationale for such legislation, it is useful to consider several models of the labor market.[13] Consider first a simple competitive labor market with many buyers and sellers of labor, in which skills of workers are completely general, in the sense that a worker's productivity is not firm-specific. In such a world, proponents of the employment-at-will doctrine argue that it is an equitable or fair form of contract since either party can terminate the contract at will. Workers can quit if they perceive better opportunities elsewhere and firms can dismiss workers if they perceive that workers' productivity has fallen below their wages. In the latter case, dismissed workers would suffer no permanent loss, since their skills would be perfectly transferable. However, since job search takes time, there would be a loss of income during the job search process. How large the loss of income would be depends in part upon whether being dismissed adversely affects the time it takes to find a job.

Proponents of employment at will also argue that it is an efficient form of contract since either party can terminate it if the other party reneges on the agreement. Knowledge that each party reserves this right decreases the chances that workers will not put forth expected levels of performance and that employers will not provide promised pecuniary and nonpecuniary forms of compensation. Thus, efficiency is promoted and monitoring costs are reduced.

If, under employment at will, an employer justly discharges a worker for malfeasance, the worker might suffer a loss of income but this loss would be deserved. Proponents claim that firms would have little incentive to unjustly discharge workers, because information that they were doing so would reduce the attractiveness of the firm to prospective future employees and increase voluntary turnover of existing employees. On both counts, employers' labor costs would go up; unjust discharges would lead to reputational costs and would be costly to the firm.

In evaluating potential losses to workers from unjust discharges, it is useful to consider four different situations. First, consider the employment relationship in casual or secondary labor markets— markets in which neither firms nor workers have incentives to maintain stable, long-term relationships. In such markets, workers frequently change jobs voluntarily or involuntarily, and the stigma from being dismissed is not likely to be a permanent one. Thus, the loss to such workers from unjust dismissal is likely to be only a short-run loss.

Next, there is the situation previously discussed—competitive labor markets with completely general skills. We know that in such a world workers bear the full costs of acquiring skills and hence firms have no investments in workers (Becker 1975). Reputational costs would discourage firms from unjustly dismissing workers; if they did, however, permanent losses to workers would occur only if information about the workers' true productivity could not eventually overcome the signal given by their dismissals.

Third is the situation in which skills are firm-specific. In this case workers and firms share the cost of training and have incentives to maintain stable relationships (Becker 1975). Firms would appear to have little incentive to unjustly dismiss workers; if they did, however, dismissed workers' losses might be permanent because their productivity with other employers would be lower.

Finally, consider the situation of general skills, where firms use earnings that increase with seniority to motivate attachment and increased productivity by employees (Lazear 1979). With such implicit contracts, workers are initially paid less than their marginal product but eventually are paid more. Here again, reputational costs would discourage firms from unjustly dismissing workers who were in the stage of their life cycles in which marginal productivity was less than wage; if they did, however, these workers would suffer permanent losses.

Proponents of employment at will essentially would argue, then, that in structured internal labor markets, where workers and firms have long-term attachment, there are strong incentives for employers not to unjustly discharge workers (the last two situations) In casual labor markets or markets where general training prevails (the first two situations), there are fewer incentives; however, in these cases it appears that discharged workers' losses would only be temporary. Given the perceived benefits from allowing employment at will, any policy recommendation should relate to short-term compensation for unjust discharge, not to restricting employers' rights to dismiss workers. Moreover, proponents would argue that once government restricts employers' rights to dismiss workers, it opens up the possibility of future restrictions on other dimensions of the employment relationship, such as promotion, transfers, and lesser disciplinary actions.

Critics of employment at will, of course, would disagree with this analysis. They would argue that labor markets are not competitive and that firms have dominant power. Worker opportunities may well be limited by the structure of labor markets, and the absence of viable alternatives implies that dismissed workers may suffer permanent losses. If worker alternatives are limited, firms need not fear any reputational costs associated with unjust dismissals. Moreover, since discharges are almost always an individual rather than a collective phenomenon, it is unlikely in any case that potential employees would be aware of any discharges—let alone unjust ones—and thus that firms would suffer any reputational costs. Viewed in this way, employment at will does not seem equitable and seems to favor employers over employees. Critics focus on modifying this policy because of the severe costs they feel it imposes on unjustly dismissed workers, costs which are much more severe than any other personnel action a firm may take (Stieber 1980a).

The case then for modifying employment at will is similar to the case for intervening in the overtime hours decision. If labor markets are not competitive, employers will not take the full marginal social cost of unjust dismissals into account in making dismissal decisions. Specifically, they will ignore the social costs of involuntary unemployment and/or dismissed workers having to accept jobs at wages that are not commensurate with their productivity. Viewed this way, the appropriate policy recommendation is to put a "tax" on unjust dismissal to increase employers' costs of taking such actions. In fact, this is exactly the policy of a number of European countries calling for severance pay if dismissals are found to be unjust (Stieber 1980b; Stieber and Blackburn 1983).

Ultimately, of course, which position is correct and which is the appropriate public policy depend upon the answers to a number of questions. What are the characteristics of people who are unjustly dismissed? Do they suffer prolonged spells of unemployment? Do they suffer permanent earnings losses from their dismissal? Not surprisingly, given that data do not permit us to distinguish unjust from just dismissals, we currently have answers to none of these questions. Some studies, however, do provide information on related questions.

First, as compared to unemployment insurance recipients, unemployed workers who are disqualified from receiving unemployment insurance benefits because they were dismissed for misconduct tend to be younger, lower wage, nonwhite, and unmarried (Felder 1979). Dismissal rates also tend to be higher at small firms than at large firms and for short-term employees than for long-term employees.[14] Together, these facts suggest that dismissed workers are often short-term employees in casual labor markets—a situation in which I argued above that unjust dismissal is likely to lead only to temporary earnings loss.

Second, survey information suggests that employers are less likely to hire an employee dismissed for cause than they are one who was laid off or who voluntarily quit (Block, Stieber, and Pincus 1983). Yet data on durations of spells of unemployment from five states suggest that in two of the states where workers dismissed for misconduct were disqualified from receiving unemployment insurance for the duration of their spell, these durations of unemployment were considerably shorter than those of otherwise comparable unemployment insurance recipients (Felder 1979). Denial of unemployment insurance benefits apparently prods discharged workers to return to employment relatively quickly; and, on average, they succeed, even if employers are less willing to hire them. For the most part these discharged workers were unemployed for only relatively short spells.

We have no information, though, on the post-unemployment earnings loss suffered by these dismissed workers vis-à-vis the losses suffered by unemployment insurance recipients; one might suspect that the lack of unemployment insurance benefits causes the former to settle for lower positions. Moreover, we do not even have any information on the absolute magnitudes of the post-unemployment earnings losses for discharged workers. Without such information for unjustly dismissed workers, it is difficult to suggest what the appropriate policy should be.

It is interesting to note, however, that public policy in European countries typically takes the form first of mediation and then formal labor court or industrial tribunal proceedings, in which workers deemed to be unjustly discharged are awarded severance pay. In most cases the severance pay is short-term, rarely exceeding six months in duration (Stieber 1980a, 159), and reinstatement is rare. This makes sense in terms of our analytical framework, in that raising the cost to employers of unjust discharges is more efficient than an outright prohibition of the action.

One possible reform, then, is to propose federal legislation on the subject. For example, one might require that discharge disputes go to arbitration or industrial tribunals and that severance pay be awarded in cases of unjust discharges. Rather than expanding the federal bureaucracy, however, it may make more sense to work within existing state legislation, specifically that dealing with unemployment insurance.

All states currently penalize unemployed workers who have been discharged due to misconduct connected with work and who apply for unemployment insurance benefits. While each state has its own interpretation of misconduct, misconduct typically includes violations of company rules, insubordination, refusal to perform work, and excessive absences. In a number of states it must be "willful and deliberate" for a penalty to occur. Fifteen states provide benefits to penalized individuals after a waiting period of typically three to ten weeks, while the remainder disqualify these individuals for at least their duration of unemployment.[15] It is interesting to note that of the fifteen states that provide benefits after a waiting period, the judiciary in only one, Nebraska, currently has adopted an implicit contract exception to the employment-at-will doctrine. Apparently the judiciary is acting as if the provision of some unemployment insurance benefits to discharged workers may reduce the pressure they feel to adopt implicit contract exemptions, although they never mention such benefits in their decisions.

Given that the provision of unemployment insurance benefits to unjustly dismissed workers would provide financial support similar to severance pay benefits, one wonders why pressure for reform does not take the form of devising ways to have state unemployment insurance systems more rigorously examine dismissals for misconduct, and to encourage them to award benefits without extra waiting periods in cases in which the dismissal was deemed excessive.[16] Even though this might require claim evaluators to hold more thorough and expeditious hearings than they currently do, in principle this type of examination is what the system should be doing anyway. The only weakness of this approach is that, to the extent that the unemployment insurance payroll tax is not perfectly experience-rated, employers would still not be bearing the full marginal social cost of their dismissal decisions.[17]

This approach essentially treats workers who are unjustly dismissed in an analogous manner to workers who are laid off permanently due to economic conditions. In both cases, through no fault of their own, they suffer economic losses which the unemployment system is meant to help alleviate. By ruling out reinstatement as a remedy, it implicitly accepts the judgment that management has the right to terminate employees at will. However, if one feels that unemployment due to an unjust dismissal is more costly to society than unemployment due to layoffs, an appropriate remedy would be to place a higher tax on unjust dismissal unemployment in the form of higher unemployment insurance.

Moving away from an employment-at-will policy would not be

costless. Suppose we moved toward a system of using labor courts or industrial tribunals to resolve discharge grievances for nonunionized employees as in many European nations. To the extent that doing so increases employers' costs of terminating workers, it should induce them to devote more resources to ascertaining the likely productivity of potential applicants and to more frequent termination of workers prior to the end of their probationary periods.[18] In a growing economy, the result would be a slowdown in the rate of growth of employment, with the lost employment opportunities concentrated among lower productivity workers (where minimum wage laws prevent employers from offering low initial wages to compensate for uncertainty about productivity). We also should expect to see increased turnover of members of this group during their probationary periods. The limited data cited earlier suggest that dismissals are currently concentrated among low-skilled workers in casual employment relationships; and it seems ironic that the very group it is hoped would be protected by the policy change would be the group that would appear to bear most of the cost of a change.

It is also not clear what the effect of moving further away from an employment-at-will policy would be on the level of unionization in the economy. European nations are much more heavily unionized than the United States and this has allowed the unions to win through national legislation many things which more typically would be part of collective bargaining agreements in the United States. Limitations on the rights of employers to assign overtime and dismiss workers are two examples. Strong national unions led to these policies in Europe, not vice versa.

Some people argue that limitations on employment at will in the United States would be a pro-union policy. They argue that unions have the skills to represent nonunion workers in cases involving unjust dismissals, and that nonunion employers' resistance to unions would diminish if nonunion workers legislatively were granted the protection that union contracts often provide. Hence, passage of such legislation might stimulate the growth of unions. Others argue, however, that legislative provision of this protection would decrease the demand for union services and hence would hurt unions.

A careful econometric study using data on unionization rates by state during the 1964–80 period found that the adoption by a state judiciary of implicit contract exceptions to the employment-at-will doctrine seemed to be associated with a decline in unionization rates, suggesting that passage of national legislation would have an adverse effect on unions.[19] However, while unions tend not to place the issue of employment at will high on their legislative agendas and have not actively lobbied for the passage of unjust discharge protection bills at the state level, in general they have been supportive of such legislation (Stieber 1984). This is not the first time that econometric evidence on the effects of labor market legislation on union growth has had little effect on the positions unions take with respect to the legislation.[20]

COMPARABLE WORTH

More than two decades after passage of the 1963 Equal Pay Act and Title VII of the 1964 Civil Rights Act—which together prohibit (among other things) sex discrimination in wages on any given job and sex discrimination in access to employment opportunities[21]—it is still common to observe that on average females earn less than males, females are distributed across occupations in a quite different manner than males, and earnings in occupations that are dominated by females tend to be lower than earnings in those dominated by males, even after one controls for traditional proxies for productivity (see Treiman and Hartmann 1981). The frustrations generated by these outcomes have led to pressure for the adoption of the principle of comparable worth, a principle that at least one participant in the debate has called "the women's issue of the 1980s."[22]

Put in simplest terms, proponents of comparable worth assert that jobs within a firm (or agency) can be valued in terms of the skill, effort, and responsibility they require, as well as the working conditions they offer. Two jobs would be said to be of comparable worth if they were comparable in terms of these characteristics. The principle of comparable worth asserts that, within a firm or agency, jobs that are of comparable worth should receive equal compensation.

Some efforts to implement comparable worth have taken place in the private sector; but the major push for comparable worth has occurred in the state and local government sector.[23] By the mid-1960s over a dozen states had passed comparable-worth legislation covering state employees, although these laws were rarely enforced. Starting with a 1974 state of Washington study, a number of states have undertaken formal job evaluation studies to see how their compensation systems mesh with the principle of comparable worth.[24] In several cases, this has led to "voluntary" implementation of comparable worth through the legislative and collective bargaining processes (such as in Minnesota, Connecticut, New York), or to court-ordered implementation (Washington).[25] By the summer of 1985, over a dozen states had begun the process of implementing some form of comparable worth in their employees' compensation systems.

Comparable-worth initiatives have also been undertaken at the local level in over 50 cities, counties, and school districts. Many of these units are in the states of California, Minnesota, and Washington. Comparable-worth wage adjustments were implemented in San José, California, after a well-publicized strike of municipal employees over the size of the adjustments; the publicity this strike received undoubtedly influenced the spread to other California units. Minnesota passed a law in April 1984 requiring political subdivisions to do job evaluations and then to revise their compensation structure in accordance with comparable worth. Finally, the early Washington comparable-worth study mentioned above attracted attention to the issue in that state.

At the federal level, hearings on comparable worth have been conducted by several congressional committees (see House of Representatives 1982). While support for the principle has been espoused by some congressional Democrats, in 1985 the U.S. Commission on Civil Rights and the U.S. Equal Employment Opportunity Commission, both dominated by Reagan administration appointees, came out against comparable worth (Equal Pay is Not Needed 1985).

Once again we can consider a simple stylized competitive labor market model to understand the cases for and against comparable worth.[26] In a competitive labor market a firm hires employees in an occupation or job category until the category's marginal product equals its real wage. A category's marginal product represents its worth to an employer. However, this is not necessarily fixed over time, but depends rather upon the number of employees hired in the category and all other job categories, the quantity of capital available to employees to work with, the production technology, and the quality of employees in the various job categories. The worth of a job then can not be determined independent of the qualifications of its incumbents and may well change over time. This suggests that job evaluation surveys cannot be one-shot events, but rather must be constantly updated; the worth of a job to an employer is not necessarily constant over time.[27]

Now move to the level of the labor market as a whole. The aggregation of individual firms' demand curves for each occupation leads to market demand curves for the occupation. The supply of labor to each occupation or job category will depend upon workers' qualifications, the pecuniary and nonpecuniary forms of compensation every job offers, and the distribution of preferences across workers for the various jobs. If there are no barriers to occupational mobility, workers will move between jobs until the net advantage perceived from each is equalized. Such movements lead to an equilibrating structure of occupational wage differentials; this depends upon the distribution of workers' qualifications and preferences for the various jobs.

In this stylized competitive world, all the factors that comparable worth advocates believe should affect wages (skill, effort, responsibility, and working conditions) would affect wages, since these factors would influence the underlying supply and demand schedules. However, the weight the market would place on each factor in determining wages would reflect the overall distribution of employees' preferences for, and employers' valuation of, each factor, not necessarily the weight assigned by a job evaluation scheme. Put another way, if workers have heterogeneous preferences with respect to various nonpecuniary conditions of employment, the relative wage each occupation would pay would depend upon employers' relative needs for the various occupations. Job characteristics would not be the only determinant of wages (Killingsworth 1985).

If, in such a world, females clustered into lower-paying occupations than males who had comparable productivity-related characteristics (for example, education), this would reflect only systematic differences in tastes between males and females for the nonpecuniary characteristics offered by the various jobs. For example, married females with children might have strong preferences for jobs that do not require travel, long hours, or work that must be brought home in the evenings. Given their preferences, males and females would have made optimal career choices and no government intervention would be required.

Of course, this conclusion presupposes the validity of the assumptions of the model and there are a number that proponents of comparable worth seriously challenge. The first is the assumption that there are no barriers to occupational mobility. If women are systematically excluded from high-paying occupations, one cannot claim that the structure of earnings is the result of voluntary choice. A market economist would respond that an appropriate long-run remedy in this case would be to break down occupational barriers through actions including rigorous enforcement of Title VII of the Civil Rights Act. However, such actions would provide only for gradual improvement of the welfare of the group discriminated against, as they would have to wait for vacancies to occur in the higher-paying "male" jobs. In addition, for jobs that require training, this policy would benefit primarily new entrants whose time horizons are sufficiently long to enable them to profitably undertake the necessary training.

In the absence of a policy that could create male jobs for all qualified females who want them, identify the older women whom historic discrimination prevented from making different occupational choices early in their lives and who now could not afford to profitably undertake the necessary investment if the barriers to entry were broken, and would provide resources to these women now so that they could undertake the training, it could be argued that a policy calling for comparable worth might make sense. Its justification would be based on equity considerations; one would have to conclude that these would outweigh any efficiency losses that might result. Some of these losses are discussed below.

The second assumption challenged is that wages in female-dominated occupations are determined in competitive markets. There is considerable evidence that employers in some female-dominated occupations, such as public school teaching and hospital nursing, appear to have monopsony power.[28] As is well known, in this circumstance there is a range over which one can legislate a higher wage without suffering any employment loss. Whether the wage that would be set under a comparable-worth wage policy would fall in such a range cannot be determined a priori and, in any case, the vast majority of females are not employed in these occupations. A remedy that insures that employers in these markets actively compete for workers might make more sense than comparable worth (Killingsworth 1985).

The case for comparable worth thus seems to rest on the argument that the current occupational distribution of female employees is based on discriminatory barriers which existing legislation has not broken down. Even if one could enforce these laws, breaking down barriers does not help experienced older workers who have invested heavily in occupation-specific training and whose time horizon is now too short to profitably undertake new occupational investments. Comparable worth is one of several policies that could provide a remedy for these workers.[29] Whether it is a desirable policy depends upon one's perceptions of how the benefits it provides contrast with the efficiency losses it induces. Just as with one's perception about the value of the minimum wage, given the trade-offs involved, ultimately one's position on comparable worth must depend on value judgments.

On the assumption that one wants to consider comparable worth as a national policy, a number of issues must be addressed. First, there are a host of questions relating to the usefulness of current job evaluation methods for comparable-worth studies. These include, but are not limited to, questions of gender bias in describing or evaluating jobs, the question of which characteristics should be valued, the statistical reliability of raters' evaluations, the correlation of ratings under alternative job evaluation methods, and whether market wages should be used in the determination of the "weights" different job attributes should receive. There is considerable debate over these issues, primarily by noneconomists, and the interested reader can pursue this debate elsewhere.[30]

Second, supporters of comparable worth are quite explicit that the concept is to apply to individual employers and that job evaluation schemes are to be establishment- or firm-specific. This immediately suggests that, like many other forms of protective wage legislation, comparable-worth legislation would have to have firm-size exemptions, because only relatively large firms would have enough employees to consider conducting formal job evaluations. Comparable worth laws would apply then only to relatively large firms.

Now to the extent that a comparable-worth wage policy succeeded in raising the wages of women in large establishments, one might be tempted to deem the policy a success. However, this ignores several market repercussions that would occur.[31] Employers in the covered sector would have an incentive to substitute male employees for female employees because their relative wages would fall; thus we should observe a decline in female employment in this sector. To the extent that scale effects outweigh substitution effects, a decline in male employment in the covered sector should also occur. If these displaced male and female workers seek employment in small firms in the noncovered sector, wages of both males and females there would fall. Hence, while some women would gain (women who keep their jobs in large firms in the covered sector), other women would lose (women who lose their covered sector jobs and women initially employed in small firms in the noncovered sector). It is unclear whether women as a group, on balance, would actually gain.

In part, the answer depends upon the magnitude of the disemployment effects. One study of Australia, where the implementation of a comparable-worth system via wage tribunals saw the average female–male earnings ratio in the economy rise from .61 to .76 over a five-year period, concluded that the policy change decreased the rate of growth of female employment by 1.3 percent a year (Gregory and Duncan 1981). This was approximately one-third the actual rate of growth of female employment during the period, so it represents a rather substantial decline. The same study concluded that the female unemployment rate was about .5 percent higher at the end of the period than it would have been in the absence of the comparable worth policy.

In the United States comparable-worth wage policies are only beginning to be implemented, and then primarily in the state and local sector. As a result, estimated disemployment effects can be obtained only from simulations that use estimated systems of demand curves for male and female employees to provide estimates of male–female substitution as relative wages change. A detailed study of the state and local sector concluded that a 20 percent comparable-worth wage adjustment for all females in the sector would lead to only a 2 to 3 percent decline in female employment in the sector (Ehrenberg and Smith 1987). While one might expect gender substitution—and hence disemployment effects—to be greater in the private sector, existing studies of male–female substitutability in the private sector are not sufficiently precise to allow one to draw this conclusion.[32]

In part, the answer also depends on whether women are employed disproportionately in the covered (large firm) or noncovered (small firm) sectors, the magnitude of the male–female wage differential in each sector, and the wage differentials between sectors. If women are disproportionately employed in small firms with large male–female wage differentials, which pay much less than large firms, on balance women as a group may lose by the policy. While it is well established that wage levels vary by firm size, evidence on the other questions is only sketchy. One study did find, however, that the proportionate representation of women in U.S. manufacturing firms declines with establishment size (Blau 1977).

Furthermore, if comparable worth is a firm-specific policy, it will do nothing to eliminate male–female wage differentials that exist because of differences in the sex distribution of employees across industries or across size classes of establishments within an industry. To the extent that women are concentrated in low-wage industries or low-wage small firms, comparable worth will have only a limited effect on the average male–female wage differential in the economy.[33]

Of course, a comparable-worth wage policy might have supply-side effects. On the one hand, it would reduce the incentive females have to obtain training for higher-paying male-dominated occupations, since increasing the wage in female-dominated occupations via comparable-worth wage adjustments would reduce the return to training investments; this would lead to another efficiency loss. On the other hand, such wage adjustments might increase the attractiveness of female-dominated occupations to males and reduce the extent to which females are excluded from male occupations. We have no information on the likely magnitudes of these responses, which further hinders our evaluation of such a policy.

PLANT CLOSING LEGISLATION

Most European nations have some form of legislation relating to plant closings or large scale layoffs (Aboud 1984). Typically the provisions call for advanced notice by employers and employer negotiations with employees and government over whether the closing can be averted. Often they require severance pay for displaced workers and some, for example Sweden, have detailed programs of labor market services (retraining, placement, public works, wage subsidies) to facilitate adjustments. Canada similarly requires advance notice. In many of these countries small establishments with less than 100 employees are exempt from the requirements, perhaps due to the greater failure rate of small businesses or the belief that a shutdown of a small business does not have a substantial effect on a community.

Plant closing legislation in the United States is much more modest.[34] As of early 1988, there was no federal law and only six state laws. Of the latter, three—Maine, Hawaii, and Wisconsin—require advance notice of plant shutdowns (with size class exemptions), and Maine also requires one week's severance pay per year of service for workers with greater than three years' tenure. Connecticut does not require advance notice, but does require nonbankrupt firms to maintain health insurance and other benefits for workers unemployed by plant shutdowns for up to 90 days. Massachusetts similarly requires maintenance of health insurance and encourages, but does not require advance notice and severance pay. Finally, South Carolina "requires" employers to give workers two weeks notice before shutting down but only in situations where employees are required to give advance notice prior to quitting.

Interest in plant closing legislation in the United States has grown since the deep recession of the mid-1970s and the relatively large number of plant closings and permanent layoffs in major manufacturing industries since then undoubtedly further stimulates this interest.[35] During the 1975–83 period over 125 bills relating to plant closings were introduced in 30 states; the majority in the Northeast and Midwest (see, for example, Bluestone and Harrison 1982). More than 90 percent of these bills had provisions requiring advance notice of shutdowns, while substantially smaller percentages required severance pay or economic assistance to either workers, employers, local governments, or potential buyers.

At the federal level, over 40 bills have been introduced into Congress since 1979. In July 1988 Congress passed the Worker Adjustment and Retraining Notification Act which requires employers of 100 or more workers to give workers and local government officials 60 days advance notice of a plant closing or a layoff that is planned to last at least six months and that involves at least 500 workers or one-third of an employer's work force. Advance notice had become an important issue during the early stages of the 1988 presidential campaign and, although philosophically opposed to the bill, President Reagan bowed to political pressures and did not veto it.

Proponents of plant closing legislation argue that advance notice provisions will ease displaced workers' shock and facilitate their search for alternative sources of employment or training. Such notice also allows employers, workers, and the community see if ways exist to save the jobs such as wage concessions, tax concessions, or seeking new ownership, including employee ownership. If plants do shut, the maintenance of health insurance provides needed service for individuals during a period when stress leads to increased incidence of physical and mental ailments.[36] Finally, payments by firms to the communities in which the plants were located would help alleviate the extra demands placed on these communities for social services that the shutdowns cause—demands that would arise at the same time local property and sales tax revenue were being reduced.

Opponents of the legislation argue that, in addition to restricting the free mobility of capital, advance notice legislation would have a number of other adverse effects on firms (see, for example, McKensie 1982). They claim it would increase worker turnover and decrease productivity, as those productive workers with the best opportunities elsewhere would leave and the morale of remaining workers would suffer. It also would decrease the likelihood that buyers of the plant's product would place new orders, that banks would supply new credit, that suppliers would continue to provide services, and that the firm could sell the plant to potential buyers.

Finally, it would depress corporate stock prices. Such a provision, plus the others that directly increase the costs of plant shutdowns, effectively increase the cost of reducing employment and thus should encourage firms not to expand operation in states where such laws are in effect. Opponents argue, then, that it is a self-defeating regional policy in that, if adopted, it would discourage creation of new jobs in the Snow Belt.

In evaluating the case for plant closing legislation, it is again useful to stress the divergence between private and social costs. Employers currently do not bear the full social costs of plant shutdowns, both because unemployment insurance is imperfectly experience-rated and because the costs these actions impose on communities are not taken into account by them. As such, imposing a tax on plant closings makes sense; it would have the effect of discouraging the action. Of course, to avoid depressing new employment growth in snow belt states, the tax would have to be nationwide; critics have inadvertently supported the case for federal instead of state legislation.[37]

Two additional points should be noted. First, the community effects of worker displacement depend partially upon the number of jobs lost relative to the size of the local labor market. In a given size market, it is hard to ascertain what the differential effects on the community would be of an establishment with 1,000 employees shutting down, of an establishment with 100 employees permanently laying off 100 of them, or of 100 establishments each laying off a single employee. Viewed this way, firm-size exemptions under the law make less sense, as does the distinction between plant shutdown and layoff. In addition, the costs the community faces for any given displacement will be higher the smaller is the local labor market and the higher is the area unemployment rate. The latter suggests that the imposed tax per displaced worker should increase as unemployment rates increase.

Second, to say that employers should pay a tax on plant closings does not necessarily imply that the revenue from this tax should go to displaced workers in the form of severance pay, just as an increase in the tax on overtime should not necessarily go to workers in the form of an increased overtime premium, as discussed earlier. However, if displaced workers' losses are greater than those incurred by other unemployed workers covered by the unemployment insurance system, and if it can be shown that these losses were not already compensated for by the market in the form of higher pre-unemployment wages, a case for worker compensation might be made on equity grounds.

To understand the losses workers suffer from a plant shutdown or permanent layoff, it is useful to again consider several simple competitive labor market models. Consider initially the situation in which all skills are perfectly general. In this case workers would accept jobs with an employer whose risk of shutdown or permanent layoff were high only if they received a wage premium to compensate them for their lost earnings during the time they expected to be unemployed searching for new employment. In such a world, worker losses would only be transitory, since their skills are assumed to be perfectly general. Their post-unemployment wages might be less than their pre-unemployment wages; however, this would reflect only that they had moved to less risky jobs. This points out that a comparison of post- to pre-unemployment wages may overstate the permanent losses workers face.

In fact, several studies suggest that labor markets do compensate workers for their risk of unemployment; jobs with higher risk of subsequent unemployment, all other things being equal, pay higher wages. While the provision of unemployment insurance indicates society believes that markets are not working perfectly, the same studies also suggest that, as expected, higher unemployment insurance benefits lead to smaller wage premiums for risk of unemployment (see Aboud and Ashenfelter 1981; Topel 1984).

Permanent losses for workers would occur, however, if workers had previously invested in firm-specific skills and they did not anticipate layoffs or plant closings. In this situation, post unemployment earnings would be less than current earnings and no predisplacement wage differential would have arisen to compensate these workers for the risk involved in their investments. When industries such as automobile and steel reach a period of decline it is likely that potential new employees (to the extent that there are any) will be aware of the risks and will demand wage premiums to compensate them. However, older workers who invested decades earlier when times were good, would be locked into the industry because of the specificity of their skills, and would receive no compensating differentials.

The notion that compensating wage differentials for risk of unemployment will arise primarily for workers with relatively short job tenure has not been tested. The study of mandatory overtime cited above did find, however, that compensating wage differentials for that unfavorable job characteristic existed only for employees with less than three years tenure (Ehrenberg and Schumann 1982). To the extent that this result carries over to risk of unemployment, permanent losses would be suffered primarily by workers with long tenure. This implies that severance pay plans and job assistance programs for displaced workers should focus on workers with relatively long tenure. As noted earlier, the Maine law requires three years' tenure for severance pay and then increases severance pay with experience. Such a structure makes sense.[38]

One must be aware, though, that since employers share the costs of investment in firm-specific training, they also will share the losses from unanticipated (at the time of the training) plant closings. To make them pay for the above programs for senior workers with specific training would increase their losses and discourage all employers from making future investments in firm-specific training; such programs might be funded out of general revenues.

The situation would be very different, however, if employees worked in structured internal labor markets where employers used upward sloping age–earnings profiles to motivate increased attachment. As noted above, in such a world workers are initially paid less than the marginal productivity but eventually are paid more. Over their expected tenure with the firm they receive an expected present value of compensation equal to their present value of productivity. Any unanticipated plant shutdown would cause permanent losses for experienced workers and the employers would not directly share in these losses. A stronger case for program costs to be borne directly by the employer can be made in this case.

The discussion so far has focused on losses that workers suffer after displacement occurs. What about possible losses in the years prior to displacement?[39] If employees anticipate forthcoming plant closings or layoffs, they will cease their investments in firm-specific training, and one should observe a flattening in their age–earnings profiles prior to the displacement. In contrast, if they fail to anticipate such displacements, they will continue their investments and no such flattening will occur. In the latter case, failure by employers to provide workers with information that displacements were forthcoming would have erroneously led workers to undertake investments that were sure not to pay off. In fact, one careful study of displaced workers found that the slope of age–earnings profiles did tend to flatten prior to displacement for permanently laid-off workers but did not for workers involved in plant shutdowns. Apparently layoffs tend to be anticipated, whereas plant shutdowns are not (Hamermesh 1984; Cordes, Goldfarb, and Hamermesh 1985).

The above finding provides a further rationale for advance notice for plant closing (but not for layoff) legislation; it would provide incentives for workers not to make wasted investments in firm-specific training. Other empirical evidence provides additional support for the policy. One study in Maine found that advance notice did appear to speed up labor market adjustments to plant closings; area unemployment rates peaked earlier in situations where advance notice took place, although long-run unemployment rates were not affected.[40] Another early study of 32 plant closings found that advance notice of closings rarely led to increased quit rates or decreased productivity.[41] To further protect against these things occurring, the receipt of severance pay and/or job assistance programs could be restricted to employees who remained with the plant until it shut down; this in fact is done in Maine. Finally, it is estimated that over tho last decade advance notice permitted about 60 cases of employee ownership to arise to avert plant shutdowns; these saved about 50,000 jobs and in only four or five cases did the firm subsequently go out of business.[42]

One should caution, however, that studies of the earnings loss suffered by displaced workers find that advance notice provisions do not appear to influence postdisplacement wage rates (Ehrenberg and Jacobson 1988). The policy may aid worker transitions but it does not seem to affect their long-run prospects. More generally, other studies concluded that workers with high education levels and general skills suffer only small earnings losses from labor market displacement.[43] In contrast, unionized workers in heavy-manufacturing industries such as steel and automobile suffer substantial earnings losses—at least 25 percent, in the first two years after displacement—and still have annual losses in the range of 10 to 15 percent after six years. Given estimated wage differentials paid to union workers of at least this amount, it is difficult to say how much of this loss merely represents that dissipation of union rent. Finally, workers in less heavily unionized industries—where turnover rates are higher, long-term attachment of workers to firms is less prevalent, and less firm-specific training occurs—suffer some short-run losses but virtually no long-run losses.

A number of studies also indicate that older workers, women, and workers with long tenure suffer the greatest losses from displacement.[44] Earnings losses also appear to be higher when area unemployment rates are high and in areas with relatively small labor markets (Jacobson 1984). These findings further support the notion that labor market adjustment policies should be targeted on older workers, and that resource allocation formulas should have area unemployment rate triggers, as various training and extended unemployment insurance benefit programs have had in the past.

These earnings losses estimates do not take account of the effects of existing income replacement programs, such as unemployment insurance and trade adjustment assistance. In cases where displaced workers were eligible for trade adjustment assistance, first-year net incomes losses were substantially reduced (Jacobson 1984; Corson and Nicholson 1981; Neumann 1978). However, these benefits did not appear to affect long-run net income losses and they did appear to increase displaced workers' duration of unemployment (Corson and Nicholson 1981; Neumann 1978). To speed up the process of labor market readjustment, any plan proposing that compensation be paid to displaced workers probably should call for lump sum payments, rather than weekly benefits while unemployed.

So far the discussion has ignored the role of unions. Workers covered by collective bargaining in the United States have some protection against plant closings. Employers must bargain with unions over the effects of plant closings (for example, severance pay, pension recall and transfer rights, seniority), although they are under no obligation to bargain over the decision to close (see Greenfield 1984). If a union wants certain rights, such as advance notice of anticipated closings, they must win them at the bargaining table. Moreover, the recent *Milwaukee Springs II* decision by the National Labor Relations Board establishes employers' rights to transfer work from union plants to nonunion plants to avoid high labor costs during the course of a contract without the union's consent unless the language in the contract specifically prohibits it. The employer, however, may still have to bargain to impasse with the union before relocating if the decision to move is based upon labor costs, and the move may be an unfair labor practice if the move is made due to the employer's "anti-union animus."[45]

A recent survey of plant closing provisions in major collective bargaining agreements (agreements covering 1,000 or more workers) found that over one-third contained some provisions relating to worker participation in decisions about the effects of plant closing or relocation decisions, with severance pay provisions being the most common (U.S. Bureau of Labor Statistics 1981). However, only slightly more than 10 percent of these contracts called for advance notice.[46] Presumably coverage in smaller agreements is less extensive.

While union protection against plant closings thus seems limited, it must be remembered that one important role unions play is to acquire information and to disseminate it to members on the true economic conditions of the firms at which they work. The study of the changes in increased earnings tied to seniority prior to plant closings or layoffs discussed above also found that the increases were lessened for union members (Hamermesh 1984). Apparently union members better anticipated labor market displacement than non-union workers, and thus were less likely to make wasted investments in firm-specific training. Furthermore, while there is no evidence that unions win larger compensating wage differentials for antici-pated plant shutdowns or layoffs than the market produces for non-union workers, there is a growing body of literature relating to other unfavorable job characteristics, which suggests that larger compen-sating differentials arise in the union sector.[47] As with overtime hours and employment-at-will legislation, the major need for plant closing legislation may well be in the nonunion sector.

Finally, it must be stressed that whatever form plant closing leg-islation takes it is subject to problems relating to bankruptcy and noncompliance. Almost by definition, bankrupt firms will not have the resources to fund benefits for displaced workers and, in the absence of substantial penalties for noncompliance, incentives for compliance are limited. If the goal is to aid both communities and displaced workers in a timely fashion, it seems clear that public insurance of benefits may be required in these cases. This leads logically to the notion of a plant shutdown benefit guarantee cor-poration, which might be financed in a manner analogous to the Pension Benefit Guarantee Corporation.

CONCLUDING REMARKS

I have focused on four areas in which protective labor legislation might be expanded in the United States over the next decade, spe-cifically the areas of hours of work, unjust dismissal, comparable worth, and plant shutdowns.[48] In each case I have tried to provide a rationale for government intervention, to discuss if empirical ev-idence supports this rationale, to discuss potential unintended side effects of the proposed policy changes that are relevant for employ-ment policy, and to discuss how proposed legislation might be struc-tured. Space and time constraints have precluded my consideration of a number of other areas of likely expansion, including disability, retirement income, health insurance, and parental leave.

Several themes emerge that are worth emphasizing in conclusion.

First, the case for legislation and the appropriate form that legislation should take often depend crucially on the empirical nature of labor markets. Are workers who are required to work overtime compensated in the form of higher wages? Do unjustly dismissed workers typically suffer permanent losses? Do wage differentials by gender arise because of occupational barriers? Have displaced workers who invested in firm-specific skills been compensated for risk of displacement by the market? Do wage profiles slope upward because of firm-specific training or life-cycle incentive compensation arrangements? We unfortunately don't have answers to some of these questions; but they are required to design policies in the areas discussed above.

Second, unionized workers, both directly through the collective bargaining process and often indirectly through winning wage differentials to compensate them for unfavorable job characteristics, appear to have much more protection in many of these areas than do nonunion employees. The major beneficiaries of legislation in these areas often would be nonunion workers. While strong protective labor legislation and strong unions coexist overseas, one wonders if the growth of protective labor legislation in the United States would decrease the demand for unions and further reduce the share of the work force that is organized.

Third, there are reasons to propose firm-size exemptions in each of the above areas. However, such exemptions stratify employment into a covered (large establishment) sector with better working conditions and a noncovered (small establishment) sector with poorer conditions. The workers most in need of protection may well be employed in smaller establishments; the design of the legislation may frustrate its objectives.

Finally, it is worth restressing that what is seen as worker protection by some is seen as sources of economic inefficiency by others (see chapter 1 by Sawhill). While I have tried to articulate many of the costs and benefits of proposed policies, and to suggest in several places ways to minimize the costs, ultimately decisions about these policies will have to involve much more explicit value judgments than are presented here.

Notes

An earlier version of this paper has been published in Research in Labor Economics 8(B). 1986. Greenwich, Conn.: JAI Press.

1. For example, higher overtime pay premiums may stimulate employment growth (Ehrenberg and Schumann 1982), while the accumulated evidence shows that higher minimum wage rates reduce employment opportunities for teenagers (Brown, Gilroy, and Cohen 1982).

2. The material in this section draws heavily from Ehrenberg and Schumann (1982) (1984).

3. The well-known preference of Congress and state legislatures for standards rather than tax-subsidy schemes may reflect only the fact that the majority of their members are lawyers who are comfortable with the standards approach.

4. Initial drafts of the legislation established outright prohibitions of long hours. The idea of instituting a penalty for overtime instead apparently arose only as a compromise during the late stages of the debate. For legislative histories of the FLSA, see Paulsen (1959); Phelps (1930); and Grossman (1978).

5. Hundreds of court decisions handed down since the FLSA was enacted confirm that Congress had the dual intent of inducing employers to reduce hours of work and increase employment, and of compensating employees for the burden of long work weeks. See, for example, Walling v. Youngerman-Reynolds Harwod Co. Ala 1945, 65 S.Ct. 1242, 1250; 325 U S 410; 80 L.Ed. 1705, rehearing denied, 66 S.Ct. 12; 326 U S 804; 00 L.Ed. 489.

6. HR 1784, introduced into Congress on 1 February 1979. This bill never reached a vote.

7. The finding that unionized workers receive compensating wage differentials for unfavorable job characteristics while nonunion workers often do not is not unique to the mandatory overtime area. Duncan and Stafford (1980) find similar results for three working conditions variables, and a number of authors (see Ehrenberg 1988 for a survey) have found similar results for wage–injury risk trade-offs.

8. See, for example, Block, Stieber, and Pincus (1983); Bureau of National Affairs (1982); Epstein (1984); Rosen (1984); Stieber (1980a) (1980b) (1984) (1985); Stieber and Blackburn (1983); Stieber and Block (1983); and Stieber and Murray (1983). A search of on-line data bases turned up almost 100 articles on the topic, primarily in law journals, during the 1981 04 period.

9. For a discussion of European policies, see Stieber (1980a) (1980b); and Stieber and Blackburn (1983).

10. See Stieber (1985) and Block and Stieber (1983) for evidence that union discharge rates tend to be about half nonunion rates. Felder (1979) similarly found that discharges for misconduct per 1,000 new spells of unemployment were much lower in highly unionized New York State than they were in four southern states with relatively low unionization. One must, of course, interpret these data with caution. One cannot distinguish whether these differences are due to the protection unions give to workers or to differences in the characteristics of workers (e.g., skilled or unskilled) or of jobs (e.g., structured internal labor market with premiums paid for a stable work force or casual unstable jobs) between the union and nonunion sector.

11. Stieber (1984). Three states—California, Massachusetts, and Montana—also have "good faith and fair dealing" exceptions which hold that while an employee may be dismissed without cause, he or she must be dealt with fairly and in good faith. So, for example, firing an employee to avoid having to pay a commission on a large sale would fall under the exemption.

12. The federal legislation, HR 7010, the Corporate Democracy Act was introduced in 1980 by Representative Benjamin S. Rosenthal of New York. It defined just cause and prohibited employees from being fired without just cause, as well as specified social policy exceptions to the employment-at-will doctrine. This bill died in com-

mittee. At the state level California and four other states are currently considering legislation to prohibit unjust dismissal (Beyond Unions 1985).

13. The material below borrows in places heavily from Epstein (1984) and Rosen (1984), although I do not always reach the same conclusions they do.

14. Stieber and Block (1983). Short-term employees were defined in this study as having six months to five years tenure and, in private communication to me, Stieber indicated he believes the majority fell in the upper end of the range.

15. UBA, Inc. (1984). In the latter case individuals often must regain employment and earn specified amounts before they become eligible for unemployment insurance benefits during future spells of unemployment. All of the above penalties are for cases of "simple misconduct"; in cases of "gross misconduct" harsher penalties are often imposed.

16. Such a policy would be less generous to workers than the policies in some European nations, where compensation for unjust discharge is often awarded in addition to unemployment insurance benefits. See Stieber and Blackburn (1983), 70, for some examples.

17. For evidence on the extent of imperfect experience rating in the unemployment insurance system and its effects on temporary layoffs, see Topel (1983).

18. European nations generally exempt employees in their first six months of employment from protection under unjust dismissal laws. See Stieber (1980a).

19. Neumann and Rissman (1984). No similar relationship was found for adoption of "public policy" exceptions. This result is to be expected; the latter exception does not relate to the services unions provide.

20. For example, a long literature on the effects of state right-to-work laws for the most part suggest they have little effect on the level of unionization or union organizing success, yet unions place repeal of these laws high on their legislative agenda. See Ehrenberg and Smith (1988, 455) for citations to this literature.

21. This section draws heavily on material in Ehrenberg and Smith (1987).

22. This statement has been attributed in a number of places to former EEOC Chair Eleanor Holmes Norton.

23. Explanations for why this occurred include that public decisionmakers are more likely to be swayed by public opinion calling for such policies than are private, profit-maximizing firms and that increases in female wages in the public sector caused by comparable worth wage adjustments are likely to lead to only small employment losses because the demand for public employees is likely to be inelastic. I discuss the evidence on the latter point below.

24. The next two paragraphs summarize information found in Cook (1983); Ehrenberg and Smith (1987, tables 1 and 2); and National Committee on Pay Equity (1984).

25. In *AFSCME v. State of Washington*. For details see Immediate Halt to Bias (1983). In September 1985, a federal appeals court panel overturned this decision. See Comparable Worth Rule Overturned (1985).

26. See Bergmann (1984) and Killingsworth (1984) (1985), respectively, for more complete analytical treatments of the cases for and against comparable worth.

27. That job evaluation scores must be reconsidered as internal and external conditions change has long been recognized by institutional economists. For a recent discussion, see Donald Schwab (1984).

28. See Ehrenberg and Schwarz (1986) for citations to this literature.

29. Another remedy would be lump sum payments specified as a function of years of service in the occupation. This would have the advantage of making the size of

the remedy a function of the magnitude of the loss and would not reduce employment of women in the occupation.

30. See, for example, Treiman (1979) (1984); Treiman and Hartmann (1981); Schwab (1984); Ehrenberg and Smith (1987); Pierson, Koziara, and Johanneson 1984); Remick (1984); and Blumrosen (1979).

31. See Oi (1985) for a discussion of this issue.

32. In the Australian data, Gregory and Duncan (1981) did find smaller disemployment effects in the public sector.

33. See Johnson and Solon (1986) for one estimate of how small this reduction might be.

34. Burchell et al. (forthcoming, chapter 9); and *Daily Labor Report* (19 July 1984, A5).

35. See Flaim and Sehgal (1985) for data on the numbers of workers who lost their jobs during the 1979–83 period due to plant shutdowns and permanent layoffs and these workers' subsequent labor market experiences.

36. See Bluestone and Harrison (1982) for citations to studies of this problem

37. A nationwide program, however, might encourage the flight of jobs overseas.

38. Flaim and Sehgal (1985) report that of the 5.1 million workers with greater than three years experience who lost their jobs during the 1979–83 period due to plant shutdowns or permanent layoffs, one-third had at least ten years job tenure and one-third had five to nine years tenure. Almost 2 million additional displaced workers had two years tenure. So where one draws the cutoff will substantially affect program cost.

39. The discussion here draws on Hamermesh (1984).

40. Folbre, Leighton, and Roderick (1984). These authors are unable to ascertain, however, whether advance notice provisions lead to faster reemployment elsewhere or faster labor force withdrawal.

41. Weber and Taylor (1963). Flaim and Seghal (1985) also found that only 12 percent of workers who received any advance notice of plant shutdowns left prior to the plant closing.

42. See Whyte (1985). The term *saved* is a bit misleading since in the event of a plant shutdown the vast majority of workers would have ultimately found employment elsewhere (see Flaim and Seghal 1985).

43. Holen, Jehn, and Trost (1981); Jacobson (1978) (1984); Jacobson and Thomason (1979); Cropper and Jacobson (1982).

44. See Gordus, Jarley, and Ferman (1981); Lipsky (1970); Stern (1972); Holen, Jehn, and Trost (1981).

45. *Milwaukee Spring II*, 268 N.L.R.B. 601 (1984), affirmed sub. nom, *United Auto Workers v. NLRB*, 765 F.2d 175 (D.C. Cir. 1985). See Schwab (1985) for a discussion of Milwaukee Springs, including whether the ruling really will affect relocation decisions.

46. This figure is somewhat misleading as advance notice provisions are probably concentrated in situations where the possibility of future plant closings exist. In fact, Flaim and Seghal (1985) found that over 60 percent of workers displaced between January 1979 and January 1983 due to plant closings had received some advance notice.

47. See, for example, Ehrenberg and Schumann (1984) on mandatory overtime and Dickens (1984) on risk of injury.

48. Between 1975 and 1981, in cases of plant shutdowns in Maine, only 23 percent of covered companies complied with advance notice requirements and only 56 percent provided required severance pay benefits. See Folbre, Leighton, and Roderick (1984).

References

Aboud, Antoine, ed. 1984. *Plant Closing Legislation.* Ithaca, N.Y.: ILR Press.

Abowd, John, and Orley Ashenfelter. 1981. Anticipated Unemployment, Temporary Layoffs, and Compensating Wage Differentials. In *Studies in Labor Markets,* edited by Sherwin Rosen. Chicago, Ill.: University of Chicago Press.

Aronson, Robert, and Robert McKersie. May 1980. Economic Consequences of Plant Shutdowns in New York State. Ithaca, N.Y.: NYSSILR.

Becker, Gary. 1975. *Human Capital,* 2d ed. New York: National Bureau of Economic Research (NBER).

Bergmann, Barbara. 1984. Why Wage Realignment Under the Rubric of Comparable Worth Makes Economic Sense. In *New Directions for Research on Comparable Worth,* edited by Heidi Hartmann. Washington: National Academy Press.

Beyond Unions: A Revolution in Employee Rights is in the Making. 8 July 1985. *Business Week.*

Blau, Francine D. 1977. *Equal Pay in the Office.* Lexington, Mass.: D.C. Heath.

Block, Richard, Jack Stieber, and David Pincus. October 1983. Discharged Workers and the Labor Market: An Analysis of Employer Attitudes and Experience. Mimeo.

Bluestone, Barry, and Bennett Harrison. 1982. *The Deindustrialization of America: Plant Closings, Community Abandonment, and the Dismantling of Private Industry.* New York: Basic Books.

Blumrosen, Ruth G. 1964. Wage Discrimination, Job Segregation, and Title VII of the Civil Rights Act of 1964. *University of Michigan Journal of Law Reform* 12:397–502.

Brown, Charles, Curtis Gilroy, and Andrew Cohen. June 1982. The Effect of the Minimum Wage on Employment and Unemployment. *Journal of Economic Literature* 20:487–528.

Burchell, Robert, et al. Forthcoming. *Plant Closings in the American Economy.*

Bureau of National Affairs. November 1982. *The Employment-At-Will Issue.* Washington.

Cahill, Marion. 1932. *Shorter Hours.* New York: Columbia University Press.

Commons, John R., and John B. Andrews. 1920. *Principles of Labor Legislation.* New York: Harper and Bros.

Comparable Worth Rule Overturned. 5 September 1985. *Washington Post.*

Cook, Alice. February 1983. *Comparable Worth: The Problems and the States' Approaches to Wage Equity.* Manoa, Hawaii: University of Hawaii, Industrial Relations Center.

Cordes, Joseph, Robert Goldfarb, and Daniel Hamermesh. June 1985. Compensating Displaced Workers: Why, How Much, How? Mimeo.

Corson, Walter, and Walter Nicholson. 1981. Trade Adjustment Assistance for Workers: Results of a Survey of Recipients Under the Trade Act of 1974. *Research in Labor Economics* 4:417–69.

Cropper, Maureen, and Louis Jacobson. February 1982. The Earnings and Compensation of Workers Receiving Trade Adjustment Assistance. Alexandria, Va.: Center for Naval Analysis. Mimeo.

———. February 1982. The Economics and Compensation of Workers Receiving Trade Adjustment Assistance, Alexandria, Va.: Center for National Analysis. Mimeo.

Equal Pay is Not Needed for Jobs of Comparable Worth, U.S. Says. 18 June 1985. *New York Times,* 12.

Dickens, William. May 1984. Difference Between Risk Premiums in Union and Nonunion Wages and the Case for Occupational Safety Regulation. *American Economic Review: Papers and Proceedings* 96:320–23.

Duncan, Gregg, and Frank Stafford. June 1980. Do Union Members Receive Compensating Wage Differentials? *American Economic Review.*

Ehrenberg, Ronald G. January 1988. Workers' Compensation, Wages and the Risk of Injury. In *New Perspectives in Workers' Compensation,* edited by John F. Burton, Jr. Ithaca, N.Y.: ILR Press.

Ehrenberg, Ronald B., and George H. Jakubson. Forthcoming. *Advance Notice Provisions in Plant Closing Legislation.* Kalamazoo, Mich.: W.E. Upjohn Institute for Employment Research.

Ehrenberg, Ronald G., and Paul L. Schumann. 1982. *Longer Hours or More Jobs?* Ithaca, N.Y.: ILR Press.

———. October 1984. Compensating Wage Differentials for Mandatory Overtime? *Economic Inquiry.*

Ehrenberg, Ronald, and Joshua Schwarz. 1986. Public Sector Labor Markets. In *Handbook of Labor Economics,* edited by Orley Ashenfelter and Richard Layard. Amsterdam: North-Holland Press.

Ehrenberg, Ronald G., and Robert S. Smith. 1988. *Modern Labor Economics,* 3d ed. Glenview, Ill.: Scott, Foresman.

———. 1987. Comparable Worth in the Public Sector. In *Public Compensation,* edited by David Wise. Chicago, Ill.: University of Chicago Press.

Epstein, Richard A. Fall 1984. In Defense of the Contract at Will. *University of Chicago Law Review* 51:947–82.

Felder, Henry E. 1979. A Statistical Evaluation of the Impact of Disqualification Provisions of State Unemployment Insurance Laws. *Occa-*

sional Paper 79–1. Washington: U.S. Unemployment Insurance Service.

Flaim, Paul, and Ellen Sehgal. June 1985. Displaced Workers of 1979–83: How Well Have They Fared? *Monthly Labor Review*, 3–16.

Folbre, Nancy, Julia Leighton, and Melissa Roderick. January 1984. Plant Closings and Their Regulation in Maine, 1971–82. *Industrial and Labor Relations Review* 37:185–96.

Gordus, Jeanne Prial, Paul Jarley, and Louis A. Ferman. 1981. *Plant Closings and Economic Dislocation*. Kalamazoo, Mich.: W.E. Upjohn Institute for Employment Research.

Greenfield, Pat. 1984. Plant Closing Obligations Under the National Labor Relations Act. In Aboud, *Plant Closing Legislation*.

Gregory, Robert, and Robert Duncan. Spring 1981. Segmented Labor Market Theories and the Australian Experience of Equal Pay for Women, *Journal of Post Keynesian Economics* 3:403–29.

Grossman, Jonathan. June 1978. Fair Labor Standards Act of 1938: Maximum Struggle for Minimum Wage. *Monthly Labor Review*.

Hamermesh, Daniel. 1984. The Cost of Worker Displacement. *NBER Working Paper No. 1495*. Cambridge, Mass.: NBER.

———. 1986. The Demand for Labor in the Long Run. In *Handbook of Labor Economics*, edited by Orley Ashenfelter and Richard Layard.

Holen, Arlene, Christopher Jehn, and Robert Trost. December 1981. *Earnings Losses of Workers Displaced by Plant Closings*. Alexandria, Va.: Center for Naval Analysis.

Immediate Halt to Bias in Wages in State of Washington Ordered. 15 December 1983. *New York Times*.

Jacobson, Louis. 1978. Earnings Losses of Workers Displaced from Manufacturing Industries. In *The Impact of International Trade and Investment on Employment*. Washington: U.S. Department of Labor.

———. December 1984. The Effect of Job Loss on Auto Workers. Alexandria, Va.: Center for Naval Analysis. Mimeo.

Jacobson, Louis, and Janet Thomason. August 1979. Earnings Loss Due to Job Displacement. Alexandria, Va.: Center for Naval Analysis. Mimeo.

Johnson, George, and Gary Solon. 1986. Estimates of the Direct Effects of Comparable Worth. *American Economic Review* 76:117–25.

Killingsworth, Mark. 1984. The Case for and Economic Consequences of Comparable Worth: Analytical, Empirical, and Policy Questions. In *New Directions for Research on Comparable Worth*, edited by Heidi Hartmann.

———. 1985. Economic Analysis of Comparable Worth and Its Consequences. *Proceedings of the Thirty-Seventh Annual Meeting of the Industrial Relations Research Association*. Madison, Wisc.: IRRA.

Lazear, Edward. December 1979. Why Is There Mandatory Retirement? *Journal of Political Economy*, 1261–84.

Lipsky, David. January 1970. Interplant Transfer and Terminated Workers: A Case Study. *Industrial and Labor Relations Review* 23:191–206.

McKensie, Richard, ed. 1982. *Plant Closings: Public or Private Choices?* Washington: Cato Institute.

National Board for Prices and Income. 1970. *Hours of Work Overtime and Shiftwork,* Report No. 61. London.

National Committee on Pay Equity. 1984. *Who's Working For Working Women: A Survey of State and Local Government Pay Equity Activities and Initiatives.* Washington.

Neumann, George. 1978. The Labor Market Adjustments of Trade Displaced Workers. In *Research in Labor Economics,* edited by Ronald Ehrenberg, 2:353–80.

Neumann, George, and Ellen Rissman. April 1984. Where Have All the Union Members Gone? *Journal of Labor Economics.*

Oi, Walter. 1985. Costs and Consequences of Comparable Worth. University of Rochester. Mimeo.

Paulsen, George E. 1959. The Legislative History of the Fair Labor Standards Act. Ph.D. diss. Ohio State University.

Phelps, Orme. 1939. *The Legislative Background of the Fair Labor Standards Act.* Chicago, Ill.: University of Chicago Press.

Pierson, David, Karen Koziara, and Russell Johanneson. 1984. A Policy Capturing Application in a Union Setting. In *Comparable Worth and Wage Discrimination,* edited by Helen Remick. Philadelphia: Temple University Press.

Remick, Helen. 1984. Major Issues in A Priori Applications. In *Comparable Worth and Wage Discrimination,* edited by Helen Remick.

Quinn, Robert, and Graham Staines. 1979. *The 1977 Quality of Employment Survey: Descriptive Statistics.* Ann Arbor, Mich.

Rosen, Sherwin. Fall 1984. Commentary: In Defense of the Contract at Will. *University of Chicago Law Review* 51:983–87.

Schwab, Donald. 1984. Job Evaluation Research and Research Needs. In *New Directions for Research on Comparable Worth,* edited by Heidi Hartmann.

Schwab, Stewart. April 1985. Collective Bargaining and the Coase Theorem: Reflections on Milwaukee Spring. Cornell University Law School. Mimeo.

Stern, James. Winter 1972. Consequences of Plant Closure. *Journal of Human Resources* 7:3–25.

Stieber, Jack. 1980a. The Case for Protection of Unorganized Employees Against Unjust Discharge. *Proceedings of the Thirty-Second Annual Meetings of the Industrial Relations Research Association.* Madison, Wisc.

———. 1980b. Protection Against Unfair Dismissal: A Comparative View. *Comparative Labor Law* 3:229–40.

———. 1984. Employment-At-Will: An Issue for the 1980s. *Proceedings of* the Thirty-Sixth Annual Meetings of the Industrial Relations Research Association. Madison, Wisc.

———. 1985. Recent Developments in Employment-At-Will. Mimeo.

Stieber, Jack, and John Blackburn, eds. 1983. *Protecting Unorganized Employees Against Unjust Discharge.* East Lansing, Mich.

Stieber, Jack, and Richard Block. March 1983. Employment Attitudes Towards Discharged Job Applicants. Paper presented at the Sixth World Congress of the International Industrial Relations Association, Kyoto, Japan.

Stieber, Jack, and Michael Murray. Winter 1983. Protection Against Unjust Discharge: The Need for a Federal Statute. *Journal of Law Reform* 16:319–41.

Topel, Robert. September 1983. On Layoffs and Unemployment Insurance. *American Economic Review.*

———. 1984. Equilibrium Earnings, Turnover, and Unemployment. *Journal of Labor Economics* 2:500–22.

Treiman, Donald. 1979. *Job Evaluation: An Analytic Review.* Washington: National Academy of Sciences.

———. 1984. Effect of Choice of Factors and Factor Weights in Job Evaluations. In *Comparable Worth and Wage Discrimination*, edited by Helen Remick.

Treiman, Donald, and Heidi Hartmann, eds. 1981. *Women, Work, and Wages: Equal Pay for Jobs of Equal Value.* Washington: National Academy Press.

UBA, Inc. 1984. *Highlights of State Unemployment Compensation Laws, January 1984.* Washington.

U.S. Bureau of Labor Statistics. February 1979. *Characteristics of Major Collective Bargaining Agreements, July 1, 1976.* Washington.

———. 1981. *Major Collective Bargaining Agreements: Plant Movement, Interplant Transfer and Relocation Allowances.* Washington.

U.S. House of Representatives, Committee on Post Office and Civil Service. 1982. *Pay Equity: Equal Pay for Work of Comparable Value.* Washington.

Weber, Arnold, and David Taylor. July 1963. Procedure for Employee Displacement: Advance Notice of Plant Shut-Downs. *Journal of Business* 36:302–15.

Whyte, William. 1985. Employee Ownership: Lessons Learned. In *Proceedings of the Thirty-Seventh Annual Meetings of the Industrial Relations Research Association.* Madison, Wisc.

Chapter Seven

INSURING EQUAL OPPORTUNITY IN EMPLOYMENT THROUGH LAW

Leroy D. Clark

In 1963 and 1964, the nation began operating under the Equal Pay Act and Title VII of the 1964 Civil Rights Act, the first federal legislation in its history to prohibit discrimination in private employment. Prior to that time, there were some minor attempts, through federal executive orders and statutory amendments, to prohibit racial discrimination by private employers who had government contracts, and racial and sexual discrimination in the federal civil service. But those efforts were largely ineffective because of a failure to commit sufficient resources or to grant genuine power to effect compliance.[1] A number of northern and western states had antidiscrimination laws in employment, prior to the federal statutes, but the state agencies that administered them were also hampered by inadequate budgets and a tendency to rely too heavily on conciliation and persuasion instead of law enforcement. None of the southern states, where racial discrimination was most prevalent, had such legislation.

In contrast, today 39 states have antidiscrimination legislation and the Equal Employment Opportunity Commission (EEOC), the largest federal agency devoted to the problem, has a staff of over 3000 persons and a budget of approximately $158 million (Hamermesh and Rees 1988).

This chapter focuses on federal laws prohibiting employment discrimination, with a view toward answering the following questions: Is employment discrimination still active today, such that a continuing federal effort at eradication is needed? What forms of inequity can federal antidiscrimination legislation most effectively confront, and are some problems unresolvable by traditional legal institutions? As federal law has developed, is it illogically or inappropriately structured, and if so, what rearrangements ought be made? Are there ways that the EEOC could be strengthened to make it a more efficient law-enforcement agency?

Current law prohibits discrimination on the grounds of race, gender, age, national origin, religion, veteran status, or handicap. This chapter discusses primarily the law as a control on discrimination against black Americans and against females. This is not to suggest that the other forms of discrimination are not active problems, but the focus on race and gender was based on three premises:

☐ An assessment of the condition of black Americans is an important barometer of legislative success in ending discrimination because of the intense and special role that race has played in American life. The historical roots of black-white interactions are unique. Blacks are the only involuntary immigrant group, having been forced into the country and enslaved, and the only group that had its citizenship right established through a civil war. Despite blacks' relatively small numerical presence, bordering on 10 percent, race helped shape the politics of a whole region (the South) and continues to play a role both overtly and *sub-silentio* on the national political scene. Most importantly, the legislative history of Title VII shows that Congress was more concerned about discrimination on the basis of race than any other form of discrimination, largely because of the very visible protest activity of black-oriented civil rights organizations. Thus it is appropriate to look at Congress's efforts to dislodge the longest standing and most entrenched form of prejudice.

☐ Another goal of the 1960s' antidiscrimination legislation was to end wage discrimination against females. To the extent that such discrimination may have been a pervasive practice, it is important to focus on gender discrimination because it involves the only "minority" that is a majority of the population and may soon be a majority of the work force.

☐ Race and gender also exhibit features found in other types of discrimination (such as unfounded myths and stereotypes) and, between them, reflect the full range of legal enforcement mechanisms utilized in antidiscrimination legislation. However, they also present an opportunity for a study in contrasts, since they are shaped by different emotional and social forces. Racial prejudice can manifest itself in distancing behavior, and may often be founded on stereotypes based on an absence of contact and limited knowledge. Attitudes about gender, however, are generated and become elaborated on the basis of contact, including contact of the most intimate sort. Thus it is important to study the law as it deals with two situations with very different variables.

THE EFFICACY OF FEDERAL LAW

Has discrimination in employment been eliminated, or even substantially reduced, since the passage of 1963–64 legislation?

Racial Discrimination

A focus on race shows that the relative occupational status of blacks has improved significantly since 1965. In the year 1980 alone, 2.46 million blacks, or 22.6 percent of the 10.98 million black work force, were in higher-paying and higher-status jobs, with a net increase in wages of nearly $9 billion more than would have been the case if minority workers were arrayed throughout the labor force in accordance with the occupational pattern of 1965 (U.S. Bureau of the Census 1981, 526).

Blacks reduced their reliance on lower-paying, unskilled service and labor jobs by 50 percent between 1960 and 1980, and the black share of higher-paying, skilled blue-collar work went up from 4.2 percent in 1960 to 8.2 percent in 1980; 10 percent would represent equal participation (Lewis 1985, 55).

Black female income increased significantly during the 1960s going from 65 percent to 82 percent of white female income. By the 1980s the median income of black females equaled that of white females although their average earnings were only 88 percent of that of white females.[2]

It is not possible to tie all employment changes to the intervention of the federal antidiscrimination law because some improvements in the occupational status of blacks was occurring before 1960 (for example, blacks had 2.3 percent of skilled blue-collar work in 1940, and 4.2 percent by 1960). However, even in the pre-1960 period, the impact of the law as an agent of change cannot totally be discounted because an increasing number of states had enacted antidiscrimination laws between 1945 and 1960. State efforts have been subjected to criticism because of weak enforcement, but many employers may have begun some degree of compliance simply because it was unlawful to function otherwise. However, with respect to the precise impact of federal law, one writer argues:

A comparison of the movement between 1950 and 1960 with that between 1970 and 1980 shows that prior to the passage of Title VII and application of a more stringent executive order, the occupational distribution of minorities did not significantly improve. This at least shifts the burden of demonstrating that the changes are attributable to factors other than the legal system to those who make the argument (Blumrosen 1984, 313, 334–35).

Another, and very significant measure of the influence of federal law is that employers with government contracts—with mandated affirmative action plans designed to improve their "minority profile"—employ more blacks, and at higher job levels, than employers not under such affirmative action obligations (Oster and Juba 1984, 218–27).

Even with all the positive movement generated by legal and extralegal forces since 1965, blacks clearly are still not on a par with whites and arguably, at least, continuing discrimination accounts for some of it. Only one-fifth (18 percent) of white workers hold jobs with low incomes, while almost one-third (30 percent) of all black workers are in these positions. Conversely, 42 percent of white employees are in higher-level positions, in comparison with 27 percent of black employees (Levitan, Johnston, and Taggart 1975). Further, black females do not attain higher levels of professional and administrative positions at the same rate as white females. This explains, in part, why the average earnings of black females are lower than for white females despite having the same median earnings. Moreover, the fact that black females work full time more often than white females contributes to their having the same median income (Hill 1981, 10).

A major source of disadvantage is that blacks, both male and female, are unemployed at twice the rate of whites. Such unemployment—a major concern of Congress in passing Title VII—has remained at the doubled rate for the entire 20 years Title VII has been in effect. Antidiscrimination law, however, does not command employers to hire the unqualified, even where the lack of qualification is due to discrimination in other areas, such as in the educational system. Title VII has protected blacks because it has been interpreted as barring credential hurdles which are not relevant to the job in question; this only underscores its emphasis on the truly qualified.[3]

Clearly, some disparities in income, occupational status and unemployment are attributable to the negatives in background that disqualify blacks for employment, including their possession of fewer of the legitimately required credentials and skills necessary for being hired or promoted. Blacks are less likely to possess high school diplomas and college degrees than whites and are more apt to be illiterate, disabled, or saddled with a criminal record. These conditions do not necessarily (or lawfully) operate as an absolute bar to employment, but they all can narrow, lawfully, the range of employment options.

Charges that the antidiscrimination laws have been ineffective because they have not improved the employment picture for the hardcore poor in the black community are misguided. Title VII countermands only racial discrimination. If disproportionate unemployment is driven by factors other than discrimination, the statute provides no protection. The hard-core poor are more likely to be handicapped by the previously mentioned employment disqualifiers. The poor, moreover, are more likely to seek unskilled work; but, during the last 35 years, the supply of laborers for such work has increased at a much faster pace than the demand. When skilled workers lose work during recessions, they further intensify the competition by accepting unskilled work.

However, even granting the presence of objective, nondiscriminatory conditions which suppress the employment and promotion opportunities of blacks, studies by the U.S. Commission on Civil Rights show that qualified blacks are still subjected to discrimination on the basis of race in employment (U.S. Commission on Civil Rights 1978). Especially problematic is the discrimination still prevalent in the higher-level positions (for example, managers and administrators in corporations) that render not only power and high income, but also the opportunity to affect employment practices below.

Choosing persons for these positions involves a large measure of subjective evaluation, and though courts have recognized the great potential for racial or sexual discrimination to covertly influence the subjective evaluation, they have constrained such subjectivity only in lower-level jobs where they think there are fewer factors in qualifying for the work. This distinction has been criticized as illegitimate (Bartholet 1984, 945, 959–78); the courts recognize their own limitations, primarily their lack of expertise in the personnel decisions of the various businesses that come before them in Title VII cases. Judicial power in this context is not one of mandatory mediation or conciliation, such that the courts can place the responsibility on the parties to arrive at some mutually agreeable compromise in high-level hiring or promotion. Judges are more likely to conceive of themselves as detectives, trying to find evidence of discrimination to support the "win" or "lose" decision they must make. The more variables that can reasonably be claimed to play a part in filling a given position, the more the courts will be reluctant to substitute their judgment for that of the employer.[4]

Gender Discrimination: Comparable Worth

What is the picture of discrimination against females? The post-1965 period presents three main features: females have entered the work force at an accelerated rate, the work force is substantially segregated in terms of gender, and there is an increasing gap in average income between males and females in recent years.

Again the precise causal connection between federal legislation and subsequent patterns in female employment is elusive. Litigation opened areas of employment to females that had traditionally been the preserve of males; it also allowed females to remain in the labor force where the custom by some employers was to treat their marriage, pregnancy, or parenthood as justification for extended layoff, discharge, or refusal to hire.[5] The majority of females probably were accepted in the work force primarily because the jobs rapidly created in the low-wage service sectors resembled the kinds of jobs traditionally held by females, such that there was little resistance to their entrance. This explanation accounts for the most salient features of employment for black and white women today: occupational segregation and annual income lower than that of males. Indeed gender appears to be a stronger factor in organizing job prospects for black females than race. While black men and women do have higher unemployment rates respectively than white men or women,[6] black males have reduced the income gap between themselves and white men since 1965, but the gap between men as a group and women as a group (ignoring race) is greater and growing (Treiman and Hartmann 1981, 16).

Given occupational segregation and the historically concomitant lower pay, the issue of comparable worth is important to black and white women. The proponents of comparable worth claim that women have been denied jobs occupied historically by men, have thus become segregated in jobs thought stereotypically to be suitable for women (such as nursing), and concomitantly that the pay for such jobs has been depressed below their intrinsic worth to the employer. Raising the pay in such gender-segregated jobs is considered necessary to correct the imbalance in pay between men and women.

Have black males suffered, as well, from artificially depressed wages through job segregation that occurred prior to Title VII? They currently experience job instability and low pay from their disproportionate concentration in marginal jobs, such as busboys, garage attendants, and messengers. Job segregation, however, has lessened considerably for them since 1965, and they do not have the additional social barrier of sex stereotypes to occupying jobs held by white males (Scales-Trent 1984, 51). Despite all of that, recent research has shown that black males are more likely than white males to occupy jobs held predominantly by females, and some depression of wages has accompanied their racially segregated jobs (Dill, Cannon, and Vanneman 1987). Females (both black and white) face a more intense problem since the socialization of females to connect femininity with helping roles still has strong currency and despite the 1964 Civil Rights Act's ban against coerced gender segregation in the workplace, it is likely that women will continue to choose, or be easily guided into, work traditional for females for the foreseeable future. Further, a large portion of the current female work force has invested many years of education and training in currently jobs and is unlikely to recommence the process in order to enter other jobs now held predominantly by males.

Given these factors, how likely is it that Title VII will be interpreted to embrace fully the comparable-worth theory as a mechanism for redressing the gap in pay between females and males? At this juncture the U.S. Supreme Court has given a bare minimum of support for a cause of action involving sex discrimination in the context of gender segregation in jobs. In *County of Washington v. Gunther* the court addressed a very limited question, namely, if it could be proven that the wages of a job had been deliberately depressed because the job holders were females, then Title VII is violated, even though the jobs held by females were not identical to those held predominantly by males. The majority opinion states that it was not deciding "the precise contours of lawsuits challenging sex discrimination in compensation under Title VII," and adds that the case before them did "not require a court to make its own subjective assessment of the value of the male and female jobs or to attempt by statistical technique or other method to quantify the effect of sex discrimination on the wage rates" (452 U.S. 161, 181 [1981]). The dissent stated more frontally that "the [majority] opinion does not endorse the so-called comparable worth theory." A number of commentators have said that *Gunther* applies only in circumstances where the plaintiffs can show intentional and conscious manipulation of job rates in order to disadvantage females. No case subsequent to *Gunther* has sustained a cause of action merely on a showing of a heavy concentration of females in jobs paying less than those held primarily by males. The major restraint on the courts in sustaining the comparable-worth theory is the charge that attempts to gauge the intrinsic worth of a job to an employer ultimately involve a degree of subjective evaluation of the factors most important for a particular job; but courts have no authority to substitute their judgment for that of the employer. (This is very similar to the problem of the court's institutional competence in assessing employer's subjective evaluation in the filling of high-level positions).

It is unlikely that any court will go further than the limited holding of Gunther because they have no authority under Title VII as it is presently drafted and interpreted to make the necessary subjective evaluations.[7] Title VII rules out only sex discrimination as a variable, and it must be proven specifically to operate in a given employer's workplace. Numerous macroeconomic studies conducted both industrywide and on a national basis, controlling for educational background, training, and seniority, show an "unexplained" disparity in income between males and females. However, some critics of the comparable-worth theory note that no study fully encompasses all the variables of nondiscrimination that could affect wages, and thus one cannot make the claim that gender discrimination is the only explanation for the gap (Livernash 1980, 44). More importantly, in a concrete lawsuit against a given employer, industrywide or national studies are not appropiate for proving that a particular employer has discriminated against female employees in setting wages.

REFORM OF ANTIDISCRIMINATION LAWS

Having looked at the current limitations in antidiscrimination law regarding unemployment, higher-level jobs, and comparable worth, we can now examine whether and how law or enforcement agencies can be reformed to meet the problems mentioned above, as well as others to be discussed.

A look at the operation of our federal laws prohibiting discrimination in employment is especially timely because the various statutes have been administered for over two decades, under both Democratic and Republican administrations, and a solid body of law, both procedural and substantive, has been developed. There have been amendments to plug loopholes, to clarify interpretations, or to extend the scope of prohibitions, and we are able to look at the effectiveness of the prime enforcement agency, the EEOC, which has functioned previously without and now with enforcement power.

Consolidation of Rights to Sue

The array of potential lawsuits regarding employment discrimination presents an enormous, confusing hodgepodge. A civil suit is now possible under a number of federal statutes other than Title VII of the 1964 Civil Rights Act. Suit can be brought under the nineteenth century Civil Rights Acts for discrimination based on race or foreign birth by private employers (sec. 1981), or for race or gender discrimination by public employers (sec. 1983). An action can be brought in federal court against a union for race or gender discrimination alleging a violation of the duty of fair representation (*Steele v. Louisville & Nashville R.R.* 1944). Complainants can also proceed against unions in an entirely different forum than the federal courts by filing an unfair labor practice charge before the National Labor Relations Board (NLRB) (*Local 12 v. NLRB* 1967). There has even been a suggestion that discrimination by employers is an unfair labor practice (*United Packinghouse v. NLRB* 1964). Statutory provisions appended to federal grant and assistance programs also permit interpretations that bar race and gender discrimination in employment, with some courts sustaining private causes of action thereunder as well.[8] Suits charging that a person has been paid less in wages than another for the same job on the basis of gender may be brought under either the Equal Pay Act or Title VII.

The various statutes have differing statutes of limitations, standards of proof, and remedies. The Age Discrimination in Employment Act reaches discrimination practiced by an American corporation in a foreign country, while all other antidiscrimination laws appear limited to conduct occurring in the United States. Under Title VII, resort to conciliation and to state antidiscrimination agencies is mandatory, and counsel fees are provided to a prevailing plaintiff who exhausts such pre-suit administrative remedies (*New York Gas Light Club v. Carey* 1980). The very opposite is true for suits under section 1981 (*Webb v. Board of Education of Dyer County* 1985). Unions are subject to money damages for sex discrimination under Title VII. But they are not so subject under the Equal Pay Act, nor for age discrimination under the Age Discrimination in Employment Act (*Richard v. Alaska Airlines* 1984).

It is unlikely that Congress carefully considered the particularized ramifications of the potential overlaps, conflicts, and inconsistencies among the various grounds for suit against discrimination at the time it passed Title VII. This is clearly true with respect to the nineteenth century Civil Rights Acts because they were revived as a basis for discrimination suit by the U.S. Supreme Court in 1968, four years after passage of Title VII (*Jones v. Alfred H. Mayer Co.* 1968). There has been some general sentiment for preserving most avenues of complaints, and a proposal to make Title VII the exclusive remedy was not adopted in the 1972 amendments passed by Congress. One amendment in 1972 did bring federal employees under Title VII; however, the law was still sufficiently unclear with respect to such employees that it took a subsequent pronouncement by the U.S. Supreme Court to find that federal employees, unlike any others covered by Title VII, are limited to Title VII for suits alleging discrimination (*Brown v. General Services Administration* 1976).

Thus a fair amount of litigation has involved the problem of the articulation and harmonizing of the various statutes and different approaches. Indeed, the end is not in sight. The current state of affairs can only induce forum-shifting by the plaintiff, the potential harassment of defendants through having to defend the same cause of action under varying labels, and the application of different remedies against defendants who have committed essentially the same kind of violations.

There does not seem to be a carefully developed rationale for continuing the multiplicity of avenues for discrimination suits. Accordingly, it is here proposed that Title VII should be the sole basis for private causes of action involving race or gender discrimination.

Combining Nongovernmental Race- and Gender-Discrimination Suits under Title VII

What adjustments would be desirable if this shift in the law were adopted? What protections should be added to Title VII to retain full protection of the covered classes? This proposal entails the repeal of the Equal Pay Act. No rights would be lost because Title VII now encompasses any violation of the Equal Pay Act and may indeed be broader to the extent that it is not limited to unequal wages, as is the Equal Pay Act, but covers all compensation (therefore pensions, which are not considered wages, would be covered). The only diminished coverage is in those rare situations where an employer has fewer than 15 employees, but meets the jurisdictional requirements of the FLSA under which the Equal Pay Act occurs. This loss of coverage could be resolved in part, by expanding Title VII to reach employers with eight or more employees.

The one amendment of Title VII necessary, should the Equal Pay Act be repealed, would be addition of a right to recover liquidated damages (which is an additional amount equal to the back wages owed). Moreover, it should be extended to all the protected classes, for there is no sound reason why females should receive double back wages for equal pay violations, and not blacks, Hispanics, or others who might suffer an identical form of discrimination.[9]

It is further recommended that liquidated damages should be available for any loss of wages occasioned by discrimination as well as unequal pay situations. For example, a person discharged discriminatorily on the basis of age can recover liquidated damages.[10] Again there is no sound basis for denying such relief to persons who are discharged discriminatorily on the basis of race or gender.

Indeed, as we limit all suits to Title VII we should consider a general strengthening of the monetary penalties to make private suits more potent and effective. It is questionable whether mere back pay is a sufficient deterrent to employers' breaches of federal employment laws. It is possible that resistant employers may come to ignore the penalty over time because of a reliance on diminished complaints resulting from employees' inertia or fear of retaliation. Indeed, some employers may want a reputation for discrimination to indirectly discourage application from members of the disfavored group. Certainly the experience under the National Labor Relations Act (NLRA) suggests that employers have engaged in calculated unlawful conduct, treating the possibility of payment of back wages to a few employees as an incidental cost of doing business because the ultimate goal of intimidating other employees is achieved. Certainly, the union establishment which pushed for enhanced monetary penalties under the NLRA, in the Labor Reform Act of 1978, thought that the current law limiting remedies to injunctions and back pay was an inadequate deterrence.[11] Therefore the following two adjustments seem appropriate: liquidated damages should be mandatory, not requiring a showing that the employer acted "willfully" as is the current law for suits under the Age Discrimination in Employment Act[12] and punitive damages for pain and suffering should be allowed. The latter would be necessary in part because our proposal would exempt employment discrimination from coverage under the nineteenth century Civil Rights Acts, which provides that remedy.[13]

Punitive damages are particularly appropriate for one form of discrimination more typically experienced by females, namely, sexual harassment. Under Title VII sexual harassment is actionable where the job atmosphere has been made particularly onerous for a woman by unwelcome sexual advances, even where there is no concrete loss of a job opportunity (Meritor Savings Bank v. Vinson 1986). The female is left with only a right to a prospective injunction against the conduct, but no right to damages for the humiliation suffered. This gap in remedies has produced another form of resort to non-Title VII suits, namely, tort actions under state law for intentional infliction of emotional distress. Again if Title VII gave full relief with punitive damages, one could then consider closing off state tort suits through preemption.[14] Title VII suits are now tried before a judge and not a jury. If plaintiffs could sue for punitive damages, the defendants would have to be given a right to demand a trial jury. If the level of prejudice against persons in the plaintiff's (disfavored) group was high in the locality, such plaintiffs might face the possibility of losing the case—even if it has sound merit—because of a hostile jury. This would simply mean that plaintiffs would have to make the strategic choice to forgo punitive damages in a situation where there is a strong likelihood of prejudice in the local populace.[15]

Employers may think the penalty of mandatory liquidated damages too harsh. However, the conditions for softening or denying them, as has been done in other labor relations statutes, do not exist when one considers the employment discrimination area. Under the Fair Labor Standards Act (FLSA), liquidated damages were granted as a matter of course against all violations, but a subsequent amendment limited such damages to employers acting in bad faith. This may have been reasonable since the employers more likely to violate the FLSA were small firms, which probably lacked regular access to counsel to keep them abreast of all of the technicalities of coverage, which are complex and changing.

In contrast the bulk of litigation under Title VII has not been against very small employers, and large employers have regular access to counsel. Moreover, the over 20 years of interpretation of Title VII have made the statute clearer in its substantive terms, thus presenting fewer problems even for small employers, and the proposals made here would simplify the legal picture even further.

It is arguable that ending employment discrimination promptly and thoroughly may be a more important goal for the society than the deterrence of small pay violations committed usually by marginal and small employers, some of whom claim that they could not stay in business if they were forced to pay higher wages. There are frequent proposals to lower the minimum wage (for teenagers) because it is said that a competing goal—increased employment opportunities—is jeopardized by trying to maintain wages at too high a level. There are hardly any public proposals to reverse current law to permit a resumption of discrimination which is now outlawed—a further demonstration that the policy direction has broad public consensus and has a higher priority than the minimum wage laws.

REFORM OF THE EQUAL EMPLOYMENT OPPORTUNITY COMMISSION

How should the EEOC be reformed? My argument here has several parts.

Cease-and-Desist Authority

A major issue with which Congress has struggled, both at the initial passage of Title VII and the revisions which have occurred in 1972, is whether enforcement authority should be lodged in the EEOC and, if so, what form it should take. As Congress first debated the legislation in 1963, senators from southern states and those concerned with the interests of the business community instituted a vigorous filibuster. Supporters of Title VII, in order to achieve its passage, had to agree that the EEOC would have no direct enforcement power. It could investigate charges and seek conciliation, but if conciliation failed, the grievant was remitted to a private action in federal court. Only the U.S. attorney general had any enforcement authority, and that was limited to proceeding against employers exhibiting a pervasive "pattern or practice" of discrimination.

The predictions that the EEOC would be a toothless tiger proved correct, for by 1971 the judgment was widespread that a commission with only authority to persuade could not be effective in confronting nationwide practices of discrimination. From 1965 until 1971, the EEOC had achieved conciliation in less than half of its 81,000 cases, and the Justice Department had brought suit in only 69 pattern-or-practice cases.[16]

The issue in 1972 was whether to give the commission authority to issue cease-and-desist orders on the model of the NLRB or to require that it seek enforcement through *de novo* actions in federal court. Civil rights groups supported cease-and-desist order authority. Representatives of the business community supported *de novo* actions in the federal courts. The latter position prevailed in the 1972 amendment of Title VII.

It is now appropriate, 15 years later, to reconsider that question. It is possible the 1972 amendment was merely a compromise with forces hostile to the act, and that cease-and-desist order authority (with other accompanying adjustments) might achieve the goals of the act more effectively and expeditiously.

Representatives of the business community opposed cease-and-desist order authority on several grounds (U.S. Senate 1971, 169–

76): (1) the courts are the traditional forum for determining guilt or innocence of a party; (2) the EEOC had developed a backlog of cases and thus would develop a larger backlog if given cease-and-desist authority, especially since the 1972 amendments covered more employers;[17] (3) administrative actions would take longer than *de novo* actions in the federal district court, thus postponing relief for plaintiffs; (4) the court's power would be limited to facts found by the EEOC which could only be rejected if there was no "substantial evidence" to support them; and (5) other civil rights are enforced solely by the federal courts (voting rights, fair housing, school desegregation, public accomodations), and the federal courts have done an excellent job in these areas.

Some of these arguments are weak or have been undermined by events subsequent to 1972 when they were made. To survey the arguments in turn: (1) The courts may be the traditional arena for determining guilt or innocence in criminal cases, but the case of *Griggs v. Duke Power* has greatly expanded and reoriented antidiscrimination litigation away from proving subjective intentional discrimination toward rooting out widely used practices and systems that have the indirect and unnecessary effect of excluding minority groups (e.g., giving I.Q. tests to applicants for truck driver jobs instead of relying on previous driving experience). Thus the focus on the moral culpability of defendant–employers, as would be the mode in a criminal case, is greatly reduced. (2) During the Carter administration, the EEOC adopted an extremely efficient rapid charge processing system which substantially reduced the outstanding backlog.[18] The EEOC under the Reagan administration began accumulating a backlog again, but it appears to have been a result of dropping the rapid charge proccessing system and cutting agency staff and funds (Norton 1988). If the agency were adequately funded and staffed and good management techniques were resumed, there should be no reason that the EEOC could not handle cease-and-desist authority. Further, one could (unlike the process under the NLRA) retain a private right to sue to aid in reducing the backlog that had developed. (3) The claims of business community spokespersons of solicitude for plaintiffs' access to a speedy remedy are suspect. The claim that administrative proceedings would take longer because of the need to resort to an appeals court for enforcement could be met by making the cease-and-desist order self-enforcing—requiring the aggrieved employer to appeal and secure a stay or be bound by the order. The time for the issuance of a cease-and-desist order by the NLRB is much shorter than the time necessary to reach judgment at a trial;

the NLRB achieves settlements in many cases before an order is issued, showing that a fair number of employers see early compliance as the most prudent course, when faced with a cease-and-desist order. (4) The more substantial claim of employers is that the federal courts ought to retain greater power than the commission under Title VII because they have been effective in other cases involving civil rights, and are likely to do so under Title VII.

It is true that, over a certain span in our history, courts were often the only forum in which minority persons subject to discrimination seemed to be able to secure redress. During periods in which Congress and the executive branch were fairly inactive, the federal courts were chipping away at the southern edifice of racial segregation as early as 1938, culminating in 1954 with *Brown v. Board of Education*, which outlawed segregation in schools.[19] It is also true that shortly after passage of Title VII the lower federal courts were giving readings favorable to plaintiffs, and in 1971 the U.S. Supreme Court decided the landmark pro-plaintiff case of *Griggs v. Duke Power*. However, subsequent to *Griggs* the critics of the federal courts and especially the U.S. Supreme Court, who align themselves with the interests of minority groups have grown more numerous and more vocal. It is claimed that the courts are now hampering plaintiffs from reaching and eradicating all of the racially or sexually discriminatory practices in an employer's business by interpretations which unduly narrow the class of persons covered by a suit (see *Vuyanich v. Republic National Bank* 1984). It is also charged that federal courts are now imposing standards on statistical proof that are extremely difficult or impossible to meet. Further, in a startling number of cases appellate courts have overturned findings of discrimination made by the lower court—despite the fact that the lower courts are normally given great deference in fact finding, since only they actually see and hear the witnesses and thus have a better vantage point in making judgments about credibility (Chambers and Goldstein 1985, 235 and 249).

It would be one thing if only the lower federal courts were reading Title VII restrictively in the post-*Griggs* era; but in a number of instances the U.S. Supreme Court (which has the last word) has been more restrictive than the lower courts. The recent trend toward giving a narrow scope to class actions was probably reinforced by the U.S. Supreme Court's decision in 1982 that a plaintiff complaining of discrimination in promotions cannot represent (and thus protect) persons discriminated against in hiring even where plaintiffs and the others were discriminated against because they were Mexican-

Americans (*General Telephone Co. of the Southwest v. Falcon* 1982). Prior to that decision, a number of lower federal courts allowed any victim of national-origin discrimination to maintain an across-the-board attack (a "class action") on all unequal employment practices committed against members of that group (*Johnson v. Georgia Highway Express Inc.* 1969). Likewise every circuit in the country had decided that when an employer had actively and openly excluded minorities from hiring prior to the enactment of the Civil Rights Act of 1964, its use of a seniority system after the act perpetuated that earlier discrimination. Only the Supreme Court thought otherwise (*Teamsters v. United States* 1977). A similar scenario has occurred with respect to one aspect of the concept of affirmative action. This is a remedy that requires or permits an employer who has discriminated in the past to consciously take account of race or gender to accelerate integration of minorities or females into the work force. While the U.S. Supreme Court has permitted affirmative action regarding hiring and promotion, it disallowed the remedy regarding layoffs where a seniority system was altered.[20] This was contrary to the ruling of both lower courts in the case, and the rulings of other lower courts that had confronted the question.

An important consideration is that President Reagan has chosen the chief justice of the U.S. Supreme Court and appointed three of its current lifetime members, and his administration is the first to disrupt the bipartisan support of civil rights over the last 20 years. It is this court that has initiated a reconsideration of a 12-year-old precedent, under the nineteenth century Civil Rights Acts, that private parties are prohibited from refusing to contract on the basis of race.[21]

The Power of Interpretation

The thrust of reform should be toward making the EEOC the central actor in the employment discrimination field. Granting the EEOC cease-and-desist powers is a first step, but others are also warranted.

At present the federal courts give some degree of deference to interpretations of Title VII developed by the EEOC, but the courts ultimately retain the power to interpret the substantive law even in the face of a contrary reading by the commission. The EEOC's interpretations have opposed most of the restrictive plaintiff-defeating rulings by the courts mentioned above, and the commission may have been more attuned to Congress' goals than the courts; following at least two Supreme Court opinions, Congress amended the statute in line with the EEOC position.[22] Further eradication of discrimination now calls for an agency actively committed to changing the previous racial and sexual status quo. The neutral-adjudicator role which is traditional for the courts is incompatible with that goal.

Congress should go one step further and explicitly obligate the courts to receive EEOC interpretations as definitive and binding, reserving to the courts a narrowly limited power to review and negate only those commission interpretations which are in flagrant contravention of the statute.[23]

The soundness of such a move rests on the fact that employment discrimination law has and will entail coping with some fairly complex and difficult issues to which a commission can devote more study, energy, and resources than are available in the federal courts. A federal court usually has a limited time period within which to resolve a problem, which is in any case one chosen by the litigants and thereafter only minimally under the judges' control. The judge is limited to only one or two law clerks to gather any information not presented by the parties. By contrast, the EEOC can give concentrated study to an issue for a year or two, can draw on multiple sources of expertise, hire consultants, and invite a wide range of public comment, both through hearings and in writing. Rule making at the EEOC thus is apt to be more informed; the federal courts cannot function in that manner.

The EEOC and the Justice Department

Another positive step would be to consolidate all litigating and enforcement power by federal agencies regarding employment discrimination in the EEOC. At present some pieces of that power are divided among the Department of Justice, the Labor Department, and other federal agencies.

Events since the EEOC was given litigating power in 1972 demonstrate that this fragmentation and dispersal of power hampers effective enforcement of the law. The situation with the Justice Department is a case in point. In 1972 the authority of the Justice Department to litigate broad pattern-and-practice suits in the private sector was moved to the EEOC; the department was limited to suing state and local governments, but the initial receipt of charges and their investigation regarding state and local governments was lodged in EEOC. This bifurcation has not worked well despite some efforts by well-meaning officials in both agencies to effect smooth coordination. The problem lies in the disjuncture between attorneys and

investigators: lawyers in the Justice Department were frequently un-
happy with the particular tack that an investigation had taken or its
thoroughness, when done by EEOC lay investigators. However, because these attorneys did not work with the investigators at the outset
of a case (a problem which chairperson Eleanor Holmes Norton cor-
rected at the EEOC during the Carter administration) and had no
authority to manage or direct the investigations, the investigations
continued in ways the attorneys often found lacking. Thus the Justice
Department had to redo the investigation or simply not institute
litigation. The lay investigators at EEOC would naturally be less
enthusiastic about cases they knew might be ignored when transferred to the Justice Department. The most visible signs of success
for the EEOC itself were the number of settlements and lawsuits
filed. Since state and local government cases were not a source of
demonstrated litigating success, and settlement was harder with a
defendant who knew that the EEOC had no authority to sue, the state
and local cases could receive lower priority among EEOC staff.

Moreover, the split of litigating authority has occasioned serious
clashes between the EEOC and the Justice Department in interpretations of the law, with the attendant confusion in the public that is
generated by such clashes. During the Reagan administration the
head of the civil rights unit in the Justice Department, William Brad-
ford Reynolds, threatened to institute litigation against municipalities who had affirmative action plans designed to correct past
discrimination. The claim was that the plans violated Title VII if the
persons who benefit from the accelerated hiring or promotion were
merely members of the group against which the discrimination had
been practiced, and not persons proven to have been refused hiring
or a promotion. The EEOC in its interpretive guidelines had previously taken a position directly contrary to that espoused by Reynolds.

It is relatively clear from the structure of Title VII that EEOC was
to be the prime generator of policy interpretations under the act, but
carving out a small piece of litigating authority for the Justice Department had set the stage for it to ignore policy developed by the
EEOC. The U.S. Supreme Court ultimately repudiated the Justice
Department's position on hiring and promotion under affirmative
action plans, but in the interim the unseemly anomaly was created
of public employers coerced to comply with the Justice Department's
new view of Title VII, while private employers, governed by the
same statute, were being moved in the opposite direction by EEOC's
guidelines. It is also to be noted that the shift in policy at the Justice
Department was pursued through a single appointee (hoping to con-

vince the courts) and not through the five-member commission that would have had to invite the more democratic and public process of comments and scrutiny by interested groups and individuals on important changes in policy. This is another sign that the commission is the place to lodge all litigating and policy development authority; it may retard precipitous and politically motivated shifts in policy.[24]

The EEOC and the Labor Department

Under the authority of the executive branch to set the terms by which it will make contracts and grants, and independent of Title VII, the Labor Department has been given jurisdiction to eradicate discrimination by employers who receive federal contracts or grants. The EEOC could become a measurably more potent and efficient agency if it received the power over federal contractors and grantees now held by the Labor Department.

Why is the present arrangement unworkable, and why might this additional authority especially enhance the EEOC's effectiveness? In the two agencies' exercise of their separate authorities, there has never been full-scale and finely meshed coordination between them. Employers who are subject to the Labor Department have been sued by private parties and by the EEOC, with the Labor Department sometimes not being informed. Conversely, the Labor Department has received individual charges that might better have been handled through the EEOC process, but were not transferred there. Employers are thus subjected to the duplicating press of two agencies, not only through investigation and reports, but sometimes in clashing interpretations of the law.[25]

The EEOC may now seek reinstatement, back pay, and prospective injunctions—including, under some circumstances indicated above, affirmative action relief. The NLRB has roughly the same kind of remedies as the EEOC to cure discrimination by employers against employees on the basis of union affiliation. These remedies have not been fully effective in deterring employers from illegal anti-union discharges and firings. Over the 50–odd years the NLRA has been in place, employers have learned that not all employees complain, that during protracted litigation some will move away, and that employers may covertly retaliate against even those who are reinstated by board orders. To avoid the weaknesses of the NLRB, the EEOC could be strengthened by having the Labor Department's authority to suspend or terminate contracts or to debar the employer in the future from contracting with the government. Employers, especially large ones, attempting to neutralize the EEOC through protracted and exhausting litigation tactics (even if the EEOC had cease-and-desist authority), would be less sanguine about that approach if they knew that loss of a major contract was a possible price. Conversely, questions have been raised about whether the Labor Department has authority to use the more tailored and individualized remedy of back pay, since it is not explicitly listed in the executive order from which its authority derives. However, it is clear that some infractions committed by an employer bound by the executive order program do not warrant the extreme remedies of termination or debarment (indeed this explains, in part, why the Labor Department has rarely invoked the full debarment remedy). The EEOC clearly has authority, under Title VII, for the more scalpel-like remedy of back pay. An EEOC, with nationwide data on all employers, could begin to identify those who might be an appropriate target for the termination or debarment remedy, thus giving a strong signal to all that the government is serious about ending discrimination.[26]

Private Suit

Another departure from the model of the NLRB is warranted: namely, the right of private suit should be maintained, and indeed strengthened. There is a host of reasons for this proposal. First, despite the growing presence of governmental litigation since 1972, the bulk of suits has been brought by private attorneys or public interest law offices like the NAACP Legal Defense Fund, the Lawyers Committee for Civil Rights Under Law, and the Women's Legal Defense Fund. Access to that pool of expertise should be preserved. These "private attorneys general" can also act as a counterweight to the efforts of any administration to reduce the level of enforcement effort, and can serve as watchdogs should the EEOC begin to propose interpretations which disserve the fundamental goals of the statute. One should naturally continue to hold the EEOC to a requirement of public participation in the development of rules. Again, the criticisms now being mounted against the NLRB are instructive. Some claim that the fact that the NLRB general counsel has exclusive control over whether an unfair labor practice will issue reinforces the tendency for the act to be easily moved in different directions during different administrations.

Are the private attorneys general an endangered species? The number of suits by private attorneys has increased each year since 1972, but the number of major class actions filed has recently diminished.

A number of practitioners for plaintiffs informally report that they find it difficult to continue to handle large-scale Title VII matters because their clients cannot underwrite the attendant expenses for experts, depositions, and interrogatories, while counsel for the well-bankrolled defendants employ diversionary tactics that delay the receipt of attorney's fees even where (or especially because) the plaintiff has a good case on the merits. Large firms are more apt to represent the corporate defendant and can engage in trench-warfare litigation tactics (within some bounds) because they bill by the hour and get paid as the litigation proceeds. Public-interest organizations, small firms, or single practitioners representing plaintiffs are usually impecunious; they lack the resources to underwrite heavy expenses or to wait long periods of time for their fees and expenses. The result is that some complainants give up after being turned away by a private attorney; and attorneys who do take cases may be under pressure to settle cases quickly for much less than the complainant would be due if given a full day in court.

A number of steps might counter these impediments to the active private attorneys general. First, one should focus on the proper articulation between the EEOC and private counsel. Some cases, massive and costly because they involve thousands of employees or the presentation of complex statistical data by experts, should be undertaken only by the EEOC. However, the less costly cases are better served by private counsel who are more decentralized and accessible to charging parties than the few offices the commission is likely to have in any given state. Further, private counsel offer an excellent backup for shifts in the ebb and flow of cases in any local area, which are hard for the commission to anticipate and respond to.

However, the EEOC should be given the financial resources and authority to establish a revolving litigation fund to be drawn on by practitioners representing plaintiffs. Loans would be repaid as cases came to a successful conclusion. Naturally guidelines would have to be developed for amounts per case and the conditions for repayment, with the more successful attorneys who were prompt in repayment receiving priority over others. The idea is akin to some "judicare" experiments now being conducted by the federally funded legal services corporations, in which private attorneys are paid to represent indigents.[27]

One might have to establish some deterrence to irresponsible counsel who might be tempted to seek attorneys' fees from the EEOC and then put in very little or no effort on losing cases. First, the agency could keep the fee below market rates for the area since the goal of the fund is to provide an interim income until the attorney collects a full fee at the successful conclusion of the case. This would discourage attorneys from relying solely on this source for compensation. Second, the courts have established that a defendant has a right to recover attorney fees if the plaintiff's claim was "frivolous, unreasonable, or groundless."[28] It is primarily the plaintiff's attorney who should bear responsibility for frivolous suits, unless the client has actively misled the attorney as to the facts. Therefore the statute could be amended to require the plaintiff's attorney, in any suit found frivolous by the court (and where responsibility could be lodged with the attorney) to surrender to the defendant any monies received from the EEOC as partial payment of the defendant's attorney's fee. The EEOC could also be empowered to recoup the funds loaned to an attorney whose suit is subsequently labeled frivolous, in the event the defendant does not seek attorney fees. Current law now holds a plaintiff's attorney responsible for attorney's fees and court costs if the attorney unreasonably prolongs proceedings. Disciplinary proceedings before the bar association are possible when an attorney takes a fee and performs no services. One might not want to go further and establish a requirement of repayment of the loan in all losing cases, for the goal is to encourage plaintiff's counsel to handle as many potentially viable cases as possible.

Recent proposals to place low caps on plaintiff's attorney fees that would discourage their continued participation should be resisted. Indeed, a useful rule of thumb, which might be adopted as an amendment to the statute, is that plaintiff's counsel should have the option of being compensated at the same hourly rate as opposing counsel on the case. This standard might go a long way toward increasing the number of attorneys in the plaintiff's bar.

A NEW SPECIAL BOARD

Two problems noted above have received inadequate judicial responses; namely, claims of race or gender discrimination in high-level positions and potential gender discrimination in female-dominated jobs. One might recognize that there is an element of subjectivity in decision making with regard to both and set up a special board, reminiscent of the War Labor Board of World War II, to handle claims in these areas.

Comparable Worth

Most responsible parties on both sides of the comparable-worth issue recognize that there is evidence at the macrolevel of discriminatory pressure on the wages of females, but the difficulty has been who is to decide in concrete cases whether discrimination has occurred. The problem in this guise resembles those faced by the War Labor Board. There the task was to prevent strikes; but in doing so, the tripartite board had to adopt general formulas to govern wage increases and could authorize special increases to remove inequities and substandard wages on occasion involving charges of sex discrimination (Livernash 1980, 205–12). The special board proposed here would function as follows: An implicit fear of management concerning comparable worth is the possibility of direct government control over wages. To allow management's continuing control over wages, therefore, a first step would require that the company retain an outside firm to evaluate the pay structure in any job categories with a designated level of concentration of females. The requirement would be imposed only on large companies because they can absorb the costs of such evaluation more easily than can small companies and, in any case, most comparable-worth litigation has been against large private employers or governmental agencies.[29]

To insure the independence of the job evaluation consultant one would require that the consultant firm have clients other than the employer. To the extent that a ranking and ordering of jobs by an evaluator ought not to be the final word on what an employer must pay, the employer would bear the burden of justifying any deviance from the views of the job evaluator who has been retained.[30] The EEOC would be given authority to represent the female employees before the board, and would have its own job evaluators to check out the employer's conclusions.

Only claims now cognizable under the Equal Pay Act would be processed by charges under Title VII. All other gender-based claims of disparate pay, the classic comparable-worth claims, would go before the board. This schematic would, in effect, reverse the surface holding of *Gunther* that Title VII encompasses pay-discrimination claims broader than the Equal Pay Act. As noted above, little is lost in the formal demise of *Gunther*, given judicial responses since that case. One can hypothesize a circumstance of intentional sex discrimination (e.g., the employer openly *says* that females, and not males, will have their pay cut by 10 percent and females occupy different jobs from males), but the overwhelming bulk of disparate pay situations will not approach such obviousness.

Panels similar to those of the War Labor Board would have representatives of management, labor, and the public. Half of the panelists would be females in light of the evidence that job evaluation is influenced by the sex of the person doing the analysis (Arvey, Passino, and Lounsbury 1977, 411–16).

As for enforcement powers, one might experiment for some years with giving the board none. Their decisions could be made public, but would be only advisory. If this initial stage proved unsatisfactory, the board's decision could then be made final and binding. A time limit of one or two years could be set on any order increasing wages, with the employer free to set wages unilaterally thereafter. Prior to the end of the wage order, the employer could petition the board for reconsideration of wage increases upon a showing of hardship. Collaterally, as was true with the War Labor Board, the executive branch of government would have the authority to withdraw government contracts, benefits, or privileges from a noncomplying employer.

High-Level Jobs

With respect to high-level jobs, Congress could amend Title VII to identify such jobs and exempt them from coverage, requiring that claims of discrimination involving such jobs go before a single arbitrator attached to the special board. EEOC or private attorneys could represent the claimant in the arbitral proceeding.

Special exceptions for high-level jobs are not unknown to the law. High-level salaried positions are exempt from the overtime provisions of the Fair Labor Standards Act, in recognition of the fact that a rigid forty-hour week is an inappropriate standard for professional work. The Age Discrimination in Employment Act also exempts high-salaried executives with protective pensions, from the prohibition on early retirement. This is a congressional judgment that more flexibility is needed in filling these positions. High-level professionals who have powers of self-governance are excluded from coverage under the NLRA on the grounds that they do not need the protection of the act. Similarly, the antidiscrimination law could extract disputes about high-level positions involving race or gender discrimination and propel them into arbitration.[31] Arbitrators could be required to have industry expertise (as with the panelists noted above) to allay management's fears that their interests would be denigrated by a nonexpert. Choosing one person for a job over another, by assessing their respective backgrounds, is the common fare of arbitration. Most high-level job litigation does not occur in the class-action form that might be inappropriate for arbitration; rather, it usually entails one or two individuals claiming denial of promotion or tenure. Moreover, the low visibility of an arbitrator's decision makes for the absence of a precedent and the "making of law," which may be the very thing that now impedes and freezes the federal courts into its current hands-off posture. The arbitrator's decision in these cases would be final and binding, whereas current Title VII law permits a plaintiff to ignore an adverse arbitral decision and to bring a fresh suit in federal court.[32] To some extent this proposal would deprive a black or female plaintiff of the right to a federal suit, but that right has become more and more illusory under current court interpretations. Naturally under this plan, the white male who loses in arbitration would also have no right to a subsequent de novo suit. It could be made clear, however, that an arbitrator could not intentionally favor a candidate for a position because of race or sex. One might permit suit only when such discrimination can be proven to have infected the arbitral decision. Arbitration decisions that directly contravene an important public policy are currently subject to reversal.[33] A reasonable guess is that such a requirement would, in practice, have little impact, especially since the arbitrator would presumably have no stake in the outcome; further, prejudice against a white male is not a widespread phenomenon. Symbolic importance can derive from such a formal check on the arbitrator; the requirement of proof of intentional discrimination by the arbitrator constitutes a sufficiently high barrier to discourage frequent or frivolous appeals of arbitral decisions.

Panelists and arbitrators at the board would need training in Title VII law and in the kind of evidence usually relevant in such cases. Such training is more pertinent for the arbitrators than for panelists, but both could be guided to some degree in their decision making by the principles derived therefrom. However, it would be clear that their authority to fashion a decision was broader than that now exercised by the courts, and could respond to what they considered the reasonable equities in the case before them.

These proposals may seem unorthodox, and to some degree they counter the process of simplification I have suggested previously. However, they recognize the legitimacy of claims that resolution of equity problems necessarily involve major element of the subjective, while suggesting a flexible structure tailored to respond to such concerns. The absence of appeal from the decisions of the panel or arbitrators recognizes the fact that their decisions are not in a substantive form appropriate for legal review. One could probably not articulate standards that would guide a court in the kind of decision making involved here. The arbitral plan is designed to preserve the independence of management and to invoke classical labor relations techniques into the resolution of problems inappropriate for the courts, in a context where most of the disadvantaged parties are not members of a union.

Notes

1. Berger (1967) 36–37 details the executive orders regarding racial discrimination. The act of 28 October 1949, ch. 782, 63 Stat. 954, Title XI, sec. 1103, prohibited discrimination on the basis of sex and marital status in the federal civil service. See U.S. Civil Rights Commission (1975), 72.

2. Lewis (1985) 48; Freeman (1973); National Committee on Pay Equity (1987). (Copies of the pay equity report may be secured from the Committee at 1201 16th Street, N.W., Washington, D.C. 20036.) The primary impetus for the narrowing of the income gap between black and white females was the improvement in occupational position by black females. The income gap is much larger between black men and white men; as of 1980 black males were paid only 73 percent of white males' earnings. It is to be noted, however, that the ceiling on white females' income results from their sexual segregation into lower-paying jobs; thus it was easier for black females to close the aforementioned gap.

3. See Griggs v. Duke Power Co. (1971), which held that employers who require a high school degree that was unnecessary to perform the job in question was illegal under Title VII, where the requirement had an adverse impact on the employment opportunities for blacks who had been blocked by racial discrimination from attaining high school degrees. However, where an employer requires a credential that is relevant to performance, he may continue its use even where there is an adverse impact on a protected group.

4. The U.S. Supreme Court did strengthen the capacity of plaintiffs to sue successfully to end discrimination, when it held that the Griggs disparate impact analysis (proof of discrimination through use of statistics without showing an intent to discriminate) was available when employees claimed they were detrimented by subjective evaluations. Watson v. Fort Worth Bank & Trust Co. 56 L.W. 4922 (1988). However this mode of attack is avilable only when a large number of adverse employment decisions are based on subjective evaluations. It will not be applicable to the circumstance where only a small number of high-level positions are filled by subjective assessment, for there will not be enough such actions to render a statement about statistical probability.

5. Phillips v. Martin Marietta Corp. (unlawful to refuse to hire females, but not males, with preschool-age children); Sprogis v. United Airlines (1971). (Title VII is violated by discharge of only females upon marriage.) An amendment to Title VII requires employers to treat pregnancy the same as any other similarly disabling condition. The U.S. Supreme Court has, however, given the states latitude beyond Title VII to

prevent pregnancy from operating to exclude females from the work force. The court held that it was permissible for a state to require employers to offer female employees reinstatement after any leave occasioned by actual physical disability due to pregnancy. The court reasoned that this was not discrimination against males, for the employer could satisfy the equal treatment demanded under Title VII by providing equivalent leave status for other (nonpregnancy) medical conditions. *California Federal Savings & Loan Assn. v. Guerra* (1987).

6. In 1980, the unemployment rate for white females was 5.6 percent, 6 percent for white males, and 13 percent for black males and females (U.S. Commission on Civil Rights, n.d., 14).

7. *Bazemore v. Friday* (1986), decided by the U.S. Supreme Court, did not involve a comparable-worth challenge, but rather was a claim that equal pay was denied for identical work. Prior to Title VII the state had an agency in which black and white personnel were segregated into separate branches, and blacks were systematically paid less than whites. When the branches were merged, the plaintiffs were permitted to prove, through multiple-regression analyses, that black and white personnel continued to have pay disparities. This proof technique may be useful in comparable-worth cases because the wages of females were sometimes depressed quite explicitly prior to the enactment of Title VII. See, for example, *IUE v. Westinghouse* (1981). A prima facie case may exist after *Bazemore* where there are continuing disparities in wages between males and females which were deliberately manipulated at one time, even though as the court in *Bazemore* acknowledged, all the possible nondiscriminatory variables were not worked into the multiple-regression analysis.

8. *North Haven Bd. of Educ. v. Bell* (1982) (a private party may sue for employment discrimination under Title IX of the Education Amendments of 1972 which prohibits sex discrimination in any educational program receiving federal financial assistance).

9. It is possible that Congress wanted a strong deterrent to a widespread practice of underpaying females; but the injury to the individual who is subjected to illegal underpayment is not diminished because it arises out of some form of discrimination other than gender.

10. Section 7(b), 5 U.S.C. sec 62(b) (1976).

11. Indeed the union's failure to achieve this reform of the NLRA may be feeding the current charges that the NLRA does not give effective protection to workers.

12. See *TWA v. Thurston* (1985) interpreting the "willfulness" requirement for recovering liquidated damages under the Age Discrimination Act.

13. *Johnson v. Railway Express Agency, Inc.* (1975). One would not want to repeal the nineteenth century Civil Rights Acts in toto because they reach discrimination in contexts other than employment.

14. Preemption is the legal doctrine that authorizes the courts not to entertain a cause of action under a state statute when a federal statute is deemed to occupy the subject matter exclusively.

15. Another area ripe for punitive damages is age discrimination, since many courts have been reluctant to grant reinstatement to successful plaintiffs.Also given the fact that average age of jurors is above the national average, the plaintiffs might cause less invidious hostility from juries than other groups.

16. U.S. Senate (1971), 53 and 126. It has been suggested that the commission was more aggressive in interpreting the statute favorably to the protected classes as a compensation for its absence of enforcement power. See Blumrosen (1971), 57–58. This conclusion presupposes that the presence of real power would have frozen the commission into a more conservative stance, but if the commission's interpretive activity was a responsible and sincere desire to read the statute properly and to achieve

legitimate goals, it is not clear why they would have done less with some minimal enforcement authority.

17. Title VII coverage was to include, for the first time, employees of educational institutions and public (federal and state) agencies.

18. The rapid charge processing system limited investigation of individual charges to the specific claims made, as opposed to the previous practice of treating every charge as a potential class action, thus warranting wall-to-wall investigation of all of the employer's practices. Complainants were also given the option of quick settlement before full findings were developed.

19. In *Missouri ex rel. Gaines v. Canada* (1938) the court required the state to admit a black applicant to a previously all-white law school.

20. *Wygant v. Jackson* (1986); *Local 93, Firefighters v. Cleveland* (1986); *Local 28, Steelworkers v. EEOC* (1986); *Johnson v. Transportation Agency*, Santa Clara County, 107 S. Ct. 1442 (1987). But see *Firefighters Local Union No. 1784 v. Stotts* (1984).

21. The court has agreed to review the precedent of *Runyon v. McCrary* (1977), in *Patterson v. McLean Credit Union* (1988).

22. Congress amended Title VII (29 Stat. 2076) to adopt the EEOC position that pregnancy be considered as other disabilities for purposes of the sex discrimination provisions. In 1972 Congress adopted the EEOC concept (Public Law 92–261) that "reasonable accommodation" was necessary to avoid religious discrimination.

23. There is an argument that the agency now has such authority. See Blumrosen (1985), 261–78. A formal amendment of Title VII could establish it beyond doubt.

24. The Justice Department also has authority to proceed against violations of the federal constitution. Any amendment of Title VII should block that as an alternative route of suits against state and municipalities.

25. At one time the EEOC took the position that it was a violation per se for an employer to pay for membership of male employees in a private club which refused membership to females. The Labor Department took the stance that it was a violation of law only if the employer claimed the membership expense as a business deduction.

26. There are a number of minor adjustments one might want to make if authority under the executive order were to be given to the EEOC. (1) The authority to publish the names of persons accused of discrimination under the executive order should be removed, and a duty to keep complaints confidential should be imposed, as under Title VII. Premature disclosure could hamper settlement efforts. (2) Unreasonable or arbitrary investigations under the executive order ought to be subject to injunction as is the case for Title VII investigations. (3) The authority to impose affirmative action programs under the terms they have been imposed in the past under the executive order program ought to be reaffirmed. See suggestions of Congresswoman Edith Green of Oregon. Legislative History of the Equal Employment Act of 1972, 68.

27. The difference is that private counsel retained to represent indigents have no obligation to replenish a fund because they typically have no recourse to securing attorney's fees and costs when they prevail, as do attorneys who represent plaintiffs in employment discrimination cases.

28. *Christiansburg Garment Co. v. EEOC*, 434 U.S. 412 (1978).

29. Ehrenberg in chapter 6 of this volume suggests that suppressed wages for females may not be characteristic of large companies. Moreover, small companies have created many of the new jobs which females have filled in great numbers in the last 20 years. If it was deemed necessary to extend the program to small companies, the government may have to underwrite the cost of retaining a job evaluation consultant.

30. See chapter 6 noting that the intrinsic worth of a job does not exhaust the factors to be considered.

31. The proposal would not include age discrimination claims although they often involve executive positions. The courts have not generally claimed they are stymied by subjective elements in resolving ADEA claims. It may be that the claimants in age discrimination cases are usually long-term incumbents who have extensive knowledge of job requirements, have been found qualified in the past, and are able to show unusual or aberrant behavior by the company in connection with their discharge, retirement, or demotion.

32. *Alexander v. Gardner Denver Co.*, 415 U.S. 36 (1974).

33. *United Paperworkers International Union v. Misco Inc.* (1988).

References

Arvey, Richard D., Emily M. Passino, and John W. Lounsbury. August 1977. Job Analysis Results as Influenced by Sex of Incumbent and Sex of Analyst. *Journal of Applied Psychology* 62(4): 411–16.

Bartholet, Elizabeth. 1984. Application of Title VII to Jobs in High Places. *Harvard Law Review* 95.

Berger, Morroe. 1967. *Equality by Statute—The Revolution in Civil Rights.* New York: Doubleday.

Blumrosen, Alfred W. 1971. *Black Employment and the Law.* New Brunswick, N.J.: Rutgers University Press.

———. 1984. The Law Transmission System and the Southern Jurisprudence of Employment Discrimination. *Industrial Relations Law Journal* 6.

———. 1985. The Binding Effect of Affirmative Action Guidelines. *The Labor Lawyer* 1:261–78.

Chambers, J. LeVonne, and D. Goldstein. 1985. Title VII at Twenty: The Continuing Challenge. *The Labor Lawyer* 1.

Dill, B., L. Cannon, and R. Vanneman. 1987. Race and Gender in Occupational Segregation. In *Pay Equity—An Issue of Race, Ethnicity and Sex*, by National Committee on Pay Equity, 13–70. Washington.

Freeman, Richard. 1973. Changes in the Labor Market for Black Americans 1948–72. *Brookings Papers on Economic Activity* 1. Washington: Brookings Institution.

Hill, Robert B. 1981. *Economic Policies and Black Progress: Myths and Realities.* Washington: National Urban League Research Department.

Levitan, Sar A., William B. Johnston, and Robert Taggart. 1975. *Still a Dream: The Changing Status of Blacks Since 1960.* Cambridge, Mass.: Harvard University Press.

Lewis, W. Arthur. 1985. *Racial Conflict and Economic Development.* Cambridge, Mass.: Harvard University Press.

Livernash, E. Robert, ed. 1980. *Comparable Worth: Issues and Alternatives.* Washington: Equal Employment Advisory Council.

National Committee on Pay Equity. 1987. *Pay Equity—An Issue of Race, Ethnicity and Sex.* Washington.

Norton, Eleanor Holmes. 1988. Equal Employment Law: Crises in Interpretation—Survival Against the Odds. *Tulane Law Review* 681:710–13.

Oster, Gerry, and David A. Juba. January 1984. *Assessing the Need for Affirmative Action: Race and Sex Inequality Among Federal Contractors.* Policy Analysis, Inc. Washington.

Hamermesh Daniel, and Albert Rees. 1988. *The Economics of Work and Pay*, 4th ed. New York: Harper & Row.

Scales-Trent, Judy. 1984. Comparable Worth: Is This a Theory for Black Workers. *Women Rights Law Reporter* 8.

Treiman, Donald, and Heidi Hartmann, eds. 1981. *Women, Work, and Wages: Equal Pay for Jobs of Equal Value.* Washington: National Academy Press.

U.S. Bureau of the Census. 1981. Money Income of Families and Persons in the United States: 1979. *Current Population Reports*, Series 60 (129).

U.S. Commission on Civil Rights. 1975. *Twenty Years after Brown.* Washington: U.S. Government Printing Office.

———. 1978. *Social Indicators of Equality for Minorities and Women.* Washington: U.S. Government Printing Office.

———. n.d. Unemployment and Underemployment: Blacks, Hispanics and Woman. Washington.

U.S. Senate. 1971. *Hearings on S.2515, S2617 and H.R. 1746 before the Subcommittee on Labor of the Senate Committee on Labor and Public Welfare, 92d Cong., 1st sess.*

Case Citations

Alexander v. Gardner Denver Co., 415 U.S. 36 (1974).

Bazemore v. Friday, 92 L.Ed.2d 315 (1986).

Brown v. General Services Administration, 425 U.S. 820 (1976).

California Federal Savings & Loan Assn. v. Guerra, 93 L.Ed.2d 615 (1987).

Christiansburg Garment Co. v. EEOC, 434 U.S. 412 (1978).

County of Washington v. Gunther, 452 U.S. 161 (1981).

Firefighters v. Local Union No. 1784, 467 U.S. 561 (1985).

Firefighters Local Union No. 1784 v. Stotts, 104 S. Ct. 2576 (1984).

General Telephone Co. of the Southwest v. Falcon, 457 U.S. 147 (1982).

Griggs v. Duke Power Co., 401 U.S. 424 (1971).

IUE v. Westinghouse, 631 F.2d 1094 (1981).

Local 12, United Rubber Workers v. NLRB, 368 F.2d 12, 5th Cir., *cert. denied*, 389 U.S. 837 (1967).

Local 93, Firefighters v. Cleveland, 92 L.Ed.2d 405 (1986).

Local 28, Steelworkers v. EEOC, 92 L.Ed.2d 344 (1986).

Johnson v. Georgia Highway Express Inc., 417 F.2d 1122, 5th Cir. (1969).

Johnson v. Railway Express Agency, Inc., 421 U.S. 454 (1975).

Jones v. Alfred H. Mayer Co., 392 U.S. 409 (1968).

Meritor Savings Bank v. Vinson, 91 L.Ed.2d 49 (1986).

Missouri ex rel. Gaines v. Canada, 305 U.S. 337 (1938).

New York Gas Light Club Inc. v. Carey, 447 U.S. 54 (1980).

North Haven Bd. of Educ. v. Bell, 465 U.S 612 1912 (1982).

Patterson v. McLean Credit Union, 108 S.Ct. 1419 (1988).

Phillips v. Martin Marietta Corp., 400 U.S. 542 (1971).

Richard v. Alaska Airlines Inc., 750 F.2d 763, 9th Cir. (1984).

Runyon v. McCrary, U.S. 160 (1977).

Sprogis v. United Airlines, 444 F. 2d 1194, 7th Cir., cert. denied, 404 U.S. 991 (1971).

Steele v. Louisville & Nashville R.R., 323 U.S. 192 (1944).

Teamsters v. United States, 431 U.S. 324 (1977).

TWA v. Thurston, 469 U.S. 111 (1985).

United Packinghouse, Food & Allied Workers v. NLRB, 416 F.2d 1126 D.C. Cir., *cert. denied*, 396 U.S. 903 (1964).

United Paperworkers International Union v. Misco Inc., 56 L.W. 4011 (1988).

Vuyanich v. Republic National Bank of Dallas, 723 F. 2d 1195, 5th Cir. (1984).

Watson v. Fort Worth Bank and Trust Co., 56 L.W., 4922 (1988).

Webb v. Board of Education of Dyer County, Tenn., 105 S.Ct. 1923 (1985).

Wygant v. Jackson, 106 S.Ct. 1842 (1986).

Chapter Eight

THE IMPLICATIONS OF INTERNATIONALIZATION FOR LABOR MARKET INSTITUTIONS AND INDUSTRIAL RELATIONS SYSTEMS

Ray Marshall

One of the most important economic trends since World War II has been the internationalization of the United States and other national economies. Between 1950 and 1980, international transactions grew from 9 percent of U.S. gross national product to about 25 percent. In 1982 over half of all profits for American corporations came from overseas, and international trade accounted for one-third of all U.S. cropland (in fact, more U.S. than Japanese land was used to feed the Japanese), one-fourth of farm income, and one-sixth of all jobs. About 70 percent of all goods manufactured in the United States now compete with imports. Similarly, an estimated 20 to 25 percent of the growth in the U.S. work force during the 1970s came from immigrants (legal and illegal) and refugees.

Internationalization of the American economy and the globalization of markets have greatly altered the context within which employment policy must operate. Internationalization has changed the effectiveness of traditional macroeconomic policies; the integration of global labor markets has transformed labor market institutions and industrial relations systems, and has subjected enterprise management practices to the requirements of international competition.

This chapter offers a brief overview of the history and nature of global interdependence. It then discusses how much internationalization and other factors have reduced America's competitiveness, and the implications of this for our industrial relations systems. The chapter thus provides a context for Daniel Burton's discussion of international competition and of American jobs, in chapter 9.

THE GROWTH OF THE GLOBAL ECONOMY

The beginnings of the internationalization of national economies came with the end of World War II, and a general consensus here and abroad that an open and expanding trading system was the way to encourage the growth of world economies. This consensus derived from the widely held belief that the virulent protectionism and trade restrictions that characterized earlier decades of the twentieth century had contributed significantly to both the Great Depression and the war that followed.

To avoid a recurrence of these disasters, the United States joined with other countries to form institutions and develop rules and policies to facilitate international trade and finance. These included the General Agreement on Tariffs and Trades (GATT), the International Monetary Fund (IMF) and the International Bank for Reconstruction and Development (the World Bank), the Organization for Economic Cooperation and Development (OECD), and aid programs for the reconstruction of Europe and Japan. This essentially free-trade system became known as the Bretton Woods system, named after the conference at which the major decisions were taken.

The Bretton Woods international economic system was founded on three basic principles: free trade, fixed exchange rates, and autonomy in domestic economic policy. Underlying this concept of the trading process was the doctrine of comparative advantage— holding that the welfare of the whole world was enlarged through a competitive, free-trade, open-market system in which each country concentrated on producing those things—with the exception of national security considerations and industries in the initial steps of development—for which it had the greatest advantage or the least disadvantage.

A major force accelerating the internationalization of national economies was the overwhelming dominance of the United States in the postwar world economy. Our economy had actually been strengthened by World War II. We emerged with a backlog of technology, much of it developed for military purposes, which provided the basis for unprecedented growth in productivity and total output. Our major competitors, in contrast, were physically devastated by the war. The dollar became the currency of international commerce and English became the language of international transactions. Our dominance made it possible for our interests to prevail—and it was in our interest to have a relatively free, open, and expanding world economy.

In addition to the overwhelming economic strength of the United States, this system was reinforced by the fact that most countries closely regulated their financial markets, capital and trade flows were relatively small, and any change was slow enough to facilitate relatively easy adjustments in domestic markets.

The Bretton Woods system facilitated the growth of the international economy throughout the 1950s and 1960s, until events began to erode its basic institutions. The first such event was the U.S. decision in 1971 to suspend the convertibility of dollars to gold. This was followed in 1973 by abandonment of the fixed exchange rate system in favor of floating exchange rates. The theory behind floating exchange rates was that free trade and capital movements would prevent persistent over- or undervaluation of currencies. An overvalued currency would penalize exports and an undervalued currency would contribute to inflation by raising the cost of imports. It therefore was assumed that the problems for countries with misaligned currencies were sufficiently serious to encourage them to adopt economic policies to produce realignment. Floating exchange rates would, therefore, be a relatively automatic mechanism that would free countries to pursue independent domestic economic policies.

Unfortunately, floating exchange rates have not had this happy outcome. Internationalization of markets and currencies have made it possible for speculators to play a larger role in a global economy with floating exchange rates, much larger supplies of money than needed for goods and services transactions, and stop-and-go national economic policies. All these combine to create considerable uncertainty. There have been particularly wide fluctuations in currency values. The dollar, for example, depreciated 17 percent against major currencies from September 1977 to October 1978, but reversed its course in 1980 and appreciated 45 percent between 1980 and 1984. By 1985 the dollar was about 40 percent overvalued relative to its purchasing power parity. Changes in the value of the dollar between 1980 and 1985 effectively raised U.S. export prices by 70 percent and lowered import prices by 40 percent. Since 1985 the dollar has again depreciated sharply relative to other currencies, especially the West German deutsche mark and the Japanese yen, but contrary to theoretical predictions, this had not done much by the summer of 1988 to eliminate the huge U.S. trade deficits.

Another major force undermining the Bretton Woods system was the massive increase in international trade. In 1965, U.S. exports totaled $27.5 billion out of a world total of $190 billion (nearly 15 percent of the total); by 1983 world exports had increased to $1,922.9 billion and those of the United States had jumped $198.8 billion (10 percent of the total). Indeed, international transactions increased much faster than the growth of national economies. Between 1960 and 1980, in real terms, exports grew at an annual rate of 6.7 percent, while gross domestic product grew at only 4.4 percent. The ratio of world trade to GDP was 12.2 percent in 1960 and 21.8 percent in 1980. Increased internationalization was not restricted to a few countries—the process was pervasive (IMF 1984, 28).

There were equally dramatic increases in foreign investment and the associated capital flows. By 1982, U.S. investments abroad were $834.2 billion, and foreign assets in the United States reached $665.2 billion. These financial flows were accelerated by the progressive liberalization of financial markets during the 1970s and 1980s. Most direct investment is by multinational corporations, whose investments doubled between 1970 and 1974. Portfolio investment almost doubled between 1975 and 1981 in the industrialized countries, and grew by two-and-a-half times over the same period in the developing countries. In the latter, portfolio investment rose from only 5 percent of capital flows in 1961–63 to 32 percent in 1981. The Bank for International Settlements (BIS) reported the short-term foreign currency assets of its reporting banks (net of redeposit) grew from $12.4 billion in September 1963 to $575 billion in 1980. On a global basis, between 1975 and 1981, capital flows increased almost tenfold, and have continued to increase since.

Another example of increased international interdependence is the growth of the Eurodollar market—which represents dollars held and traded abroad—primarily in Europe. This huge part of the international capital market—which is very volatile because it is largely uncontrolled by public entities—originated in the late 1950s. It has subsequently grown by leaps and bounds, reaching over $1 trillion in 1983.

There has also been a huge increase in debt, especially of the United States and the non-oil-producing developing countries. In 1982, U.S.-owned assets abroad exceeded the assets owned by foreigners in the United States by about $150 billion. In that circumstance, earnings on these net foreign investments allowed the United States to run substantial trade deficits without alarm. During the 1981–85 period, however, the United States financed its huge trade and budget deficits with massive inflows of capital from abroad. Its investment position, built up over 65 years, was wiped out in just over two years. By mid-1987, the United States was the world's largest net debtor nation with debts of about $340 billion, and rising.

The U.S. labor market has been substantially affected by this internationalization. Economists traditionally have assumed that labor does not move among countries. This was never literally true; workers always have migrated in response to income and employment opportunities. The process has greatly accelerated, however. For example, some consider the postwar economic miracles in Europe, especially in West Germany, to be due in some significant measure to the labor market flexibility made possible by the importation of "guest workers" from eastern and southern Europe. During 1965–85 there were large-scale international movements of workers, some legal, some illegal. Indeed, the contribution of immigrants to the American labor force has been estimated as high as 20 percent or more. Worldwide, there were an estimated 20 million migrant workers in the late 1970s, 12 million of whom were from developing countries. These migrants were heavily concentrated in certain regions: North America, 6 million; the Middle East, 3 million; and Western Europe, 5 million[1] (the consequences of worker immigration to the United States are discussed in detail by Daniel Burton in chapter 9).

CONSEQUENCES OF INTERNATIONALIZATION FOR EMPLOYMENT POLICY

The internationalization of markets has a number of important implications for employment policy. On the positive side, the increased efficiency and expanding knowledge that has accompanied international economic integration has promoted higher standards of living for many of the world's people. But on the negative side, internationalization has brought many destabilizing influences. Indeed, the nature of many economies has changed to such an extent that international economic rules that appeared to be effective in the 1950s and 1960s are no longer applicable.

One important aspect is the enormous fungibility of world markets, causing a ballooning effect for countries that are relatively open to imports and people. To cite one example, when European countries limited their imports of Japanese automobiles, the excess was diverted to the United States and other relatively open countries. To cite another, at a time when most countries have greatly restricted immigration, population surpluses are diverted to the United States, whose borders are relatively open, and whose policies toward illegal immigration were relatively permissive until 1986. To cite a third, when the United States attempted to embargo wheat or pipeline equipment sales to the Soviet Union its efforts were negated because it sold wheat and equipment to other countries which then sold these products to the Russians.

Not only are countries able to direct their international policy making less effectively than in the past. Even more important, the effects of domestic economic policy making have changed.

As the experiences of the United States in the late 1970s and France in the early 1980s demonstrate, traditional Keynesian demand-stimulus policies have been weakened by international leakages. Stimulus at a time when most major economies are depressed tends to limit domestic economic expansion by increasing foreign imports. This was a particularly serious problem for the United States in the recovery from the 1981–82 recession, when foreign imports offset a large part of the increased demand. It was especially important for American capital goods markets during the 1981–84 business cycle, when almost all of the increased demand during the recovery was met by imports.

The consequences of our budget deficits are also no longer under our control. The 1981 U.S. tax cut and the ensuing recession created huge budget deficits, greatly increasing the federal demand for money. The fact that the federal government's borrowing requirements offset most of net private domestic savings put strong upward pressure on real interest rates. High real interest rates attracted foreign capital, which, as noted, greatly increased net foreign debt. Since debts ultimately must be repaid in goods and services, this debt will bring reductions in potential future American living standards—to the extent to which our present consumption exceeds our present production and has to be paid for by future production. It may also bring inflation. Inflationary pressures are moderated by an expensive dollar, which reduces the cost of imports; but this process is reversed when the dollar is devalued, as it was during the 1970s and after 1985. Then the inflation we were able to export during the early 1980s will be brought back into the United States in the form of more expensive imports. At the same time, high interest rates in the United States not only limited job-creating investments in the United States, but also caused serious trouble for European countries, which were forced to keep their interest rates high because lower interest rates would have accelerated the flight of capital to the United States. These high interest rates abroad caused rising unemployment abroad, reducing European demand for American exports.

The destabilization of the international economic system has necessitated a reconsideration of the theoretical underpinnings, institutions, and practices of the Bretton Woods system. Under the classic conditions of comparative advantage—that international trade took place on the basis of competition between private profit-maximizing companies; that physical capital and labor were relatively immobile; that conditions within a country were governed by competitive markets, so that no resources were involuntarily unemployed; that adjustments were instantaneous; and that change was gradual—it is easy to show that all countries gain by an open trading system in which each country specializes in those things for which they have the greatest advantage or the least disadvantage.

As with the theory of freely fluctuating exchange rates, however, reality has been different. Competition does not govern domestic markets, so countries do experience unemployment; similarly, governments and transnational oligopolistic enterprises and cartels are now heavily involved in international markets. Almost all governments except the United States have active trade polices to support national economic objectives. Following the Japanese practice, many countries, especially the newly industralizing countries, have adopted the theory of *dynamic* comparative advantage, meaning that they adopt strategies to create comparative advantage and improve industry mix rather than simply having comparative advantage revealed by markets. Further, economic activity is based on national and enterprise strategies, not just on the interplay of short-run market forces and profit maximizing. Free trade usually is justified in the United States on the basis of maximizing short-run profits and consumer satisfaction; Japan and the "little Japans" are more interested in strengthening national power, productive capacity, and market share than in short-run profit maximizing. Finally, in the internationalized information world, change is no longer gradual. Trade is not just in goods at the margin; whole technologies are exported, and production of a particular product is shared between different countries.

The consequence of these changes for the United States and other high-wage industrialized countries is that jobs can, in fact, be lost, and wages and working conditions can be reduced by international competition. How much danger the United States is in from these changes depends on what has happened to its international competitiveness. In the next section I discuss the effects of internationalization on U.S. competitiveness. I then discuss the implications of this for the U.S. industrial relations system.

IS INTERNATIONALIZATION CAUSING US TO LOSE OUR COMPETITIVE EDGE?

No one doubts that there have been major structural changes in the American economy. There are two schools of thought, however, about whether these changes are associated with a loss of international competitiveness, as the President's Commission on Industrial Competitiveness charges in its February 1985 report. According to the commission the ability of American business to compete in world markets has been slipping for 20 years or more, even in high-tech industries.

An Optimistic View

Two representative studies giving the optimistic view are by Robert Lawrence of the Brookings Institution (Lawrence 1984) and by the New York Stock Exchange (NYSE 1984). The major points of their argument are as follows:

☐ Most of our present economic problems are not due to a loss of competitiveness but are caused by the overvalued dollar. This results, in turn, from huge U.S. budget deficits that require the federal government to absorb a large proportion of net earnings to service the debt. When, in this view, the budget is balanced, things will return to "normal"—whatever that is. Some economists, including the Reagan administration's Council of Economic Advisors, consider the 1970s to have been normal and the booming 1950s and 1960s to be abnormal.

☐ Trade was responsible for a net increase in jobs during the 1970s. Although 100,000 jobs were lost because of trade between 1970 and 1980, trade raised jobs by 390,000 between 1972 and 1980, during which time total manufacturing employment increased by 1.14 million.

☐ American exports increased by 101.5 percent in constant dollars during the 1970s, while imports increased by only 72 percent. Thus, we gained more in employment from trade than we lost in employment to trade.

☐ Trade was not the main reason for declining employment even in most declining industries: (a) in 6 of 9 industries where employment fell by 10 percent or more, employment due to trade actually increased; (b) employment from trade was positive in 14 of 21 industries in which total employment fell. The only industries where employment losses due to trade were greater than those from domestic causes were radios, televisions, and automobiles.

□ U.S. industrial performance was strong relative to other countries. U.S. manufacturing growth during the 1970s was about the same as for the average major industrial country and was greater than that of Germany, France, or the United Kingdom. U.S. manufacturing employment grew more than that of any other industrial country. Indeed, U.S. manufacturing employment growth was greater than that of Japan in every major industry.

□ The United States was first or second in the world in 22 of 40 manufacturing industries in 1972 and 23 of 40 in 1982. The main losers were automobiles, steel, textiles, and shoes, but American performance was strong in computers, office equipment, aerospace, appliances, and others.

□ Most of the job losses were concentrated in these four key depressed industries, which account for only 20 percent of total manufacturing output. The 36 industries that dominate manufacturing output actually added jobs and even expanded at a faster rate than the overall economy between 1977 and 1982.

□ One of the most significant indicators of the poor performance of the U.S. economy is the slowdown in productivity growth since the 1960s. After having grown at over 3 percent during the 1950s, annual productivity growth dropped to 2.2 percent between 1965 and 1973 and was a meager .8 percent between 1973 and 1979. However, there was a pickup in productivity growth to 1.1 percent between 1979 and 1983 and about 2.7 percent for 1983, 2.5 percent for 1984, and 1.0 percent in 1985. Manufacturing productivity growth in the United States has been particularly strong. After having declined from 3.2 percent a year from 1960 to 1973, to 1.4 percent a year betweeen 1973 and 1979, manufacturing productivity was 3.1 percent a year from 1979 to 1986, reaching annual rates of 4.4 percent in 1985 and 3.5 percent in 1986.

These optimists believe that the poor productivity performance during the 1970s was an aberration caused by the energy price shocks, inflation, and economic uncertainty—all of which are behind us—and that the country is now strengthening its competitiveness. The positives for productivity growth, according to the optimists, are strong expansion of real plant and equipment spending, rising outlays for research and development, increased efficiency because of the accumulated work experience of the baby boom generation, a slowing of the pace of increased regulatory costs, a better-educated work force, and a significant improvement in labor–management relations because of the recognition by both management and unions of their need to become more competitive in international markets. The optimists also believe the United States has entered a new era, where managers are forced to increase productivity through greater pressure on workers because they can no longer increase profits by raising prices. In this view, the problems of the 1970s induced fundamental structural changes that will cause the U.S. economy to be much more competitive during the 1980s.

A Pessimistic View

The optimistic view has many critics, among the most vehement being Bruce Scott of the Harvard Business School (Scott 1984a, 1984b), and a group of analysts called the Berkeley Roundtable on the International Economy (Cohen, et al.; see Cohen and Zysman 1987). The major points of their rebuttal are as follows:

☐ A more realistically valued dollar will not necessarily solve the competitiveness problem because the structure of trade has changed: the recovery from the 1981–82 recession caused a slower growth of U.S. exports and a faster growth of imports than in previous recoveries. Even during the 1970s, when the dollar was considered to be undervalued, productivity was falling and U.S. producers were forced to make defensive price cuts in order to hold their markets, resulting in declining real wages and profits. According to Scott, during the 1970s the return on business assets failed to keep up with the rising cost of capital: "roughly from 1975 onward U.S. manufacturers would have earned more on their assets investing them in corporate bonds than in production of goods."

☐ Energy prices played a role in the U.S. merchandise trade deficits of the late 1970s and the 1980s, but there has been a decline in nonenergy trade balances as well. Unlike Germany and Japan, the United States was unable to offset its mounting energy trade deficit with mounting surpluses in manufactured goods despite a large depreciation in the value of the dollar during the 1970s.

☐ The structure of U.S. trade has changed. The recovery from the 1981–82 recession caused a slower growth of U.S. exports and a faster growth of imports than in previous recoveries.

☐ Market share in constant dollars is not the only, or even the most important, measure of performance. Competitiveness is determined also by the relative values of exports and imports. Even though our exports increased proportionally more than our imports during the 1970s, our share of total world exports declined from 17.4 percent to 15.4 percent.

□ America's share of high-tech exports fell between 1962 and 1980. Between 1965 and 1980 the United States expanded its share only in aircraft, computers, and agricultural chemicals.

□ The recent pickup in productivity growth was mainly cyclical. A return to 2 to 3 percent productivity growth over the longer run would have required the 1983–84 productivity figures to have been about double what they actually were. In any case, U.S. productivity growth in our best years (1983–84) was far below that of our competitors, even though their ecomomies were still very depressed.

The pessimists point out that most of the "positives" cited by the optimists actually have very little relationship to increased productivity: the baby boom generation has been gaining experience for some time but productivity has not improved much; the absence of oil price shocks will help cause actual and potential productivity to converge, but will have minimal effects on productivity growth; research and development has improved only slightly and has never had a very strong impact on productivity growth. Finally, the pessimists concede some improvements in labor–management relations but say the evidence for this improving productivity is not very powerful. Nor is there much evidence, in this view, that either capital–labor ratios or capital investment have had much effect on productivity growth.

Indeed, the evidence shows that in manufacturing, productivity growth deteriorated during the 1970s despite improvements in both capital formation and capital–labor ratios.

An Overall Assessment

There is some truth in both the pessimists' and optimists' arguments. On the optimistic side, the United States is still the strongest economy in the world. We also probably still have the highest average productivity levels, though we are rapidly losing our advantage— even with more rapid growth than our main competitors our overall productivity improvement is below theirs. The optimists also are correct in stressing the importance of macroeconomic policy and the expensive dollar. It clearly was inevitable that the United States would lose the position it held in the 1950s.

One's judgment about competitiveness depends upon the definition used. The optimists define it as maintaining overall market position regardless of industry composition, profits, real wages, and what is happening to key industries. Indeed, they argue there are no key industries. The pessimists are concerned about maintaining market positions without sacrificing return on assets or real wages and incomes. I think the pessimists are right and we are clearly losing our ability to maintain real wages and living standards. The pessimists are also correct in comparing our performance with our strongest competitors, especially Japan and the "little Japans," and not with the average of Western Europe.

A key problem for the American economy is declining productivity growth. We are unlikely to maintain real wages and living standards in a competitive world without substantial improvements in productivity growth to make unit labor costs more competitive at higher wages. I do not believe present trends will restore long-run productivity growth rates of 2 to 3 percent. The rate of productivity increase in 1985 (1.0 percent) was only about half as large as needed to restore the 1960–73 trend rate of between 2 and 3 percent. Moreover, production did not increase at all during 1985–86. However, there was a significant improvement in manufacturing productivity growth during 1985; indeed, at 4.4 percent the United States for the first time had faster manufacturing productivity growth than any other country in the OECD. It is, however, too early to know whether the 1985 performance was an aberration or, as optimists predict, the long-awaited recovery of productivity growth—at least in manufacturing. Figures for 1987 are not available but the 1986 rate fell to 3.5 percent. Without greater improvements in overall productivity to maintain and widen our average productivity advantage, it will be difficult to sustain high wages and profits.

The composition of industry also is important because some industries are more important than others—a fact that is likely to be concealed by studies that merely count industries with increases or decreases of export shares without weighting them. There are dynamic and symbiotic relationships between production activity and technology transfer. Technology has externalities that cannot be incorporated into particular firms; therefore, free markets will not necessarily achieve the desired outcomes. Moreover, the linkages between economic activities and technology are cumulative. A lack of competitiveness in key industries can cause a country to lose them and in so doing deny its remaining businesses the technological externalities, learning, and linkage advantages needed to stay competitive in international markets.

How do we arrest the slippage in our international competitiveness in a world where the Bretton Woods system is no longer adequate to ensure that international trade benefits people in most countries? One answer that is being increasingly advanced is to restrict the growth of the international trading system. This is the wrong answer. Trade restrictions in an interdependent world could exacerbate our economic problems by eliciting retaliation, as well as through unintended feedback effects such as described earlier. The right answer is to promote an open and expanding trading system within the framework of internationally acceptable and enforceable rules, policies, and institutions (see discussion by Burton in chapter 9). Also required are coordinated macroeconomic efforts to avoid an overvalued dollar and other economic distortions, and reforms of our industrial relations system which—through its effects on labor costs, productivity, product prices, and inflation rates—can have major influences on economic stability, employment, and unemployment.

I have already reviewed the major macroeconomic problems that have adverse effects on our international competitiveness. I now turn to a description of the U.S. industrial relations system as it was during the heyday of the Bretton Woods system, and to a discussion of the kinds of changes that will make it better suited to our global economy.

THE TRADITIONAL INDUSTRIAL RELATIONS SYSTEM

The U.S. industrial relations system that worked so well in the 1950s, 1960s, and into the 1970s—and is still in effect to a large extent—is characterized by a Keynesian demand–management approach to macroeconomic policy and a commitment to a free labor movement.[2] These were well suited to the earlier consensus view that the main domestic economic problem was to achieve adequate aggregate demand to maintain high levels of growth and relatively low levels of unemployment. Growth helped companies and unions, and the existence of unions was justified partly on the grounds that the fruits of collective bargaining—along with unemployment compensation, social security, and other income support systems—helped prevent recessions or moderate their impact by sustaining purchasing power.

The primary objectives of the system were establishing work rules and assuring flexibility in response to changes in the basic forces affecting the system, especially technology, budget or market constaints, and the power status among those involved in the system. The system's ideology (body of common ideas) involved management's recognition of the right of workers to organize and bargain collectively, and the unions' acceptance of the prevailing economic and political system.

These features of the system were not unique to the U.S. industrial relations system, but were shared with other industrial nations. Other features of the industrial relations system, however, were unique to the United States:

☐ Exclusive representation, whereby the union recognized as the bargaining agent has bargaining rights for all employees, whether or not they are members of the union. The legal right of workers to vote for or against unions in government-supervised elections has had a strong influence on the American industrial relations system, creating competition between the union and nonunion sectors and between unions and employers for the workers' allegiance.

☐ Decentralized bargaining, with heavy emphasis on wages, hours, and working conditions in particular firms, industries and labor markets.

☐ Hostility on the part of U.S. employers to unions. This surprises some people in other countries because the American labor movement has been unique in embracing the capitalist system and has demonstrated relative flexibility in accommodating employers' interests.

☐ Authoritarian management and adversarial, confrontational relationships between labor and management. This system was rooted in the "scientific management" system developed in the beginning of America's industrial revolution for relatively uneducated and inexperienced (often immigrant) workers in goods-producing activities. It subdivided work into discrete tasks, and assumed that management's responsibility was to determine the best way to do a given task and to impose it on employees. This model provided little security for, or participation by, workers; left workers with little commitment to, or identification with, the enterprise; and tended to produce a detailed system of rules for such matters as job content, promotion and layoff procedures, and management's rights and prerogatives.

☐ Lack of class consciousness in union politics. American unions are unique in not having formed a labor party. This lower degree of class consciousness has caused the American labor movement to be organized mainly around the job for economic purposes rather than around the working class for political purposes.

American unions have been strongest in large oligipolistic firms, urban areas, regulated industries, and among male, blue-collar workers and workers who occupy strategic locations in the economy (such as transportation). Other industries that were unionized but had limited competition because of regulations (such as trucking and transportation) existed where unions and companies accommodated each other—within the framework of adversarial relations. By limiting wage competition, the unions helped companies regulate markets, companies recognized the right of workers to organize and bargain collectively, and free collective bargaining helped legitimize the free enterprise system. Moreover, management's right to lay off workers during economic recessions was justified by unemployment compensation and the assumption that Keynesian policies would cause the layoffs to be temporary. This was an informal social compact that had broad public support, not only as a part of the Keynesian economic rationale, but also because of the prevailing assumption that unfettered labor market competition was not good for workers or the economy.

The traditional American industrial relations system—together with the Keynesian economic policies to which it was closely related, and the expanding international economy facilitated by the Bretton Woods institutions—contributed to a long period of relatively high growth in productivity and total output. Collective bargaining made it possible for most union members to achieve middle-class incomes.

ADAPTABILITY TO CHANGE

The American system also has been more flexible than most European industrial relations systems in adjusting to change. The main indications of flexibility in the American system relative to the European were the greater decline in real wages and increase in employment in the United States during the 1970s, and the greater increase in long-term unemployment in Europe during the 1970s and 1980s. The characteristics of the system providing for greater flexibility in the United States than Europe included: the principle of exclusive bargaining rights; a more decentralized bargaining system; lower degrees of unionization and the resulting competition between union and nonunion companies; and the greater ease with which U.S. employers could close plants and lay off workers. These factors were helped by the U.S. economy's greater openness to immigration and imports, and the greater internal displacement of labor from American agriculture, which created pools of underemployed workers.

The traditional industrial relations systems in the United States, however, contained inflationary biases that became apparent with the oil price shocks of the 1970s. Its decentralized bargaining was conducive to whipsawing (raising wages by playing one employer off against another) and leapfrogging (union leaders escalating wages in competition with each other); long-term contracts with cost-of-living adjustments and annual improvement factors which tended to allow temporary factors to increase the wage base and therefore ratchet the compensation base upward; the safety nets of unemployment compensation and income maintenance programs for those who were unemployed or not expected to work, which reduced the impact of labor supply on wages, as did the growth of families with multiple wage earners; and the full-employment policies, which reduced incentives for employers to resist wage increases or for unions to hold wages down, since wage and price increases were likely to be offset by government monetary and fiscal policies.

These characteristics of the system led to inadequate attention being given to productivity and efficiency. It was not that the U.S. (or European) industrial relations systems lacked the participatory features that improve productivity. The existence of such features is one of the reasons many studies tended to show higher productivity in union than in nonunion firms in the same industry. But productivity increases alone do not make industries more competitive. This occurs only if increases in costs are less than increases in productivity.

The inflationary pressures in the U.S. system are conspicuously absent in Japan. The main indications of this are higher growth in Japanese productivity, total output, and real wages than in either the United States or Europe; and greater ease in bringing down inflation without generating high levels of unemployment after the oil price shocks of the 1970s. Large Japanese enterprises have adjusted to declining demand by maintaining output and reducing labor compensation and prices.

The factors that create flexibility in the Japanese system highlight the major differences between it and the traditional U.S. system. These include:

☐ highly interrelated consensus-based economic policies that have emphasized the upgrading (in terms of productivity and value added) of the Japanese industry mix

□ an enterprise management system stressing labor–management co-operation, participation, and consensus

□ mechanisms within enterprises to absorb shocks in demand, including a bonus compensation system, production sharing (whereby low-wage work is done in third world countries), subcontracting, and the use of temporary workers

□ one of the world's most effective positive adjustment programs to shift resources from noncompetitive to more competitive industries

□ an industrial relations system that stresses lifetime employment, continuing education of an already well-educated work force (education and training make individuals more flexible), the concentration of collective bargaining at the enterprise instead of the industry or sectoral levels, and the annual adjustment of wages through a "spring wage offensive" that minimizes whipsawing and leapfrogging

□ heavy reliance on consenus mechanisms at every level rather than the detailed regulations that characterize the American and European systems

□ a bonus wage payment system, which prevents wage increases based on temporary factors from becoming imbedded in the wage base, thereby avoiding the American practice of ratcheting wages up, and

□ flexibility in job assignments and training made possible by the lifetime employment system; which a) causes workers to have employment security rather than job security and hence to be less concerned about protecting particular jobs, and b) makes companies more willing to finance long-term education and training for their employees.

While the Japanese system has received a lot of attention, it is not superior across the board; after all, productivity and living standards are still higher in the United States than in Japan. Moreover, whereas most American companies (outside the basic industries dominated by oligopolies) have been fairly competitive, some Japanese sectors like agriculture and consumer distribution are not very efficient, and only about 15 to 20 percent of the work force has "lifetime" employment to age 55. Older workers and women have less security than prime-aged males. Nevertheless, the Japanese have developed a very competitive system in the industries they have targeted—such as automobiles, steel, consumer electronics, and computer chips. The Japanese system likewise provides rising real incomes and security to all, even though some people have more security than others. Moreover, the Japanese system is much more egalitarian than the American, in the sense that the income differentials between managers and workers are much smaller. The Japanese also have developed a system where workers perceive their benefits to be much more closely related to productivity improvements than is the case with American workers. For example, a Public Agenda survey found that only 9 percent of American workers thought that increasing productivity would benefit them; 93 percent of comparable Japanese workers thought they benefited from increased productivity.

It must be acknowledged here that the Japanese also provide an economic environment for their enterprises that is conducive to flexibility and productivity growth. Coordinated economic policy based on public–private cooperation and consensus creates greater stability and predictability, as well as flexibility. Japanese public policy socializes much economic risk, making it possible for enterprises to be satisfied with lower rates of return. The Japanese financial system is particularly beneficial: the consumer credit, social security, compensation, consumer price, and tax systems all encourage a high level of savings; the government has kept interest rates relatively low to producers; and Japanese corporations rely much more heavily on debt financing than their American counterparts, who rely more heavily on equity; bank financing relieves the Japanese of the need to be concerned about short-run stock market quotations, enabling them to develop longer-term strategies based on the latest technologies. Moreover, Japanese banks and related companies are likely to be the enterprises' main stockholders. These related companies are less likely than individual or institutional investors to be concerned about short-run returns on their stock; they are more interested in their long-term business relations with the enterprise than in their stock dividends.

Coordination of economic policy, therefore, is an important adjunct to the industrial relations system in Japan. An economic policy with low interest rates, high savings, research and development, and information sharing protects domestic producers. The Japanese keep prices and interest rates low and encourage flexible systems in order to absorb shocks, while maintaining output and employment. Small, open European systems (like the Austrians') have developed wage and price policies that keep prices competitive in the sectors that depend on exports, as well as those that are most affected by import competition. The lack of coordinated trade and economic policy in the United States makes it difficult to sustain low levels of unemployment at stable prices. Our macro- and microsystems are too likely to let real output and employment absorb demand shocks.

Possible reforms to our macrosystems are beyond the scope of this chapter. Possible reform to our industrial relations system are discussed in the next section.

THE IMPLICATIONS OF THE INTERNATIONALIZATION OF THE U.S. ECONOMY FOR THE TRADITIONAL INDUSTRIAL RELATIONS SYSTEM

The American system—as it was established in the 1930s, 1940s, and 1950s—was justified at least in part as a stabilizing system that took wages out of competition, thus reducing product market competition. The main impact of internationalization has been to transform a system that was geared primarily to the U.S. product and labor markets into one that must address the requirements of international competition. This has called into question the effectiveness of our traditional management and industrial relations system.

In a relatively open trading system with increased international competition, labor cannot be as insulated from competition as it was during the 1950s. Because technology can be standardized, and capital and material prices are determined mainly by international markets, unit labor costs become a more important and strategic element in the viability of economic enterprises. Union bargaining for wage premiums becomes less tenable, as do long-term contracts, pattern bargaining, and fragmented work assignments.

Weaknesses in flexibility, productivity, and quality output, which previously had been concealed by economic growth, become more obvious in a slow-growth global economy. Competition with the more flexible and productive Japanese industrial relations system reveals weaknesses in the American system. The lessons learned from the Japanese (as well as more competitive American enterprises) include the following:

☐ The importance of quality to productivity. Quality affects management and worker morale, market share, the ability to maintain steady production, and therefore optimal resource mixes and utilization levels.
☐ The potential of employee-owned enterprises to be more competitive. The Japanese approach of increasing market share rather than

profits suggests that employee-owned enterprises could possibly be a more competitive form of structure. Higher productivity might result from greater employee involvement, and there might be lower profit requirements because workers would be more concerned with employment preservation than profit maximization.

□ The relationship of cooperation and consensus building (labor–management, and public–private) to productivity, quality, flexibility, and stability.

□ The correlation between employment security, worker commitment, and good management. Employment security provides greater flexibility. With labor as a fixed cost, education, training, and job rotation allow more flexibility. As some American companies have discovered, providing employment security makes it more difficult to shift the costs of change to workers in the form of unemployment, and forces management to better plan production and labor utilization.

□ The adversarial–confrontational mode of labor relations places American enterprises at a disadvantage when competing with more cooperative models like those in large Japanese firms. Adversarial–confrontational relations make it difficult for labor and management to establish the kind of cooperation and mutual trust required for quality output, productivity, and flexibility in adjusting to change. In the internationalized information world where workers have higher levels of education, authoritarian, adversarial management systems deprive enterprises of the productivity and creativity of workers who know their jobs better than anyone else in the organization. Strong visible links have been established between the viability of enterprises, labor–management cooperation, employment security, and worker participation. In this new environment, unions must give greater attention to the enterprises' economic viability, and management must give greater attention to workers' security and involvement in decision making.

Notes

1. Labor migrations have even been important for some Communist countries, especially Yugoslavia and, more recently, the People's Republic of China. As a means of earning foreign exchange for its modernization program, China stepped up its export

of labor in the early 1980s. Labor contracts brought in $937 million in 1983, an increase of 95 percent over 1982. Contracts for 1984 were for over $1 billion.

2. A labor market is called free when it is not controlled by outside political or religious organizations and emphasizes democratic control by its members and the right to strike.

References

Cohen, Stephen, Daniel Teece, Laura Tipou, and John Zysman. Competitiveness. Working Paper for the President's Commission on Industrial Competitiveness. Berkeley, Calif.

Cohen, Stephen, and John Zysman. 1987. Manufacturing Matters. New York: Basic Books.

International Monetary Fund. 1984. The Realities of Economic Independence. *Finance and Development*. Washington.

Lawrence, Robert Z. 1984. Can America Compete. Washington: Brookings Institution.

New York Stock Exchange. 1984. *U.S. International Competitiveness: Perception and Reality*. New York: NYSE.

Scott, Bruce. March–April 1984a. National Strategy for Stronger U.S. Competitiveness. *Harvard Business Review*.

———. 25 November 1984b. Toward Greater U.S. Competitiveness. *New York Times*.

Chapter Nine

INTERNATIONAL COMPETITION AND AMERICAN JOBS

Daniel Burton

The ragged push and pull of American workers over the extremes of recession and recovery during the 1980s have led to a sustained search for policies that will ease job dislocations. Just how successful this policy search has been is an issue of some debate, as earlier chapters in this volume have made clear. There is, however, broad agreement on one issue: U.S. labor markets have become inextricably tied to international markets. If we hope to understand our jobs problems, we must begin to address their international dimensions.

The international dimension of our current jobs problems stems from two powerful trends. First, U.S. economic linkages with the rest of the world have expanded dramatically over the past two decades. Second, many of the economic policies of the Reagan administration have resulted in increased global competitive pressures on U.S. workers and industries. These two trends have forced U.S. companies to improve their competitiveness and flexibility, but have also resulted in widespread labor dislocations.

As Richard Cooper has pointed out, the "involvement linkages" of the U.S. economy with the rest of the world are now extensive. Twelve and one-half percent of U.S. gross national product stems from the export of goods and services, and one-third of our cropland is devoted to exports. Over one-half of after-tax U.S. corporate profits result from overseas operations, not including profits from exports, and 10 percent of U.S. bank loans are overseas. Furthermore, the U.S. labor market has been internationalized. One-sixth of our manufacturing jobs owe their existence to exports, and immigration (both legal and illegal) has accounted for a substantial part of the increase of the U.S. labor force in recent years. The internationalization of commodity and capital markets, the decline of transport costs, the removal of trade barriers, and the spread of English as the international language of business mean that the distinction between domestic and foreign transactions is rapidly disappearing (Cooper 1984).

The economic policies of the Reagan administration have exacerbated the vulnerability of American workers and companies to international competition. Although these policies have spurred U.S. firms and their employees to make necessary adjustments to increase efficiency and competitiveness, these policies have also had costly side effects that have caused many U.S. industries severe problems in international markets. As a result, many American firms, especially in the manufacturing sector, have reduced the size of their work force. Furthermore, many U.S. manufacturing companies have shifted production and jobs overseas. From the viewpoint of the U.S. labor market this development has made the problems worse. This strategy may protect balance sheets, but it does little for the U.S. labor force.

During most of the postwar period the United States welcomed the trend toward the globalization of markets and production. American workers and industries were the most competitive in the world, and the policy of free trade was a powerful tool with which to enhance economic growth and prosperity. During the late 1970s and early 1980s, however, American trade deficits and unemployment escalated to high levels and sparked a rethinking of U.S. international economic policy. The U.S. recovery that began in 1983 has greatly eased the jobs pressures stemming from heightened foreign competition and an expanded U.S. foreign trade sector, but it masks the fact that American workers, even in companies that were leaders in their industries only a few years ago, remain critically vulnerable to international economic pressures.

Although global competition and U.S. jobs are inextricably linked, the United States has no coherent policy for dealing with the international vulnerability of American workers and firms. Individual policy measures are important, but they will have little impact unless they are part of a broader, strategic effort. In order to arrive at the necessary package of policy measures, changes in both targeted, firm-level (microeconomic) policies and broader, federal (macroeconomic) policies will be required. The chapter focuses first on efforts at the firm level that can enhance international competitiveness, ease jobs dislocations, and contribute to job creation. It then examines three major economic issues: immigration, trade, and monetary and fiscal policy. It ends by proposing a policy agenda that addresses the micro- and macroeconomic issues. Some critical issues, such as employment subsidies, training, and equal opportunity, will not be addressed since they are the subject of other chapters in this volume (see Burton, et al. 1985).

FIRM-LEVEL POLICIES

U.S. macroeconomic policies and intense international competition have put tremendous pressure on U.S. companies, workers, and unions. Although the performance of U.S. firms has been very uneven, the past few years have been a time of extensive experimentation, and many new ideas are emerging about how to ease job dislocations and improve U.S. competitiveness. For purposes of discussion, I group actions at the firm level under two major headings: buffer systems and labor management relations.

Buffer Systems

Three kinds of buffer systems have been used in order to limit or avoid work-force reductions: attrition and transfer, which seeks to achieve necessary staff reductions by reallocating labor resources; work sharing, which seeks to minimize job dislocation by spreading reductions in work time throughout the labor force; and flexible systems management, which seeks to introduce ways to enhance efficient employee adjustment to fluctuations in the demand for labor.

Attrition consists of freezing recruitment and filling all vacancies through internal promotion and transfer. Attrition is often encouraged by increased severance allowances and early retirement provisions that allow for income maintenance until entitlement to full pension. In the United States transfers of workers are usually linked to internal job vacancies created by attrition; but in Japan transfer extends well beyond the individual firm to subcontractors and the wider corporate group (Yemin 1982).

Work sharing seeks to spread available work among the existing labor force by reducing the number of hours worked. Generally, overtime and extra shifts are eliminated before work sharing is instituted. Work sharing can take the form of fewer daily working hours or reductions in the number of days worked per week. It is attractive since it allows firms to distribute work reductions throughout their overall staff rather than target an isolated group of employees for dismissal or layoff.

Flexible systems management can be broadly defined as the effort to improve a company's ability to respond and conform to changes in the competitive environment that affect labor requirements. Private sector efforts to increase flexibility can be divided into three approaches: functional, which allows employees to be redeployed quickly; numerical, which enables the number of people employed to be varied to meet short-term changes in demand; and financial, which allows labor to be hired and discharged as inexpensively as possible.

One of the most important developments in the effort to maximize flexibility is the increased use of temporary and part-time workers. The Organization for Economic Cooperation and Development (OECD) has called the increase in the use of part-time workers one of the most important structural shifts in the industrial world's labor markets. Over the past decade the proportion of part-time workers has increased in all 24 OECD countries, and in the United States it is now over 14 percent. Part-time workers provide a particularly attractive means for companies to control the cost of benefits and closely match labor supply with fluctuating demand.

Many companies in Japan and increasingly in Europe have increased the flexibility of their work force by separating employees into a core and periphery. Managers, marketing personnel, technicians, and other skilled employees with career opportunities constitute the core. They enjoy a certain amount of employment security and in exchange are expected to learn new skills, switch to different jobs if necessary, and move from one plant to another. Workers in the periphery include full-time employees who perform routine tasks, part-time workers, and employees from supplier industries. Skill levels in the periphery are generally lower than in the core, and career opportunities are limited. In addition, workers in the periphery often do not enjoy as much employment security, training, or benefits as workers in the core.

Despite their convenience and cost-cutting advantages, flexible labor arrangements imply a long-term risk for the work force since they can lead to the creation of a new tier of peripheral jobs with little stability, social protection, or career prospects. Many of the workers with part-time jobs need the income from full-time jobs; and those who accept casual, part-time work in the periphery will find it difficult to make the transition to better full-time jobs. This is a particularly serious problem for women, young people, and minorities who must often accept low-level jobs in order to enter the labor market. Those with full-time but low-status, low-paying jobs that provide little serious, continuous work experience or training reduce their chances of being absorbed into more skilled jobs later on (see OECD 1982). This problem highlights the fact that some of the measures meant to increase the flexibility of the firm and security of the core work force do so at the expense of secondary workers. Such a system can add to the competitiveness of the firm; at the same time it can create a new tier of workers who not only fail to enjoy a full range of opportunities and work benefits but also bear the brunt of any economic shocks.

Labor–Management Relations

International competition has significantly altered U.S. labor–management relations. During most of the postwar period U.S. dominance in world markets permitted collective bargaining to focus on how to share gains, rather than on how to share losses, improve efficiency, or increase flexibility. The dominant position of American companies in world markets permitted U.S. wage levels to rise without undermining U.S. competitiveness or threatening job security for the majority of workers. Management was able to provide these benefits without sacrificing profits or conceding to workers any substantial decision-making power in the management of the firm.

Today there is a need not only to share gains, but also to maximize competitiveness and distribute the burden of losses. Genuine cooperation can help U.S. companies and workers adapt to the new economic setting. However, two important impediments to greater labor–management cooperation exist: lack of union responsiveness to the success of the enterprise, and lack of company responsiveness to the employment security of its workers.

The indifference of some unions to the success of their companies has made management reluctant to accept unions as legitimate partners. But the indifference of many companies to the employment security of their work force has served to block workers' identification with company performance. As long as management regards labor as a variable cost and fails to take into account its legitimate needs and aspirations, workers will continue to have a limited identification with the success of their company. If workers are to regard the long-term economic health of their company as more important than immediate increases in wages and benefits, employers must accept greater responsibility for the employment security of their work force.

Worker participation programs are perhaps the best example of the efforts of management and labor to forge a more cooperative relationship. Whereas some worker participation programs have failed fully to involve employees in the exchange of information and decision making, other programs have succeeded in promoting genuine cooperation (see Economic Policy Council 1983).

Labor market developments in the past few years attest to the extreme pressures facing American workers and managers. The prohibitive export cost and lucrative import strength of the dollar in the early to mid-1980s had a powerful effect on employment in the U.S. foreign trade sector. U.S. companies boosted their imports and shifted production and jobs overseas, while American workers stepped up their demands for greater protection from imports and more employment security. Jobs in the U.S. manufacturing sector have been especially vulnerable to recent trade developments.

Developments in the American automobile industry, which is closely tied to world markets, represent a microcosm of many of the changes taking place in U.S. labor markets as a result of increasing international competition. U.S. automobile companies have streamlined their work forces and are providing some form of job security for their remaining workers, such as the Job Opportunity Bank-Security Fund at General Motors. The U.S. automobile industry is also trying to improve labor–management relations and the quality of work life through such efforts as the Employee Involvement (EI) program at Ford. Finally, automatic annual wage increases have been reconsidered and new compensation packages are being introduced, such as two-tier wage systems and lump-sum payments or bonuses in lieu of wage increases.

For their part, foreign companies are also changing the way they approach the U.S. market. They are recognizing that they cannot simply export but must also produce cars in the United States (discussed in more detail later in the chapter). This is especially true of Japanese companies. Honda, Nissan, Toyota, and Mazda are producing nearly a million cars and trucks a year in U.S. factories and employing some 12,000 workers. And this figure will increase in 1989 when Mitsubishi gets its operations underway. However, these plants may actually hold down employment potential in the U.S. automobile industry since they will get about half of their parts and components from Japan.

Efforts at the firm level to cope with the new kinds of jobs problems stemming from international competition come in many different forms and have met with mixed success. However, it is important not to overlook the very real difference these actions can make. Although they cannot substitute for national economic policies, they have important advantages since they can be implemented quickly and can be tailored to the needs of individual companies and workers. As such, they can provide a first line of defense against job dislocations resulting from international pressures.

IMMIGRATION

As the United States has become more tightly linked to the global economy and as the international mobility of labor has increased, immigration has come to have an increasingly important impact on the U.S. labor market (see Economic Policy Council 1981). Net U.S. immigration, both legal and illegal, amounts to approximately 1 million people per year, which means that the United States accepts twice as many immigrants and refugees as the rest of the industrialized world combined. The great difference between today's immigrants and those of earlier periods is that most arrive illegally and subsequently live here outside the protection of U.S. laws. Perhaps even more sobering is the fact that the inflow of illegal immigrants into the United States is likely to accelerate. The world's population, which was 4 billion in 1975, will increase to 6.5 billion by the year 2000. Most of the population growth will take place in developing countries that already have serious unemployment problems. These nations will need to create between 600 and 700 million new jobs just to keep unemployment from rising. To put the magnitude of this increase in perspective, this represents more jobs than existed in the combined industrial world in 1980.

This problem is brought closer to home when it is realized that the population of Mexico alone is expected to double—from 70 million in 1980 to 140 million—by the year 2000. In order to accommodate all the new entrants into the labor force, absorb its present unemployed and underemployed, and reintegrate those who would otherwise be employed in the United States, Mexico would have to create 31 to 33 million jobs over the next 20 years. Even if Mexico were to sustain a 6.5 percent growth in GNP a year, only about 20 million jobs would be created—and the wage differential across the U.S. border is such that many Mexicans would continue to be drawn into the United States.

The Immigration Reform Act that was signed into law on 6 November 1986 demonstrates that the United States is beginning to recognize the magnitude of the problem of illegal immigration. Nonetheless, there is no clear consensus on the impact that illegal immigrants have on the U.S. labor market.

There are two schools of thought about the effects of illegal immigration on the American economy. Those who believe it has a positive impact stress that undocumented workers take jobs that are unacceptable to U.S. citizens, and therefore benefit U.S. workers, employers, and consumers. Those who believe that illegal immigration should be subject to greater control stress that undocumented workers compete for jobs with U.S. citizens, especially minorities, young people, and low-wage workers. According to this view, illegal immigrants displace U.S. workers, depress wages, and perpetuate low-wage, low-productivity jobs. (U.S. Commissioner of Immigration and Naturalization Alan Nelson estimated in 1984 that there were about 6 million illegal immigrants in the United States—4 million of whom held jobs—and concluded that this represented some 3 million fewer jobs for U.S. citizens.)

It is impossible to resolve this controversy definitively, but the evidence appears to support the following conclusions: illegal immigrants do displace American workers, but the displacement is not one-for-one; during periods of rapid economic growth there is little displacement, but with uneven growth and high unemployment, displacement clearly increases; illegal immigrants depress wages and working conditions in low-wage jobs where they are usually concentrated; and, as they learn English and acquire more work experience, illegal immigrants move into successively higher-paying jobs. Low-income legal U.S. residents are the clear losers from illegal immigration. U.S. employers probably gain, and consumers of the goods and services produced by illegals also gain, at least in the short run.

If employers did not have recourse to undocumented workers, they would have three options: raise wages, improve management, and make their jobs more attractive to legal residents; mechanize and maximize the productivity of individual employees; or shift jobs to low-wage developing countries. This three-pronged approach is the strategy adopted by Japan, and a look at Japanese immigration policy reveals just how closely it is linked to its overall labor strategy.

The dilemma facing Japan is the same one confronting all advanced industrial countries. During times of rapid economic growth, Japan has experienced shortages of low-skilled labor, which could be efficiently met by importing unskilled workers. But during times of slow growth, imported labor can pose serious economic and social problems. Japan weighed the European and U.S. experiences and contrasted them with its wartime decision to import 2 million Koreans to do low-skill, low-wage work. As a result, Japan adopted very stringent immigration laws after World War II.

Japan's decision to limit immigration has had an important impact on its labor market. With limited immigration, internal labor markets were forced to adjust to available resources. With no imported labor to do low-skill, low-wage work, Japan was prompted to upgrade jobs whenever possible. In some cases, technology was introduced to eliminate menial jobs. In other instances, menial jobs were combined with other responsibilities. (For example, in schools the students and teacher in each class are responsible for the maintenance of their classroom, and in factories each unit is responsible for cleaning its own area.) Furthermore, menial jobs were often structured so that they were only one step in a career pattern rather than permanent dead-end occupations. Finally, when Japanese companies invested overseas, they tried to insure that low-skill, assembly jobs were performed in the host country while the skilled, high-wage, value-added jobs remained in Japan. As these initiatives demonstrate, Japanese immigration policy is closely tied to the effort to create and upgrade jobs for Japanese

The United States is not Japan. From our beginnings we have been a nation of immigrants, and successive waves of new arrivals have enriched our culture, history, and economy. The challenge before us is not to arrest completely the flow of immigrants. Not only is this undesirable, it is wholly impractical given the geography and diversity of the country. However, sooner or later, the United States must confront the tremendous impact that illegal immigrants have on U.S. labor markets. Unless we can more successfully control the flow of illegals, U.S. workers could face mounting jobs problems, especially during times of uneven economic growth and high unemployment.

TRADE

The *other* deficit, as the U.S. trade imbalance is often called, has grown to unprecendented levels, and has resulted in the loss of many U.S. manufacturing jobs. From 1982 to 1985 the U.S. trade deficit nearly doubled each year. In 1982 it was $36 billion; in 1983 it rose to $61 billion; and in 1984 it climbed to $123 billion. By 1987 it was more than $170 billion. For manufactured goods the U.S. trade imbalance is especially serious. In 1983 U.S. manufactured imports exceeded manufactured exports by $38 billion. In 1984 the manufacturing trade imbalance surged to $88 billion—an increase of $50 billion in one year. And by 1987, the U.S. manufacturing trade deficit had risen to over $140 billion.

The collapse of U.S. trade has been virtually worldwide. Latin America, Asia, and Europe all have increased their trade surplus with the United States in recent years. In 1986 our largest trade deficits were with some of our biggest trade partners—$15.7 billion with Taiwan, $26.4 billion with the European Community, $23.3 billion with Canada, and $58.6 billion with Japan. The trade deficit with Japan was the largest U.S. trade deficit ever recorded with any one country.

Large U.S. trade deficits mean lost U.S. job opportunities. Estimates vary as to the number of American jobs lost in recent years as a result of trade. Data Resources, Inc. estimates that from 1981 to 1984, the widening U.S. trade deficit cost the U.S. economy some 2 million export-related jobs; international economist C. Fred Bergsten believes that the number could be even higher. The New York Stock Exchange estimates that 1,109,000 gross jobs were lost as a result of foreign trade in 1982, but 525,000 trade-related jobs were added, so the net loss was only 584,000 jobs. Whatever yardstick is used to measure the job loss due to trade, there is no question that it has cost the U.S. economy significant numbers of jobs in recent years, and these losses have escalated as U.S. trade deficits have increased.

The U.S. manufacturing sector is bearing the brunt of the trade deficit. Record levels of manufactured imports combined with sagging U.S. manufactured exports have meant widespread job losses for U.S. manufacturing industries. In 1984 the U.S. trade deficit in textiles and apparel was $16 billion, and from 1980 to 1985 U.S. employment in textiles and apparel declined from 2.2 million to 1.8 million. In 1984 steel imports accounted for 26.7 percent of the U.S. steel market, and from 1981 to 1985 employment in the U.S. steel industry declined by some 200,000. Even electronics had a $12 billion trade deficit in 1985, compared with a $7.4 billion surplus in 1980; without that trade reversal it is estimated that there would have been approximately 150,000 more electronics jobs in the United States.

The Reagan administration's search for policies to arrest the hemorrhage of jobs in the U.S. foreign trade sector has taken place within the constraints of the commitment to free trade. Policy responses have been largely "voluntary," that is, designed so that they do not contravene the General Agreement on Tariffs and Trade (GATT). They have also been sector-specific and applied only after the industry in question has suffered serious difficulty.

Automobile trade restrictions are perhaps the best known example. The United States imposed voluntary trade restrictions on Japan in 1981 after the U.S. automobile industry had lost $4 billion, Japanese imports had increased to 23 percent of the U.S. market, and 300,000

American automobile workers had been laid off. Japanese automobile exports to the United States were initially limited to 1.68 million units per year under this agreement. This ceiling was raised to 1.85 million in 1984, and in recent years U.S. automobile companies have posted record profits.

The voluntary trade restrictions had several effects. Japan shifted its automobile exports to higher priced units and increased its foreign investment in the United States; U.S. companies were given a breathing spell in which to retool their operations and rebuild their profits; and the layoffs of U.S. automobile workers were slowed. Although profits in the U.S. automobile companies recovered under these import restrictions, employment still remains below its 1979 peak.

Policy Limitations

U.S. trade officials have a limited range of options open to them since the bulk of our current trade problems stem from macroeconomic imbalances (see discussion of monetary and fiscal policy later in the chapter). Furthermore, some analysts argue that trade policy is ill-suited to the task of protecting U.S. jobs since the cost can far outweigh the wages for each job saved. For example, Robert Crandall of the Brookings Institution estimates that the recent U.S. automobile quotas cost American consumers $160,000 for every job they saved. However, advocates of trade restrictions argue with some justification that the United States cannot simply abandon workers to international competition, emphasizing that the employment security of American workers is a valid concern. Our policy choices are further complicated by the fact that no single committee in Congress deals with both trade and employment, and therefore these two issues tend to be treated as separate agenda items.

Trade Proposals

Trade policy options can be broadly classified as efforts to open foreign markets; efforts to restrict foreign access to U.S. markets; and recourse to the GATT. The United States has pursued all these avenues in recent years, but not aggressively enough to prevent the U.S. trade deficit from rising precipitously or to significantly stem the tide of trade-related job losses.

Efforts to open foreign markets to U.S. exports are by far the most desirable alternative. Not only are they consonant with the U.S. commitment to free trade and comparative advantage; they entail little cost, have limited international repercussions, and do not interfere with domestic economic management. Recent efforts to open foreign markets to U.S. exports have been aimed primarily at Japan and Western Europe. However, these initiatives have met with limited success. Between 1980 and 1986 Japan unveiled seven "market-opening" packages, yet the U.S. trade deficit with Japan steadily increased. Futhermore, key sectors of the Japanese economy in which U.S. firms are highly competitive—such as telecommunciations, medical and pharmaceutical supplies, lumber processing and paper products, and electronics equipment—remain effectively closed to many U.S. exporters. U.S. efforts to open markets in Europe have been primarily aimed at the Common Agricultural Policy (CAP) and have also met with little success.

U.S. import restrictions have been exercised cautiously since they can lead to serious international complications. The United States imposes antidumping and countervailing duties in the event of unfair international competition, and Title II of the Trade Act of 1974 permits the U.S. government to restrain imports temporarily, even in the absence of unfair trade practices, if American producers are harmed. In addition, the United States has instituted voluntary trade restrictions to help industries such as autos and steel adjust to foreign competition.

One frequently discussed means of controlling imports and increasing U.S. employment in the foreign trade sector is domestic-content legislation, which requires foreign producers to include a certain level of U.S. components in those products that they sell in the United States. The purpose of this legislation is to spur foreign investment in the United States. Domestic content was encouraged by the U.S. automobile industry in the early 1980s, but now that many foreign automobile companies have established production facilities in the United States and American automobile companies' profits have recovered, there is less urgency to the demand for local-content laws.

Another trade policy option is a surcharge on U.S. imports. A surcharge could come in many different forms. Among the most frequently discussed are a 10 percent levy on all imports, 20 percent on manufactured imports, or 20 percent on U.S. imports of Japanese products. This would make U.S. products relatively more price competitive with imports and provide the U.S. Treasury with a new source of revenue. However, an import surcharge could also lead to some significant problems. It could invite retaliation by our trading partners, undermine the competitiveness of U.S. industries that depend on imports for inputs into their products, penalize U.S. consumers, exacerbate the debt problems of the developing world, set back the European recovery, and slow global economic growth. In short, stringent import controls are a "black box" that could provide domestic relief, but could also invite a series of serious international repercussions.

Current U.S. trade policy pays homage to the GATT, but in recent years has been increasingly bilateral and sectoral in nature. The United States has called for a new round of trade talks to follow up the trade liberalization accomplished by the Kennedy and Tokyo rounds, but it is uncertain whether the new GATT round will result in any highly significant new achievements. First, the easy problems of quotas, tariffs, and some nontariff barriers have already been dealt with, what remain are more difficult trade barriers that arise from different national approaches to economic organization. Second, the political will is lacking. With a $171 billion merchandise trade deficit in 1987, the United States is not interested in liberalizing its imports but in opening foreign markets for it exports. And Japan and Western Europe are unlikely to come forward with major trade liberalizations of their own. Third, many of our trade problems are with developing countries that claim special trading privileges. Fourth, and perhaps most importantly, many of our current trade problems stem largely from macroeconomic imbalances, as noted, and it is highly unlikely that trade policy can correct these imbalances.

If efforts to open foreign markets to U.S. exports have little effect, if import restrictions have many potential undesirable side effects, and if GATT has important limitations, what is left? The answer is that given the current set of micro-imbalances, trade policy has a limited capacity to resolve U.S. trade-related jobs problems. But that does not mean that U.S. trade policy is totally ineffective and that the United States should resign itself to large trade deficits and subsequent job losses.

MONETARY AND FISCAL POLICY

The tremendous impact that U.S. macroeconomic policy has on jobs in the international sector of the U.S. economy has never been more evident than in the past five years (see Economic Policy Council 1984). Although U.S. macroeconomic policy has had a mixed impact on U.S. labor markets as a whole—first inducing recession that pushed

U.S. unemployment to postwar highs, then sparking a recovery that added over 12 million jobs—U.S. macroeconomic policy has had a distinctly negative impact on jobs in the U.S. foreign trade sector.

The bulk of our current trade problems are due, not to the lagging international competitiveness of U.S. firms, but to the insurmountable obstacles created by macroeconomic imbalances. The precipitous rise in U.S. trade deficits since 1981 and their impact on U.S. labor markets has already been described. There are three main reasons for the sudden deterioration in the U.S. trade balance, and all three can be traced to U.S. macroeconomic policy: the rise of the dollar, the debt crisis, and the nature of the recent international recession and recovery.

The Rise of the Dollar

When U.S. monetary policy tightened in late 1979, the dollar began a sharp appreciation in foreign exchange markets. Since 1980 the dollar has fluctuated by more than 60 percent in value against an average of the world's other major currencies. At the beginning of 1985, it was widely recognized that the dollar was overvalued by about 35 percent, which is equivalent to placing a 35 percent tax on all U.S. exports and giving a 35 percent subsidy to all foreign exports to the United States. On 22 September 1985 five industrial nations—France, the Federal Republic of Germany, Japan, the United Kingdom, and the United States—announced a program to bring down the foreign exchange value of the dollar. Although this program has been highly successful in bringing down the value of the dollar against the currencies of our major industrial trading partners, the dollar remains strong vis-à-vis the currencies of many of our developing-country trading partners.

The major cause for the high dollar in the early 1980s was high real U.S. interest rates. If real U.S. interest rates are higher than those of other countries, U.S. assets pay a higher real rate of return than foreign assets and become attractive to foreign investors. During most of the 1970s the average real U.S. interest rate was actually negative, while that of our major trading partners was about zero. However, in late 1980 the interest rate differential between the United States and its major trading partners swung sharply in favor of the United States, and the dollar began its steady rise.

It was not until 1981 that the dollar's negative impact on the U.S. trade balance became apparent, and it was not until 1982 that the U.S. trade balance on goods and services (as opposed to simply merchandise trade) swung into deficit. This pattern is consistent with historical experience and reflects the fact that there is a slight time lag before markets react to significant swings in foreign exchange rates. The immediate impact of the rise in the dollar's value was to improve the U.S. trade balance because fewer dollars were required to purchase a given quantity of imports. However, over time consumers in the United States and abroad began to realize that a stronger dollar was making U.S. goods and services more expensive than foreign goods and services, and as a result they began to purchase fewer U.S. products and more foreign products. Consequently, U.S. exports failed to match the increase in U.S. imports, and the U.S. trade balance deteriorated. Between 1980 and 1986 U.S. exports remained practically unchanged, while U.S. imports rose by over 50 percent.

U.S. industry has taken several steps to compensate for the competitive disadvantages stemming from the overvalued dollar. One of the ways that U.S. industry has tried to compensate for an overvalued dollar has been to cut prices. However, prices can only be cut so far without seriously reducing profit margins. A second response has been to institute currency hedging practices; but no matter how sophisticated these are, they can have only a marginal impact on the price competitiveness of U.S. exports. A third reaction has been to engage in more countertrade. Countertrade has long been popular among communist bloc countries, but often complicates existing trade relationships and can serve to limit the range of goods and services that are traded. A fourth response has been to resort to out-sourcing, which entails importing less expensive, foreign-made parts and components for use in U.S. products destined for export. Closely related to this practice has been the decision to engage in more joint ventures. Joint ventures allow U.S. companies to circumvent the negative impact of a strong dollar on exports by producing overseas. Like out-sourcing, however, joint ventures can result in a shift of U.S. jobs and capital overseas at the expense of American workers and the U.S. economy.

There are several reasons why the decline in the dollar's value since 1985 has had a limited impact on the U.S. trade deficit. First, there are always substantial lags between a change in exchange rates, a change in import process and a change in demand. In part, the fall in the dollar's value has been uneven. Approximately 40 percent of U.S. trade is with Canada, Mexico, Brazil, Korea, Taiwan, Hong Kong, and Singapore; the currencies of these countries remained relatively unchanged vis-à-vis the dollar through the end of 1986.

Second, foreign competitors have reacted more aggressively to the dollar's fall than expected. Foreign firms have chosen to reduce profit margins rather than lose their market share in the United States. In particular, Japanese and German firms have not raised their dollar export prices nearly as much as the shift in currency values would suggest. Instead, many have initiated major steps to cut costs and improve productivity. They also have allowed their substantial profit margins to erode in an effort to hold the market shares they won during the period of dollar appreciation. Having established a presence in the United States, foreign firms will not easily give up their hard-won distribution networks, name recognition, or market share.

Third, the protracted era of a high dollar appears to have significantly altered supply and demand patterns. Many foreign suppliers have expanded their capacity to serve the U.S. market. Many domestic suppliers have moved offshore or subcontracted more of their production abroad. Domestic consumers now prefer new, previously unknown, and unavailable foreign goods. For these reasons, a change in exchange rates is likely to have a smaller impact than before the dollar's rise. American purchasers have come to associate imports with quality, reliability, service, and state-of-the-art technology. They may require a very large increase in import prices or a changed perception of the quality of U.S. products before they are willing to switch back to domestic substitutes.

The Debt Crisis

The second way that U.S. macroeconomic policies have affected international trade and jobs in the U.S. foreign trade sector is by creating an environment that contributed to the onset of the world debt crisis. U.S. monetary and fiscal policy fueled the debt crisis in three ways. First, tighter U.S. monetary policy led to a rapid increase in U.S. interest rates and a decline in inflation. Because most third world debt carried floating interest rates and was short term, the rise in interest rates was immediately translated into significantly higher debt-service payments for developing countries. Second, tighter monetary policy in the United States induced a recession in 1981 that quickly spread throughout the world economy. As a result of this recession, demand for exports from the developing countries declined and the export earnings that they relied on to service their debt fell off sharply. Third, as has been discussed, U.S. macroeconomic policy sparked a sustained rise in the value of the dollar. A stronger dollar sharply increased the debt burden of the developing countries since a significant portion of their debt must be repaid in dollars.

This is not to say that the debt crisis was not also influenced by poor economic management in many of the debtor nations; but the net impact of these three developments was to increase debt-service requirements of developing countries while reducing the amount of foreign exchange they had to service their debt. The resulting liquidity crisis caused developing countries with large external debts to completely reorient their trade policies. In order to generate enough foreign exchange to pay the interest on their towering debts, many highly indebted third world countries drastically cut their imports and pushed their exports. Import barriers, import substitution schemes, and export incentives were used as part of the attempt to maximize third world trade surpluses. This reorientation of third world trade policy has meant that the United States has been flooded with exports from developing countries and has found that its exports to them are often unacceptable at any price.

Recession and Recovery

The third way that U.S. macroeconomic policy has affected U.S. trade flows since 1981 is by influencing the cyclical business pattern. Tight U.S. monetary policy and large U.S. federal budget deficits forced up U.S. interest rates and sparked a deep recession in the United States in 1981 and 1982. Since economic activity was more robust in other industrial nations than in the United States during 1981 and 1982, the recession tended to reduce U.S. demand for the exports of other industrial countries more than it reduced foreign demand for U.S. exports. What was extraordinary about the 1981–83 recession was that despite the positive impact that the relatively deeper American downturn had on U.S. trade flows, the U.S. trade balance continued to deteriorate. The continued deterioration was because any positive impact that the relatively deeper U.S. recession had on the U.S. trade balance was overwhelmed by the effect of the overvalued dollar and the debt crisis.

In 1983 U.S. fiscal policy sparked a sharp U.S. recovery while most of the rest of the world remained mired in recession. As a result, U.S. demand for imports grew more rapidly than foreign demand for U.S. exports, adding yet another drain on the already anemic U.S. trade balance.

The overvalued dollar, the debt crisis, and the nature of the recent international recession and recovery were in large part due to U.S. macroeconomic management. Combined, they not only resulted in increased U.S. imports, but also eroded the price competitiveness of U.S. goods and seriously cut foreign demand for U.S. exports. The resulting trade deficits have meant millions of lost jobs in the U.S. foreign trade sector. Unless U.S. macroeconomic policy is systematically handled with greater attention to its impact on the foreign trade sector—including its impact on real U.S. interest rates and the foreign exchange value of the dollar—U.S. companies and workers will continue to face serious competitive disadvantages.

POLICY AGENDA

Each of the following policy proposals, taken individually, would have beneficial short-term effects. Taken as a whole, they would also contribute to an economic environment that could achieve long-term gains for American workers. The agenda follows the same sequence as the discussion.

Firm-Level Policies

Three policy proposals should be considered. The first addresses the long-term need for greater worker participation. The second and third address the need for worker protection during temporary periods of unemployment.

U.S companies should expand worker participation programs that improve the quality of work life, since these programs enhance the economic efficiency that leads to greater competitiveness. The following guidelines are important to the success of worker participation programs. Employees (and in the case of a union, the union's leadership as well as its rank and file) should be involved in worker participation programs from the outset. Participation in these programs should be voluntary. Employee involvement should be adopted as a long-term commitment. Programs should first focus on workers' needs and product quality, and should not be disguised speed-up programs designed solely to increase productivity. Managers should continue to move from an authoritarian to a more participative style of management. Adequate training and education programs are essential. Where unions represent workers, they should be involved as an equal partner for planning through implementation and evaluation. And worker participation programs must make every effort to ensure employment security (see Economic Policy Council 1983.)

Firms should adopt temporary buffer systems as a means of increasing flexibility during cyclical downturns. Hiring freezes, elimination of extensive overtime, moving work in house, shifting employees to nontraditional jobs within firms, helping workers to find employment in outside companies, and using temporary or contract workers may all be parts of this buffer system. In this context, U.S. firms should explore the feasibility of the Japanese practice of intercompany transfers, since detaching workers to the extended corporate group during periods of falling demand is an important way of avoiding dismissals in Japan. Workers who are transferred to other companies retain their initial employment relationship, and their original employer usually makes up any difference in wages. They have the option of either returning to their original employer when conditions permit or assuming permanent employment in the new enterprise.

Buffer systems have a limited role in industries facing structural decline, but they can be highly successful in helping firms and workers adjust to temporary setbacks. A key to their effectiveness is to make every effort to integrate temporary and part-time workers into the core work force. By reducing employment insecurity, buffer systems can enhance the flexibility of both individual workers and firms over the course of the business cycle.

States should pass legislation to allow companies to establish short-time unemployment compensation. Short-time unemployment compensation gives individual firms the opportunity to reduce the work schedule of their overall work force instead of laying off a group of workers altogether. The unemployment compensation that would normally go to a few laid-off workers is then distributed over the entire work force. Short-time unemployment compensation should be voluntary for companies and unions and should not substitute for other private and public adjustment polices. California, Arizona, Florida, Illinois, Oregon, Washington, and Maryland have already passed legislation for short-time unemployment compensation, and approximately one-fifth of all collective bargaining agreements contain provisions for dealing with shorter workweeks to cope with the prospect of unemployment. The federal government should continue to study the effects of short-time unemployment compensation in those states where it has been enacted and should encourage those states that have not done so to pass legislation providing for short-time unemployment compensation.

Immigration

The Immigration Reform and Refugee Act of 1986 (Public Law 99–603) represents a significant step in the effort to control illegal immigration. Two of its most noteworthy features are a general amnesty program and employer sanctions. Given the fact that this act only became law in November 1986 and was phased in gradually, it is premature to make any broad recommendations for U.S. immigration policy until the impact of this law can be assessed.

Trade

The omnibus trade bill passed into law in 1988 should strengthen U.S. trade policy. The program for a $1 billion worker-adjustment program to assist all dislocated workers, not just those affected by imports, is clearly a step in the right direction. In implementing U.S. trade policy, the following recommendations should be kept in mind.

The United States should persistently press Japan and other countries to open their markets to U.S. exports. If these actions are to be productive, they must be part of a coordinated, continuous effort rather than a series of sporadic overtures. And U.S. companies must follow up these market-opening inititatives with sustained export drives. An open world trading system must be a two-way street. Other countries cannot expect to continue to benefit from the openness of U.S. markets while keeping out U.S. exports.

When voluntary trade restrictions are implemented, they should focus on value as well as volume, so that foreign producers will not simply move into upscale exports and thereby increase their dollar volume while limiting the number of units exported.

When U.S. industries are given government trade assistance in the form of voluntary trade restrictions, clear performance criteria should be spelled out. For example, wages and bonuses in the protected U.S. industry should be limited as long as trade restrictions remain in place.

Fiscal and Monetary Policy

U.S. monetary and fiscal policy should be treated as part of a carefully coordinated program rather than two separate exercises that are frequently at odds with each other. Overly expansive fiscal policy puts undue pressure on monetary policy to discipline economic growth, and it is important for the United States to adopt a more evenly balanced monetary and fiscal policy package. More responsible fiscal management allows for more flexible monetary management.

U.S. fiscal policy should be revised by altering both outlays and receipts, and American labor and management should join together to insist on a reduction of U.S. budget deficits. Defense, medicare, social security, and interest on the national debt account for two-thirds of government spending. The programs constituting the remaining one-third of the budget have already been cut considerably, and it is clear that major savings can be achieved only if spending is reduced in the two-thirds of the budget that has not already been subject to deep cuts. On the revenue side, the primary cause of the structural deficits were the phased tax cuts of 1981, 1982, and 1983. The arithmetic of spending cuts leads to the conclusion that tax revenues will also have to be increased if the deficit is to be substantially reduced.

The Federal Reserve System should continue its current pragmatic approach to monetary targeting and should identify the trade-weighted value of the dollar as one of the key variables that guide U.S. monetary policy.

The United States should also work with other countries to achieve greater international macroeconomic policy coordination. Economic coordination is intrinsically difficult among industrial democracies, but the disparities among the macroeconomic policies of OECD nations must be narrowed. The answer is not to create new international bodies, but to achieve a political commitment at the highest level to use existing institutions for their original purpose—cooperation in framing economic policy. The annual summit meetings of seven of the OECD countries should not be merely public relations exercises but serious attempts to develop coordinated policy packages. An independent commission of international experts should be charged with the responsibility of reporting on the extent to which summit countries are implementing these agreements.

References

Burton, Jr., Daniel F., John H. Filer, Douglas A. Fraser, and Ray Marshall, eds. 1985. *The Jobs Challenge: Pressures and Possibilities.* Cambridge, Mass.: Ballinger Publishing Co.

Organization for Economic Cooperation and Development. 1982. *The Challenge of Unemployment*. Paris: OECD.

Cooper, Richard N. 1984. Linkage Effects. In *The Global Repercussions of U.S. Monetary and Fiscal Policy*, edited by Sylvia Ann Hewlett, Henry Kaufman, and Peter Kenen. Cambridge, Mass.: Ballinger Publishing Co.

Economic Policy Council of the UNA-USA. 1981. *Illegal Immigration: Challenge to the United States*. New York: EPC of the UNA-USA.

————. 1983. *The Productivity Problem: U.S. Labor–Management Relations*. New York: EPC of the UNA-USA.

————. 1984. *The Global Repercussions of U.S. Monetary and Fiscal Policy*. New York: EPC of the UNA-USA.

Hewlett, Sylvia Ann. Winter 1981/82. Coping with Illegal Immigrants. *Foreign Affairs* 60:358–78.

Yemin, Edward, ed. 1982. *Workforce Reductions in Undertakings*. Geneva: International Labor Organization.

Chapter Ten

AN EFFECTIVE EMPLOYMENT POLICY: THE MISSING MIDDLE

Forrest Chisman

Previous chapters in this volume have documented troubling trends in U.S. unemployment over the past decades. They have discussed the macroeconomic constraints on the potential of direct labor market intervention to affect overall employment. They have considered a series of macro- and microeconomic strategies that, if pursued in a coherent, systematic way, hold the promise of reducing the bleakness of our employment landscape. They have also suggested areas where we really do not know what is an effective policy, and have called for further research and experimentation to provide that knowledge.

I would like to put the employment issue in a wider context by arguing that we need an effective employment policy, that such a policy can attract wide support and, finally, that such a policy can be economically feasible. In my view, the issue is essentially one of commitment. If we, as a people, have the will to support a full employment policy, we can find the means to create one.

THE PLACE OF EMPLOYMENT POLICY IN THE FEDERAL SOCIAL ROLE

In one sense, employment has always been central to activist government in the United States. Americans have always believed that they and everyone else should work. This has led them to favor policies that provide public and private benefits largely as a matter of earned right rather than entitlement. Policies to promote economic development, for example—the outstanding priority for public policy at the federal level during the first century of our public life— are intended to improve the lives of Americans by providing them

249

with opportunities to make a living through good jobs. Policies to provide economic security—the outstanding federal priority in the second century of our public life—depend on a history of steady attachment to the work force. Job subsidies, tax preferences, and even much of our business regulation are intended to help people make a good living and enjoy the fruits of their labors.

American public policy is ungenerous—relative to policy in other developed countries—to those who work but whose efforts fail to lift them above the poverty line, to the long-term unemployed, to mothers on welfare, and to poor children. Such policy makes sense if we accept a certain rather American assumption—that people can earn a decent living from work if they want to. It is only a slight exaggeration to predict that, if everyone had a good job, the under-class would disappear, the working poor would rise to the economic condition of middle-income Americans, public and private programs would protect us against the costs of ill health and old age, economic growth would overcome the problems associated with population aging, working families would have the necessary income to solve their problems, and so forth. And our individualist values would be satisfied, because all of us would have solved our most serious problems by our own efforts. Federal employment policy would make perfect sense.

But, of course, we do not have the assurance of earning a decent living from work because the United States does not have a full employment policy. As chapters 1 and 2 have indicated, these are major substantive problems to be tackled in designing such a policy. But this is not the major reason we lack such an employment policy in this country. The fundamental reason is that the United States has not made a real commitment to the effort. The architects of the New Deal recognized the need for one. The evidence is clear that they realized their design would only meet the nation's needs if employment problems could be overcome. Indeed, the first recommendation of the Committee on Economic Security of 1935 was for a full employment policy (The Report of the Committee 1935, 23). The committee expected that, even in times of economic recovery, large numbers of people would be without work; and they realized that neither social insurance nor other public protections would be adequate by themselves to sustain those people at a decent level or maintain overall prosperity for long. Only jobs would do, because only jobs would provide continuing security in the prime of life and access in times of distress to the kinds of programs designed by American social activists. The New Deal architects did not take employment for granted: they called for measures to ensure that it was available.

But attempts to introduce a full employment policy were deferred in 1935, and defeated by the business community in a monumental battle over the Full Employment Bill in 1945.[1] Opponents were successful in arguing that full employment would be too costly, too disruptive of the labor market, and, in general, un-American, and socialistic. The Humphrey-Hawkins Act of 1978 was the nation's most recent review of the issue. It resulted in a statement of laudable goals but no mechanism for achieving them.

As a result, we are left with a system of public policy and a set of social values that are based on the assumption that virtually all Americans can and do hold good jobs, when this is clearly not the case. This is the sense in which a full employment policy is the missing middle of the American social policy structure.

THE EXTENT OF THE EMPLOYMENT PROBLEM

As previous chapters have made clear, employment in fact has become less secure in the last decade, and the things that we must do to gain and hold jobs are becoming more difficult. We must develop and maintain a high level of skills, follow the ever-changing labor market, and protect ourselves against a wide range of other threats to our wages, benefits, and conditions of employment.

As Johnson pointed out in chapter 2, unemployment rates exceeded 10 percent during the last recession, and have recovered only to about 5 to 6 percent—an all-time high for a period of economic recovery. Thus, even when the economy is working well, it is less able than it used to be to absorb the available work force. It is also the case that these statistics understate the problem. Official government figures do not count people who want to work but are so discouraged that they have stopped looking for jobs. Most estimates indicate they would add at least 1 percent to the overall unemployment rate, and their numbers have been growing in recent years.

Nor is unemployment spread evenly across regions or across population groups. In some areas, where troubled industries or failing farms make up a large part of the local economy, unemployment rates have been at least 50 percent higher than for the nation as a whole, even during the recovery. In these pockets of depression, workers laid off during the late 1970s and early 1980s have never come back. The Bureau of Labor Statistics (BLS) estimates that over 5 million Americans who had been employed for over three years lost their jobs between 1979 and 1983 as a result of plant closings or slack work, or because their positions were abolished.[2] The BLS also estimates that over half of these people were unemployed for 26 weeks or longer. According to other sources, as many as 11 million have been displaced over the last five years, and there are over 5 million "permanently" unemployed people in the United States—a number roughly equal to the population of Missouri (Pear 1986).

Although authorities differ on the severity of the structural or long-term unemployment problem, there can be no doubt that millions suffered the shock of sudden and prolonged unemployment as they saw their jobs vanish in the last recession. And a large portion of those who found work again ended up in jobs that pay less than their previous employment. Moreover, many of these people had worked in troubled basic industries where job opportunities have continued to decline. We are likely to have more displaced workers in the future.

The other large category of the long-term unemployed are teenagers and young adults trying to enter the labor force. Although there is a shortage of young workers for certain sorts of jobs in some parts of the country, nationwide the unemployment picture is bleak. Among men 16 to 24 years of age, the unemployment rate was about 14 percent in 1985, and among women it was about 13 percent (U.S. Department of Labor 1986). It was also nearly three times as high for blacks as whites (U.S. Department of Labor 1986). But the aggregate numbers are deceptive. The unemployment rate for teenagers ages 16 to 19 was far higher than the rate for young adults ages 22 to 24. The vast majority of teenagers are enrolled in school and looking for or holding parttime jobs to supplement their personal or family resources. But about 725,000 unemployed teenagers are looking for full-time work—which presumably means that they must live on their earnings. The unemployment rate for this group is over 20 percent for whites and over 40 percent for blacks.

Together, young people struggling to enter the work force and displaced workers form the hard core of unemployment in the United States. They account for about half of total unemployment, and they are far more likely than most Americans to suffer the hardships of being out of work for prolonged periods of time. Can we, therefore, dismiss them as special cases, as many observers are inclined to do? Can we comfort ourselves by saying that, aside from these special cases, American business has accomplished the remarkable feat of absorbing most of the 76 million members of the baby boom generation into the work force over the last two decades?

I think we run a great risk if we take such comfort. It is at least worth considering the possibility that the experiences of the hard-core unemployed may be straws in the wind for many more Americans. Here is the argument.

Many of the displaced workers formerly held low-skilled, blue-collar jobs, and many unemployed young people have lower manual and intellectual skills than are needed in today's labor market. There simply is less of a market for low-skilled workers today than there was 10 or 20 years ago. Most jobs today call for higher levels of education and training, and greater flexibility than the blue-collar jobs of the past. If this trend continues, as it seems certain to do, an even larger number of the jobs of the future will call for still higher levels of expertise.

Most new jobs are in the service sector, which now accounts for 70 percent of total employment. The popular image that service sector work is typically low-paid and low-skilled—janitorial work or serving in fast food restaurants—is wrong. On average, wages are as high as those in manufacturing, and the fastest growing areas of the service sector are jobs as nurses, accountants, and other specialists. These jobs pay well, but they require high levels of specialized training.

The problem for the hard-core unemployed, therefore, is not that there is a shortage of jobs. There are plenty of opportunities in the service sector. The problem is that displaced workers and young people often lack the skills and the specialized training needed to seize those opportunities.

The experiences of the hard-core unemployed of today may be an omen for the rest of us. We face the danger that the demand for increasingly high levels of skill in the workplace that handicaps them may limit the opportunities of millions of other Americans in the years to come. In addition, many people now employed in blue-collar jobs either may see those jobs vanish in coming years or may have less chance of advancement.

And it is not only blue-collar workers who may face limited prospects. All employees of a firm are threatened when it shifts operations to take advantage of the opportunities of a service economy. The experiences of a firm headquartered in the Washington, D.C., area are a microcosm of what is happening to the economy as a whole. In the early 1980s the firm concentrated its operations on uranium mining. A few years later it shifted into machine tools and oil exploration. Finding the opportunities limited in that field, it changed operations again to concentrate on maintenance of jet engines (Area Businesses 1986). Obviously, with each of these changes, the firm required a different set of skills in its employees, all the way from the hands-on worker to top management. It stands to reason that many people must have lost jobs in the process of change from basic industry to the service sector in this firm because new lines of business called for skills they did not have.

Within the white-collar world of the service sector, good jobs are also becoming increasingly specialized. An accountant or a nurse today must have more sophisticated skills to deal with new information or medical technology, respectively, than their counterparts were expected to have some years ago. As a result, an increasing number of service sector workers run the risk of being left behind in their jobs.

Employees who are middle-aged or older often face especially serious problems. Firms that employ them are likely to promote younger workers with more up-to-date training. Companies are also increasingly prone to get rid of their older workers by one means or another. And if older workers lose their jobs, they stand a far higher chance than any other group in the work force of being unemployed for long periods of time—no one else wants a worker whose skills are outmoded.

Finally, many people get trapped by their own specialization. The days of the generalist are over—even in the professional world. A pediatric nurse may find it increasingly difficult to switch to surgical nursing if the demand for workers in her field diminishes. She may have to settle for a less lucrative job at general-practice nursing.

At the extreme, one measure of the mismatch between the skills of American workers and the jobs available is provided by recent estimates that up to 20 percent of Americans read at or below the fifth-grade level (Kozol 1985). A large proportion of the service sector jobs available are not open to someone who cannot read, write, and compute at more than an elementary level. Moreover, as Sawhill pointed out in chapter 1, it is unrealistic to expect industry to train people in these basic skills or to provide a great deal of the more specialized education that is essential to gaining and holding a job in today's labor market.

Suppose, for a moment, that we neither deny the likelihood of this outcome, nor throw up our hands in helplessness. Suppose, instead, that a group of committed public servants are appointed to a Committee on Human Resources to consider the problems of society, and suppose they come out with a set of recommendations that include a call for an effective full employment policy. What might such a policy look like? I will sketch a possible scenario, in order to set the stage for a discussion of the likely political support for such a policy and the arguments that are certain to be raised against it.

A FULL EMPLOYMENT POLICY SUITED TO OUR TIMES

The committee might begin by pointing out the obvious—that we should make a national commitment to full employment and ratify that commitment by a program of public jobs because all our existing social programs would be more effective if it could be achieved. It would be the one achievement that, more than any other, would ease the strains caused by social and economic change.

A plausible basis for the committee proposal would be the observation that most of the unemployed already fall into two natural catchment areas of public policy: Aid to Families with Dependent Children (AFDC) and unemployment insurance (UI). That is, sooner or later most people who are experiencing hardship from unemployment end up applying for benefits from one or the other of these programs. At present, the programs simply tide them over for a period of time, in the expectation that they will find jobs on their own. And most do. But, at present, those who remain unemployed are dropped by UI after a period of time and are maintained indefinitely by AFDC. This is waste.

There are probably many sound ways to combat the waste that results from unemployment. A fairly direct approach that combines ideas from a variety of recent discussions of employment problems runs along the following lines.

The first step would be to raise AFDC and UI benefits in low-benefit states to at least the national average or above, so that the unemployed can concentrate on finding jobs rather than on coping with immediate financial emergencies. After a reasonable period of time, mandatory job search, placement, and, if necessary, retraining assistance would be provided to those who remain unemployed. Finally, if, despite their best efforts, some individuals cannot find employment at a decent wage, public service jobs would be offered. We can debate endlessly about what sorts of jobs they should be. There is no end of public improvement—both physical and social— required in our society on which we can put people to work. We might expand recruitment in the armed services. Or adopt the simple expedient, once suggested by Senator Daniel Patrick Moynihan (D-N.Y.), of creating jobs by reinstating twice-a-day mail delivery. In the end it matters less how we do it; what matters is that a nation with a strong work ethic should live up to its principles.

The second step would address the problems of unemployed young people, who often are not eligible for UI or AFDC. A simple expedient would be to make any young person living in poverty who applies to a federal job search center automatically eligible for UI, if that person can demonstrate that he or she has actively sought employment for a certain period of time. The same progression of job search, placement, and training, followed by the offer of a public service job, if all else fails, could be made available to unemployed youth as to UI and AFDC recipients. In some cases, such a system could be used to pay school dropouts to continue their education.

To increase the chances of success in placing the unemployed, and to ease labor mobility generally, the third step would be to develop an improved job search information system. As noted in chapter 4, the U.S. Employment Service, which is currently responsible for performing this function, lists only a small percentage of all job openings, and the openings it lists tend to be either highly specialized or minimum wage jobs in the service sector. Also Employment Service offices often lack the information needed to refer applicants across state lines. Either the capabilities of the Employment Service should be upgraded or private firms should be offered head hunter fees for placing the long-term unemployed.

The fourth step might be to create a program to retrain people now on the job, particularly those working in troubled industries and middle-aged employees whose skills are becoming outmoded by changes in technology and structural transformations in the work place. Ideally, skills should be upgraded whenever possible. But workers who have reached a dead end in their present fields should be offered the chance to gain training in new technical specialities where there is an increasing demand for labor.

Many approaches are possible. Greater tax incentives to employers or regulations mandating retraining of employees about to be terminated in some circumstances would place much of the responsibility in the hands of business. A revolving loan fund, retraining vouchers, or a direct grant program organized along the lines of the GI bill would place responsibility on individuals to take the initiative in upgrading their skills. Because many displaced workers have been employed in troubled industries which tend to be unionized, support for unions to provide stronger retraining and placement services to their members should also be considered. In all likelihood, the right approach is a combination of these different ideas. At present the federal government does little to help solve the retraining problem: surely some more adequate response can be devised.

To summarize: what I have sketched is a four-part program, involving uniform nationwide benefits for AFDC and UI recipients accompanied by mandatory job search placement and retraining assistance as necessary; automatic UI eligibility for young persons in poverty who can demonstrate that they have actively sought employment, followed by the same progression of mandatory job search, placement, training, and public service employment as necessary; an improved job search information service; and retraining program for persons in troubled industries or in dead-end jobs.

Each of these components sounds sensible. But taken together and talked about in national terms as I have done, the proposals sound almost outrageously grandiose in the context of the current political debate. But are they so implausible? In the next sections I argue that they are not.

Potential Support for Such a Program

What is the basis for expecting a full employment policy such as the one sketched above to attract any substantial public support?

The most obvious reason is that the American people are consistently worried about the problem. Public opinion polls show that concern about unemployment is near the top on people's lists of leading domestic policy issues.

More importantly, a program such as I have sketched, which is aimed at enhancing the abilities of each of us to function more effectively in today's complex society, is more than just a response to problems of employment and related economic and social concerns. It expresses a larger social ideal: what theorists have called the value of individual autonomy.

For centuries, advocates of democracy have stressed the central importance of the individual as a social, political, economic, and moral being. According to this view, the success of a democratic society and government can be measured in large part by whether it creates conditions that will enable all citizens to make choices and engage in the activities that allow them to lead their lives successfully, by their own lights and up to their own capacities.

To put it differently, democratic government and social life are in serious jeopardy when people are blocked from pursuing options that are within their abilities—when there are second-class citizens of any sort.

This view of democratic principles has two implications. The first is that institutions—governments, businesses, families—are means to the end of individual self-fulfillment. It is to the well-being of individuals, not institutions, that we owe our first allegiance. Our primary goal must be to create conditions that will allow all citizens to lead autonomous, self-directing lives. The second is that individuals are responsible for making their own best efforts to avoid dependence on government, charity, or other sources of help.

There is every indication that this version of democratic principles—an emphasis on autonomy, opportunity, and responsibility—fits well with the values that Americans actually hold. Recent studies of American belief systems by sociologist Sidney Verba and political scientist Jennifer Hochschild reveal that equality, fairness, freedom, and many other positive words in the democratic vocabulary tend to be equated with opportunity.[3] Americans generally do not condemn unequal outcomes in the race of life, but they do believe that everyone should have a fair and equal chance. This is what we would expect from a nation of individualists: everyone is expected to make it on his or her own, but no people should be held back by circumstances beyond their control.

A full employment policy should stand a good chance of winning public acceptance in part because these are goals to which we all aspire. Using government to achieve them would be harnessing its energies to some of our most strongly felt common values.

These mainstream American values resonate throughout our history. It was Lincoln who argued that "the leading object" of our form of government should be "to lift artificial weights from all shoulders; to clear the paths of laudable pursuit for all; to afford all an unfettered start, and a fair chance in the race of life" (1861). And Theodore Roosevelt urged us to use government in the same way. "Help any man who stumbles," he declared. "If he lies down, it is a poor job to try to carry him; but if he is a worthy man, try your best to see that he gets a chance to show the worth that is in him" (1910, 34).

Advocates of both political persuasions have always argued that their agendas would lead to greater opportunity for individual self-reliance. Liberals have sought to reach this goal by measures that enhance individual security. Virtually every major extension of the federal social role in this century—from the time of Theodore Roosevelt, to the New Deal, to the Great Society—has been justified, at least rhetorically, as a way of enlarging opportunity. Conservatives have sought to reach the same goal by clearing away needless government interference with individual choice.

But neither liberals nor conservatives have fully come to grips with the fact that, through no fault of their own, large numbers of people are unable to achieve their full potential. As a result, there is a tendency for liberal policies to reduce to the promotion of security of and by itself and for conservative policies to promote freedoms that many people find empty.

A full employment program could reach beyond traditional liberal and conservative measures to open up greater opportunities and help individuals develop the capacity to take advantage of them. This is a common ground on which both liberals and conservatives can meet. By directly confronting the barriers to individual opportunity, such a program should help the nation to achieve goals that adherents of both political persuasions have sought by indirect means.

But how, it may objected, can a strong federal program such as I have sketched here gain widespread support when it would extend the federal role into an area that traditionally has been dominated by other levels of government and by business? In a nation that values institutional diversity, a program of this scope might be expected to meet with opposition, as have other attempts to impose stronger federal priorities. But there is no reason why such a policy should obviate the need for other institutions to play an active role. On the contrary. The nation's needs are too great and too many to squander either public or private means. The federal government must do what it does best, and other institutions must perform the roles to which they are suited if we are to improve the opportunities of all our people. There are, in fact, tangible straws in the wind that indicate such an initiative would meet with strong support.

Private Sector Moves toward Job Security

Many of our largest and best-managed businesses are already turning their attention to the benefits they can reap from improving the prospects of their workers, and from a national work force that has greater opportunities. In recent years, many companies have been trying to enhance the prospects of their employees by improving retention, equal opportunity, retraining, and benefit plans, and by allowing greater participation in workplace management. They believe they can boost production by developing a more loyal, more highly skilled, and more stable work force. Through placement, training, and relocation programs, companies have also shown increased concern for workers who have lost their jobs. The favorable attention being paid to Japanese labor-relations techniques (as described by Marshall in chapter 8) is another indication of the growing concern for more creative use of human resources.

Progressive corporate managers are also looking for partnerships with states, communities, and the voluntary sector to develop programs that will improve the skills of young people and meet the midcareer needs of older employees. Many states and communities, in turn, have acted vigorously to upgrade schools, colleges, and other institutions that help enhance human resources. In virtually every state efforts have been made to give disadvantaged people—typically poor children, welfare mothers, and displaced workers—a second chance to become self-sufficient. In the last few years, counseling, retraining, placement, public employment, and other activities intended to get people off welfare and to help them become self-sustaining have been emphasized at all levels of government.

Individuals have responded enthusiastically to corporate and governmental initiatives. Programs offering training, opportunities for greater involvement in company decision making, and a second chance for the disadvantaged have found no shortage of would-be participants. Individual Americans clearly are willing to assume their share of responsibility for achieving success in life, if given the opportunity.

CAN WE DO IT?

Let me assume my political argument is convincing. Three objections will still be raised: we do not know how to do it; we cannot afford it; and it will stimulate inflation.

It is true that, in a great many cases, we do not know all we need to know about how to help individuals become more self-sufficient. This is one reason why policymakers have backed away from some efforts under the umbrella of human resource policy in the past. Abandonment of some of the more ambitious programs of the War on Poverty is a case in point. It is simply very hard, for example, to help a teenage mother who has been reared in a culture of poverty— who has few skills, low self-esteem, and a defeatist attitude—to become a self-supporting member of society. We must realize that, because of limits on our present knowledge about human behavior and how to make social programs work, there are practical limits to how much a human resource program can accomplish in the near term at least.

But we must also recognize that we have learned a substantial amount about how to design programs with the correct incentives, and we have quite a good idea about where our major employment problems are and where we should put the most effort, at least initially. It is certainly possible to keep measures aimed at enhancing human resources within the bounds of our other public values to improve our social technology, and to focus federal initiatives on the areas of greatest need.

To solve long-standing problems and meet the challenges of economic and social change we not only can but must overcome these difficulties. But we will never do so unless we both admit that the difficulties exist and make a firm commitment to overall directions of policy that require us to come to grips with them.

What does it mean to say that we cannot afford it? It is certainly correct that we have a huge federal budget deficit that must be reduced to manageable proportions over the next several years. But this does not, of course, mean that we cannot afford to spend on a social program we decide is important. It simply means that we must order our spending priorities and if these priorities require additional spending we can raise taxes to cover them. Here again, the issue is one of commitment. If our society is committed to the goal of full employment we can find a way to afford it.

To the extent that economic growth does not provide the resources we need, we can reexamine the priorities embedded in our tax code and credit policies. Should we continue to forgo tens of billions of dollars through tax exemptions that support, for example, state and local bonding authority and subsidies to large corporate farms? Now that the Internal Revenue Service exempts most low-income people from taxation, is there any reason not to tax social security benefits fully? We can find the money, if we can find the will.

It is, of course, possible that the privileged institutions of our society, as well as ordinary taxpayers, will balk at this type of expense. But it is a mistake to assume the worst on this score before we even try the idea.

In the end, whether the investments should be made will depend on the American people. The federal government is their government, to do with as they want. It is the task of public leadership to help them find where their interests lie and to appeal for their support. And it is also the task of leadership to find combinations of policies that close and open doors in ways that make it easier for both the privileged and the rest of the public to act on the interests they have in common.

There is still, however, a ghost at the banquet: renewed inflation.

Because the idea of full employment is not new, ample arguments have been mustered both for and against it over the years. The most telling opposition in recent decades has come from economists, who argue that full employment would result in increased inflation. As Isabel Sawhill, a friend of full employment, points out in chapter 1, it would be relatively easy to increase employment if there were no worries about inflation.

The economist's argument takes two forms: a concern about labor supply and a concern about consumer demand. The supply argument in essence is that, in a situation of unemployment, the number of job openings available at current wages may be less than the number of qualified employees looking for work. Hence, if employers were forced to hire everyone who is without a job, they would have to raise their prices to cover the increased cost of labor. The demand argument, in an equally simple form, is that if everyone were suddenly employed at a good wage, there would be such a massive increase in purchasing power that the existing supply of goods and services would be used up. Prices would rise as the newly employed competed with everyone else for a limited pool of consumption items.

Both concerns are justified and lead to the inescapable conclusion that an effective full employment policy would result in some inflationary pressure. It is impossible to say how strong those pressures would be, however, because that depends on a host of details that change over time about the general state of the economy and the work force. Conceivably, inflationary effects could be trivial. In any event, the ways to minimize those effects are also among the ways to create full employment, in the broadest sense of the term: creating an environment that fosters economic growth, training workers to fit the jobs available, helping them find jobs, and giving special priority to people who are living in poverty or hard to place. And, in addition to a well-designed employment policy, we have other means to fight inflation: federal monetary policy, better enforcement of antitrust policies against oligopolies, and, if necessary, price and wage constraints, administered either by regulatory means or through the tax system. It is also possible that we can reduce the trade-off between inflation and employment by encouraging firms to link wage increases more closely to increase in productivity. This idea has been elaborated by economists Martin Weitzman and Lester Thurow in their proposals for developing a share economy (see Weitzman 1984; Thurow 1985).

By all estimates, however, full employment would lead to some increase in inflation, at least in the short run. Is this any reason to oppose a full employment policy? In the end that question comes down to a moral issue. Inflation is, in effect, a tax—like a sales tax— that increases the price of everything we buy. If the only way that we can avoid paying that tax is for some of our fellow citizens to be doomed to idleness, then it is a tax that we should feel morally obliged to pay. Otherwise, our prosperity is attributable to their distress. We are standing on their shoulders, holding them down.

Most of us are willing to accept some level of taxation to support the indigent. We live in a country that that spends billions of dollars on welfare payments to tide people over periods of financial distress. An inflation tax that would result from these same people working and contributing to the economy and that would also increase our own prospects and security would seem more worthwhile.

It is not clear that the tax needs to be large, and certainly every effort should be made to keep it as small as possible. Obviously high, sustained rates of inflation would wreck the American economy and, like any excessive tax, should not be paid. But we have no solid grounds for believing that an inflation tax resulting from full employment must be excessive. As mentioned, we can moderate it by a variety of means. And, in the end, if not paying a moderate inflation tax allows us to prosper while others are left helpless, then it is a tax we should gladly pay.

Notes

1. The classic description of that battle is in Bailey (1950).

2. Flaim and Seghal (1985); Office of Technology Assessment (1986). For a discussion of various estimates of the number of displaced workers see Stone and Sawhill (1986).

3. Verba and Orren (1985); Hochschild (1981). See also Mead (1985); McCloskey and Zaller (1985).

References

Area Businesses Trimming the Fat. 14 September 1986. *Washington Post.*
Bailey, Stephen Kemp. 1950. *Congress Makes a Law.* New York: Columbia University Press.

Flaim, Paul O., and Ellen Seghal. June 1985. Displaced Workers of 1979–83: How Well Have They Fared? *Monthly Labor Review*. Washington.

Hochschild, Jennifer L. 1981. *What's Fair*. Cambridge, Mass.: Harvard University Press.

Kozol, Jonathan. 1985. *Illiterate America*. New York: Doubleday.

Lincoln, Abraham. 11 July 1861. Message to Congress.

Mead, Lawrence M. 1985. *Beyond Entitlement*. New York: Free Press.

McCloskey, Herbert, and John Zaller. 1985. *The American Ethos*. Cambridge, Mass.: Harvard University Press.

Office of Technology Assessment. February 1986. *Technology and Structural Unemployment: Reemploying Displaced Adults*. Washington.

Pear, Robert. 16 March 1986. Millions Bypassed as Economy Soars. *New York Times*.

The Report of the Committee on Economic Security. 1985. In *The 50th Anniversary Edition of the Report of the Committee on Economic Security of 1935*. Washington: National Conference on Social Welfare.

Roosevelt, Theodore. 1971. *The New Nationalism*. Reprint. Gloucester, Mass.: Peter Smith.

Stone, Charles F., and Isabel V. Sawhill. 1986. *Labor Market Implications of the Growing Internationalization of the U.S. Economy*. Washington: National Committee for Employment Policy.

Thurow, Lester C. 1985. *The Zero Sum Solution*. New York: Simon and Schuster.

U.S. Department of Labor. January 1986. *Employment and Earnings* 33(1): 155–56. Washington.

Verba, Sidney, and Gary R. Orren. 1985. *Equality in America*. Cambridge, Mass.: Harvard University Press.

Weitzman, Martin. 1984. *The Share Economy*. Cambridge, Mass.: Harvard University Press.

ABOUT THE CONTRIBUTORS

Burt S. Barnow is a senior economist and Vice President at Lewin/ ICF, a research and consulting firm in Washington, D.C. His recent publications include "The Uses and Limits of Social Experiments" (1988), *Developing Models to Predict State AFDC Caseloads: A Guide for States* (1988), and *Using Performance Management to Encourage Services to Hard-to-Serve Individuals in JTPA* (1988).

Marc Bendick, Jr. is a principal in Bendick and Egan Economic Consultants, Inc., Washington, D.C., specializing in employment, economic development, and the evaluation of programs serving low income populations. He is a consultant to the U.S. Department of Labor on development of the Employment Service for the year 2000. His recent publications include *Jobs. Employment Opportunities in the Washington Area for Persons with Limited Employment Qualifications* (1988) and *Business Development in the Inner City: The Community Development Link* (forthcoming, 1989).

Daniel F. Burton, Jr. is Vice President of the Council on Competitiveness, a policy group of CEOs from American business, labor, and higher education. Prior to joining the Council, he was Executive Director of the Economic Policy Council, UNA-USA. He has written extensively on trade, technology and international economics. He was coeditor of *The Jobs Challenge: Pressures and Possibilities* (1985). His latest book is *Vision for the 1990's: U.S. Strategy and the Global Economy*, edited with Felix Rohatyn and Victor Gotbaum (1988).

Forrest P. Chisman is director of the Washington Office of the Southport Institute. From 1983 to 88, he was director of the Project on the Federal Social Role. Previously he was an official in the Commerce Department and program officer of the John and Mary Markle Foundation. He is the author (with Alan Pifer) of *Government for the People: The Federal Social Role* (1987) and of numerous articles on public policy and communications.

Leroy D. Clark is professor of law at Catholic University and former general counsel of the Equal Employment Opportunity Commission. Among his publications are an article entitled "Drug Abuse in the Workplace: Arbitration in the Context of a National Solution of Decriminalization" which appears in *Arbitration 1987—The Academy at* 40 (1987) and *Employment Discrimination Law—Cases and Materials*, third edition (1988), a coauthored volume.

Ronald G. Ehrenberg is Irving M. Ives Professor of Industrial and Labor Relations and Economics at Cornell University and a research associate at the National Bureau of Economic Research. His research has focused on the evaluation of labor market programs and legislation, public sector labor markets, wage determination in regulated industries, resource allocation issues in education, and analyses of compensation policies. His recent publications include *Modern Labor Economics*, third edition (1988) and *Advance Notice Provisions in Plant Closing Legislation* (1988).

Robert Eisner is William R. Kenan Professor of Economics at Northwestern University and past president of the American Economic Association. He is the author of *The Total Incomes System of Accounts* (forthcoming, 1989), *How Real is the Federal Deficit?* (1986), *Factors in Business Investment* (1979), and many professional articles and other volumes on monetary and fiscal policy, depreciation, employment, and economic growth.

George Johnson is professor of economics at the University of Michigan and a research associate at the National Bureau of Economic Research. He was director of the Office of Evaluation in ASPER in the Labor Department and a senior economist with the Council of Economic Advisers. His research has focused on the analysis of labor market behavior and on a variety of labor market policies. His current research concerns the puzzling causes of the dramatic changes since the 1970s in the structure of wages in the United States.

Ray Marshall is Audre and Bernard Rapoport Centennial Professor of Economics and Public Affairs, University of Texas at Austin. He was Secretary of Labor in the Carter administration, and is a widely published author on issues related to industrial organization and the labor market. He recently authored *Unheard Voices: Labor and Economic Policy in a Competitive World* (1988) and coedited *The Jobs Challenge: Pressures and Possibilities* (1985).

Isabel V. Sawhill is senior fellow of the Urban Institute and director of the Changing Domestic Priorities project. Her areas of research include human resources and economic policy. She has directed several of the Institute's research programs and has held a number of government positions, including that of director of the National Commission for Employment Policy. Her most recent book is *Challenge to Leadership: Economic and Social Issues for the Next Decade* (1988), an edited volume.

ABOUT THE EDITORS

D. Lee Bawden is director of the Human Resources Policy Center of The Urban Institute. A former professor of economics at the University of Wisconsin-Madison and senior fellow of the Institute for Research on Poverty, he has published extensively on social policy issues. Recent publications include *The Social Contract Revisited* (1984), an edited volume.

Felicity Skidmore, until her recent appointment as managing editor of The Urban Institute Press, was a freelance editor and writer on social policy issues. Among her publications are *Social Security Financing* (1981), an edited volume, and *Economics* (1983), a co-authored textbook.